Otis Tuflon Mason

Woman's Share In Primitive

Otis Tuflon Mason

Woman's Share In Primitive

ISBN/EAN: 9783742836731

Manufactured in Europe, USA, Canada, Australia, Japa

Cover: Foto ©Andreas Hilbeck / pixelio.de

Manufactured and distributed by brebook publishing software (www.brebook.com)

Otis Tuflon Mason

Woman's Share In Primitive

AT THE FOOT OF THE LADDER—A PUEBLO WOMAN OF HOPI.
(After Wittick.)

WOMAN'S SHARE

IN PRIMITIVE CULTURE

BY

OTIS TUFTON MASON, A.M., Ph.D.

CURATOR OF THE DEPARTMENT OF ETHNOLOGY IN
THE UNITED STATES NATIONAL MUSEUM

WITH NUMEROUS ILLUSTRATIONS

"Dux femina facti."
AENEID, 1, 364.

LONDON
MACMILLAN AND CO.
AND NEW YORK
1895

EDITOR'S PREFACE.

The word Anthropology in its broadest meaning includes several subordinate sciences, such as Somatology or Physical Anthropology, Ethnology, Ethnography, Prehistoric Archæology, and Culture History. In the Anthropological Series, of which this is the first volume, it is planned to publish books dealing with special topics in these various fields. The work is undertaken in the hope that through this series the grandest and newest of all the sciences, Anthropology—the science of man—may become better known to intelligent readers who are not specialists and who do not desire to become such. At the same time the series will be one which no special student can afford to ignore.

For, while the works are intended to be of general interest, they will in every case be written by authorities, and scientific accuracy will never be sacrificed to popularity. Leaders in anthropological study in America and Europe have expressed an interest in the undertaking and have promised their co-operation. Besides books expressly written for the series by workers in the Old World and the New, the plan includes translations of valuable works from the French and German.

The editor is particularly glad that the series begins with this book by Professor Mason upon Woman's Share in Primitive Culture. In many minds it will awaken new thoughts. Division of labour began with the invention of fire-making, and it was a division of labour based upon sex. The woman staid by the fire to keep it alive while the man went to the field or the forest for game. The world's industrialism and militancy began then and there. Man has been cunning in devising means of killing beast and his fellowman—he has been the inventor in every murderous art. The woman at the fireside became the burden bearer, the basket-maker, the weaver, potter, agriculturist, domesticator of animals—in a word, the inventor of all the peaceful arts of life. Professor Mason traces the story for us in these chapters.

Arrangements have already been made for other volumes, which will be issued soon. Still others will be undertaken if the success of the early numbers warrants it.

CONTENTS.

CHAPTER	PAGE
I.—Introduction	1
II.—The Food Bringer	14
III.—The Weaver	41
IV.—The Skin Dresser	70
V.—The Potter	91
VI.—The Beast of Burden	114
VII.—The Jack-at-all-Trades	140
VIII.—The Artist	161
IX.—The Linguist	186
X.—The Founder of Society	206
XI.—The Patron of Religion	241
XII.—Conclusion	272

LIST OF ILLUSTRATIONS.

FIG.		PAGE
	At the Foot of the Ladder—A Pueblo Woman at Home. (After Wittich.) . . . . *Frontispiece*	
1.	The Primitive Farmer and Burden-bearer, South Africa. (After Livingstone.)	0
2.	Division of Labour under New Conditions—A California Scene. (After Henshaw.) . . . . . *facing*	7
3.	Reciprocity—A California Family at Home. (After Henshaw.) . . . . *facing*	11
4.	The Primitive Farmer—California Woman assorting Food. (After Henshaw.) . . . . . . *facing*	15
5.	Bean Granary, Mohave Indians, Southern California. (After Henshaw.)	17
6.	The Primitive Miller—California Indian Woman using Metate and Muller	22
7.	The Pemmican Maker pounding Cherries and Dried Buffalo Meat—Sioux Indians, Dakota. (After Jungling.)	28
8.	Tuscan Vintners—Carrying on the Head, the Shoulder, and the Side	31
9.	Moki Fruit Picker's Basket, Arizona. (After Mason.)	43
10.	The Basket-maker—California Woman at Work. (After Henshaw.) . . . . *facing*	45
11.	Twined Weaving by Hupa Women, Northern California. (After Mason.)	46
12.	Coiled Weaving by Ute Women, Utah. (After Mason.)	50
13.	Mohave Cradle Frame, showing the Shredded Bark Bed, the Framework, and the Geometric Patterns in Weaving	56
14.	The Primitive Loom Weaver—Navajo Woman, Arizona. (After Matthews.)	61
15.	Impressions of Twined Weaving on Ancient Pottery. (After Holmes.) . . . . *facing*	63

LIST OF ILLUSTRATIONS.

FIG.		PAGE
16.	Eskimo "Scraper," made to fit the Woman's Hand. (After Mason.)	73
17.	Eskimo Fat Scraper of Reindeer Antler and Rawhide. (After Mason.)	74
18.	Eskimo Fat Scraper of Walrus Ivory, made to fit the Fingers. (After Mason.)	75
19, 20, 21, 22.	Tools of the Primitive Tanner—Implements of Bone, Antler, and Iron used by Sioux Women in dressing Hides . . . . facing	83
23.	Modelled Vase, with Buttles in the Legs. (After Holmes.)	96
24.	Making Coiled Ware in Basket Bowl. (After Cushing.)	98
25.	Basket Bowl as Base Mould for Large Vessel, showing also the Smoothing Process after Coiling. (After Cushing.)	100
26.	The Processes in building up the most Finished Type of Jar. (After Cushing.)	102
27.	Clay Vessel Modelled after a Shell Vessel. (After Holmes.)	110
28.	Vessel of Shell as Model for one in Clay. (After Holmes.)	111
29.	California Cradle Frame. (After Mason.)	116
30.	Eskimo Mothers. (After Healy.)	117
31.	Turkish Beggar in the Streets of Washington. (After Thomas Lee.) . . . . facing	119
32.	Indian Men and Women delivering hay to the Government . . . . facing	121
33.	Ute Children carrying Water in Basket Bottles. (After Powell.) . . . . facing	123
34.	The Knapsack in Woman's Work.—German Peasant Woman.	124
35.	The Danish Fish Woman.	133
36.	Florentine Wood Gatherers. (After Gioli.) . facing	132
37.	German Bread Woman supporting the Sinews of War	134
38.	German Market Women	135
39.	Hod Carriers in Nuremberg	137
40.	German Women as Housewives, Gardeners, Domesticators, Draught Animals, and Merchants. (After Chandler.)	140
41.	The Primitive Shelter or Home—A Bannok Family, Montana . . . . facing	156
42.	"The Matron of Isleta, New Mexico." (After Wittich.)	159
43.	The Origin of the Scroll. (From ancient Pueblo pottery, after Holmes.)	168
44.	Elucidation of Decoration on Tusayan Dipper. (After Holmes.) . . . . facing	173

LIST OF ILLUSTRATIONS. xiii

FIG.		PAGE
45.	Ancient Tusayan Dipper, Arizona. (After Holmes.)	173
46.	The Pretty Girl—A Noki Beauty. (After Wittich.)	180
47.	The Ute Standard of Beauty, Utah. (After Wittich.)	181
48.	The Yuma Fine Lady, Southern California. (After Wittich.)	facing 182
49.	Manner of piercing the Ear—Seminole Indian Woman	184
50.	The Mother of the Caryatides—Low Caste Indian Woman	186
51.	The Maiden in Savagery	facing 207
52.	The Founder of Society, the Primitive Social Unit	214
53.	The Ganowarian Family, Havasupai, Southern California	facing 217
54.	The Australian Family	facing 219
55.	Mexican Indian Family	222
56.	Zuñi priestess Praying for Rain on the Young Corn which she planted	240
57.	Moslem Water Carrier, Cousin of the Nixies	246
58.	Sioux Women cutting themselves for the Dead. (After Yarrow.)	facing 252
59.	Atropos drawing out the Thread or Weft of Life	facing 266
60.	Kwan-yin, the Chinese Female Buddha	282

WOMAN'S SHARE IN PRIMITIVE CULTURE.

CHAPTER I.

INTRODUCTION.

Of the billion and a half human beings on the earth, one half, or about seven hundred million, are females. What this vast multitude are doing in the world's activities and what share their mothers and grandmothers, to the remotest generation backward, have had in originating and developing culture, is a question which concerns the whole race. The answer to this inquiry will benefit the living in many ways, especially if it can be shown that the achievements of women have been in the past worthy of honour and imitation and have laid the foundation for arts of which all are now justly proud. Dr. Hermann Ploss, just before his death in 1891, finished his monumental work, Das Weib, which leaves little to be desired concerning the natural history of woman. In this work her anatomy and physiology, in health and disease, in savagery and civilization, from the cradle to the grave, are clearly traced. The girl, the maiden, the wife, the matron, the widow, pass before us one after another to absorb our attention. In the present work these subjects are ignored or lightly passed over, and the effort is made to set forth woman's share in the culture of the world by her works.

The woman and her works have reacted one upon the other, as every one knows. But the point of view adds new pleasure to the vista.*

Militancy and industrialism—these are the two periods into which Herbert Spencer divides the life history of civilization. First came the period of militancy, of savagery and barbarism, of warring between man and man, between man and Nature. After that succeeded the period of industrialism, when peoples settled down to the great occupations that dignify the most advanced nations.

Without calling in question this classification, the inquiry is here made whether these two words, in the early history of our species at least, did not mark a sexual division—whether, instead of an *age*, we should not rather say a *sex* of militancy and a *sex* of industrialism. Certainly there was never an age in which there was a more active armament, larger battle ships, more destructive explosives and cannon, and vaster establishments for the creation of engines and implements of death than in our own. From all these women are excluded, save now and then a few poor girls may be allowed for a pittance to fill cartridges; save that, as in the days of Tacitus, women carry food and cheers to their husbands on battlefields; save that the good sisters of the Red Cross bind up the wounds and minister to the wants of the unfortunate victims. In contact with the animal world, and ever taking lessons from them, men watched the tiger, the bear, the fox, the falcon—learned their language and imitated them in ceremonial dances.

But women were instructed by the spiders, the nest

---

* Ploss, Das Weib in der Natur- und Völkerkunde, Leipsic, Formm; also consult Lester F. Ward, Our Better Halves, Forum, N. Y., 1888, vol. vi. pp. 266–275; Cecilia Seler, Die Frau im Mexico, Berlin, 1893; and O. T. Mason, Am. Antiquarian, Chicago, 1889, xi, pp. 1–13; Havelock Ellis, Man and Woman, London, 1894, Scott.

builders, the storers of food and the workers in clay like the mud wasp and the termites. It is not meant that these creatures set up schools to teach dull women how to work, but that their quick minds were on the alert for hints coming from these sources."* Even though we disarm our soldiery, we do not seem to be able to dissociate men from the works that bring violent death. It is in the apotheosis of industrialism that woman has borne her part so persistently and well. At the very beginning of human time she laid down the lines of her duties, and she has kept to them unremittingly.

How comfortless, however, was the first woman who stood upon this planet! How economical her dowry! Her body was singularly devoid of comfortable hair, her teeth and jaws were the feeblest, her arm was less powerful than that of any creature of her size, she had no wings like the birds, she could not see into the night like the owl, the timid hare was fleeter of foot than she. Her inventive genius and cunning fingers had not yet devised the sheltering tent or the comfortable clothing. As yet she had no tools of peaceful industry nor experience. Society had not then formed its body politic around her as a nucleus. She had poor ways of expressing her thoughts or her sense of beauty. She had no theory of the life below and poorer conceptions of the heavenly world. Nature mocked her. The food and textile plants withheld their productions from her. The mountain sheep fled away to their fastnesses with their fleece and milk. So many secrets were held back from her by Nature, who knew so much and told so little. As yet her magic touch had not even begun to cover the earth with waving grain.

---

* Cf. Payne, History of America, New York, 1899, vol. i, p. 307, quoting Lucretius (v. 1057). On the conduct of the bees in the honey industry, see Riley, President's Address, Biological Society, Washington, 1894.

fields or golden cornfields, or luscious fruit. As we in imagination behold these women primeval, the words of Lear rise spontaneously in the memory:

> Poor naked wretches on the edge of time,
> That bide the pelting of this pitiless storm,
> How shall your houseless heads and unfed sides defend you
> From seasons such as these? KING LEAR. III, 1.

The road from her to my fair reader in the midst of many comforts is long indeed. But even this poorly equipped woman had more brain than was sufficient to meet the demands of bodily existence, and in this fact lay the promise of her future achievements. The maternal instinct, the strong back, the deft hand, the aversion to aggressive employment, the conservative spirit, were there in flower.

Her shop was ample enough, for it was the vaulted sky; but her tools and materials and methods were of the simplest kind. What we do in hours she accomplished in years. But if you could from some exalted position take in the exploitation of the earth and sea, the transformation of raw material into things of use, the transportation of these products in all directions, the commercial transactions involved in the sale of these commodities, you would be astonished to know how many of these wheels were set agoing by women in prehistoric times.

Furthermore, as the method of living in each age of the world survives and is propagated into the succeeding ages, one would not have to go far from any of our great cities to find women still, in a small way, practicing these same arts in competition with the products of machinery. Her patient face may also be seen in the midst of our flying wheels, so that in Ezekiel's vision the rims that were full of eyes remind us of a modern cotton factory. The spirit of the living creature in the wheels is the genius of industrialism originated and fostered in the world by women.

In the year 1888 the United States Commissioner of Labour published his fourth annual report, devoted to working women in large cities. There are three hundred and thirty-six occupations mentioned in the book. In some of them the women were simply working with men at men's trades. Other employments, such as rag picking and a few more, are peculiar to civilisation and are not hinted at in savagery. Again, the differentiation and specialization of trades found in this list do not exist low down in culture or even in our own farmhouses. For instance, a great many of them are merely the needle-woman making a variety of things. But it is most interesting to run the eye up and down the columns and see what a large proportion of the working women in our cities are still following the paths trodden long ago by dusky savages of their own sex.[*]

Now, Jules Simon is not altogether satisfied with what the nineteenth century has done for the millions of toiling women in cities. Says he: "And what shall we say of women? Formerly isolated in their households, now herded together in manufactories. . . . From the moment when steam appeared in the industrial world, the wheel, the spindle, and the distaff broke in the hand, and the spinsters and weavers, deprived of their ancient livelihood, fled to the shadow of the tall factory chimney. The mothers have left the hearth and the cradle, and the young girls and the little children themselves have run to offer their feeble arms; whole villages are si-

---

[*] Report of Commissioner of Labour, Washington, 1889, Government Printing Office. Also H. Ditmar, United States Consular Report, 113, March, 1890, p. 431; Popular Science Monthly, xxiii, p. 598; North American Review, cxxxvi, p. 478; ibid., cxxxv, p. 487.

lent, while huge brick buildings swallow up thousands of living humanity from dawn of day to twilight shades."*

In many books of travels woman among savage tribes is pictured to us as an abject creature born under an evil star, the brutalized slave of man, to be kicked or killed at his pleasure. This can scarcely be true of any advancing people. Savages as they are now visited are not in a normal condition. It does not need to be urged, for instance, that a tribe of Indians on a reservation, the same tribe running at large but environed by whites, or, thirdly, in its unmolested condition before the discovery, presents different states of social health.

Fig. 1.—The Primitive Farmer and Burden-bearer, South Africa. (After Livingstone.)

It is not reasonable to suppose that any species or variety of animals would survive in which the helpless, maternal half is subjected to outrageous cruelty as a rule. According to the law of survival of the fittest, a tribe or stock of human beings in which brutality of this sort has place simply chooses the downward road and disappears. It is one way to account for the great industry and patience of

---

* M. Jules Simon, quoted by Bessie Rayner Parkes, Essays on Women's Work, London, 1865, p. 92. Also U. S. Consular Reports, p. 109, 1890.

savage women, that the best have been educated through their trials, and in the "good old days" of summary execution the vixenish and the worthless were weeded out by their disgusted lords and masters.

Again, cruelty does not breed refinement either of manners or of taste. Where women adorn themselves with flowers, and produce with skilful fingers work that will excite the admiration of the most refined, their home can hardly be the abode of cruelty. Of one of the most primitive peoples E. H. Man says: "It is incorrect to say that among the Andamanese marriage is nothing more than taking a female slave, for one of the striking features of their social relation is the marked equality and affection which subsists between husband and wife. Careful observations extended over many years prove that not only is the husband's authority more or less nominal, but that it is not at all an uncommon occurrence for Andamanese Benedicts to be considerably at the beck and call of their better halves." *

A charming confession is made by the same writer with reference to the moral influence of woman's presence. He says: "Experience has taught us that one of the most effective means of inspiring confidence when endeavouring to make acquaintance with these savages is to show that we are accompanied by women, as they at once infer that, whatever may be our intentions, they are at least not hostile."

From Africa we have the testimony of Livingstone upon the same subject. He offered one of Nyakoba's men a hoe to be his guide, which the man agreed to, and went off to show the hoe to his wife. He soon returned

---

* The Andamanese Islanders, London, 1883. The foot-notes abound in contradictions of disparaging remarks about these people by superficial observers. Also Trotter, Proc. Roy. Geog. Soc., London, 1882, p. 791.

and said his wife would not let him go. After much chaffing the doctor was told: "Oh, that is the custom in these parts—the wives are masters." *

We do not stop to inquire into the veracity of Nyakoba's man. If he was sincere, there was at least one henpecked husband in the Dark Continent. If he was lying, he had not forgotten a very ancient subterfuge of laying the blame on his wife.

Among the Guiana Indians, says Im Thurn, an excellent observer, there is an equal division of labour, though that of the men is accomplished more fitfully than that of the women. No different distribution ever entered into the thoughts of Indians, and the women do their share willingly, without question and without compulsion. The women in a quiet way have a considerable amount of influence with the men; and even if the men were—though that is contrary to their nature—inclined to treat them cruelly, public opinion would prevent this. Moreover, the women, just because they have been accustomed to hard labour all their lives, are little weaker than the men. If a contest arose between an average man and an average woman, it is very doubtful with which the victory would be.† Even on a hunting trip women were not to be despised, according to Warburton Pike.

"I now saw what an advantage it is to take women on a hunting trip of this kind. If we killed anything we had only to cut up and cache the meat, and the women and small boys would carry it in. On returning to camp

---

* Travels in South Africa, New York, 1858, p. 607.

† Im Thurn, Indians of British Guiana, p. 215. Consult also Dall, American Naturalist, Philadelphia, 1878, vol. xii, p. 5, note, and Murdoch, Ninth Annual Report of the Bureau of Ethnology, Washington, 1868, quoting Parry, Nordenskjöld, and Simpson. See also Bancroft, Native Races, New York, 1874–'76, sub voce, vol. v, p. 737.

we could throw ourselves down on a pile of caribou skins and smoke our pipes in comfort, but the women's work was never finished. The rib bones have all to be picked out, and the *plat côtés* hung up in the smoke to dry; the meat of haunches and shoulders must be cut up into thin strips for the same purpose, and the bones have to be collected, pounded down, and boiled for the grease, which is in such demand during the cold weather about to commence. But the greatest labour of all lies in dressing the skins, cutting off the hair, scraping away every particle of flesh and fat, and afterward turning them into soft leather for moccasins, which are themselves no easy task to make. Many skins, too, have to be made into parchment or carefully cut into babiche for snowshoes, and again there are hair coats to be made for each member of the party."*

The work of the men among the Omahas, according to Dorsey, was regulated essentially by that of the women, who were to them a sort of calendar. The summer hunt was undertaken after the women had planted the corn and the pumpkins and the beans had been gathered. They returned on the ripening of the sunflower. They went on the fall hunt when the hair on the game was thick and warm, out of which the women made the clothing. The women buried in caches whatever they wished to leave. Food, etc., was placed in a blanket, which was gathered at the corners and tied with a thong; then the bundle was allowed to fall at the bottom of the cache. Then the women went over the cornfields to see that all the work had been finished. They prepared pack-saddles and litters and mended moccasins and other clothing. The day for the departure having arrived, the

---

* Warburton Pike, Barren Grounds, etc., London, 1892, Macmillan, pp. 75, 100.

women loaded their horses and dogs and took as great weights on their own backs as they could conveniently transport.*

Another popular error concerning the division of labour in savagery is the assertion that all woman's work is degrading to men and all man's work tabooed to women.

It is not denied that the taboo is in full force among primitive races. There are occasions in all aboriginal tribes when it would be fatal and ill-starred for a woman even to touch or to look upon objects to be used in men's activities. There are also occupations of women in which men think themselves degraded to engage. But nothing is more common than to see the sexes lending a helping hand in bearing the burdens of life. Men were the hunters and fishermen, but women went hunting and fishing. Women have been the spinners and weavers the world over, but there are occasions when men have to weave. Indeed, the taboo of which we have been speaking compels them to weave the blanket to be worn by the man in the next prayer ceremonial for rain or in the tribal dance. Hence, among the Navajo, and in some of the Pueblos, men are among the best weavers.

Yet this co-operation in one another's employments, unless demanded by religion, must always have been a matter of friendly help and never of compulsion. The feeling never seems to be absent that it is a reflection upon the ability and skill of a woman, however weak she may be, to have her husband bearing her burden. When the woman engages in the man's occupation it is to help him out in those matters that are not tabooed.

---

* Cf. Dorsey, Omaha Sociology. Also Bartram, Travels, etc. London, 1792, p. 461; Rev. Asher Wright, quoted by Morgan, Anct. Society, New York, 1877, Holt, p. 455; J. G. Garson, J. Anthrop. Inst., London, 1886, p. 145; and Boas, Fifth An. Rep. Bur. Ethnol., p. 485.

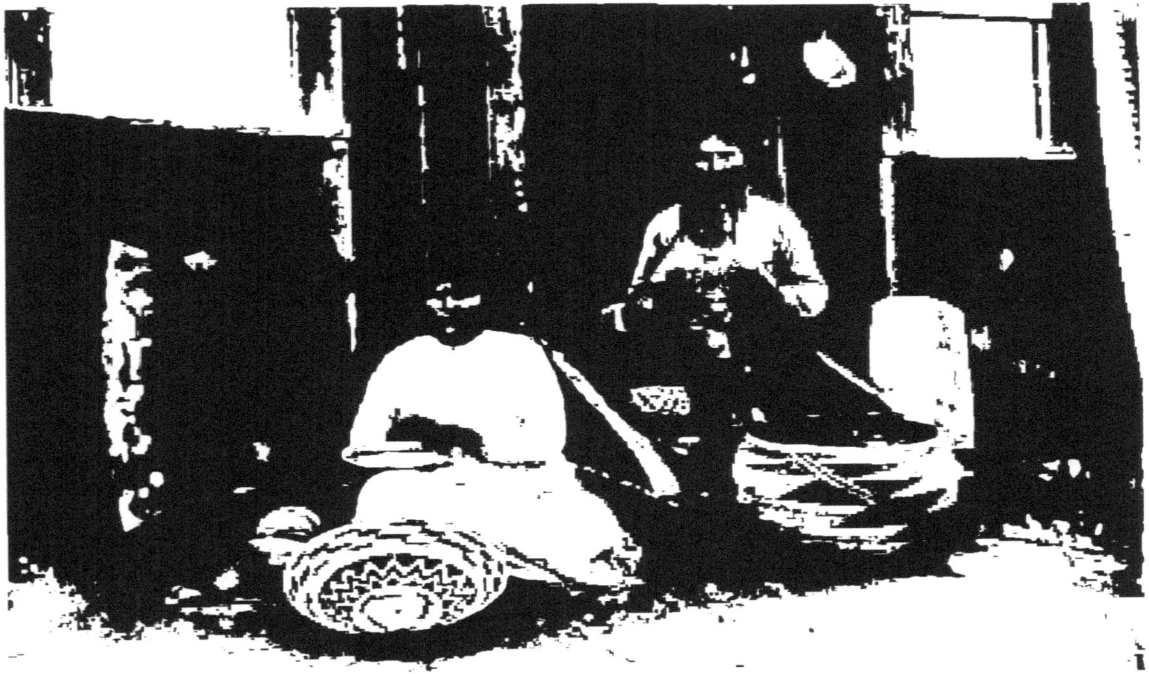

Campbell[*] says of a Corean woman: "To make matters worse, the head man upon whom I had relied for assistance in hiring the men I wanted was absent, but his wife proved a capable substitute, and seemed to fill her husband's place with unquestioned authority. Between bullying and coaxing, she rapidly pressed twenty reluctant men into service. . . . The subjection of women, which is probably the commonest of accepted theories in the East, received a fresh blow, in my mind. Women in these parts of the world, if the truth were known, fill a higher place and wield greater influence than they are credited with."

For a correct knowledge of primitive woman's activities there are five witnesses to take the stand. The first is Clio, Muse of history. Her memory runs backward three or four thousand years, and recalls the childhood of nations now grown old and decayed. Her faithful servants put on record many things by the way of tribes that lingered in the pristine culture, and these she hands to us.

The second witness is Language, feminine in gender among all races. Already has her testimony brought Aryan peoples into a common brotherhood and showed the status of the common ancestress before the separation.

The third witness is Archæology—or Archaiologia, as Pinto wrote it. She wears an apron, and in her hands she carries a very ancient digging stick, by means of which she opens the graves of the dead and points to this one as of a man, to this one as of a woman. The skulls and bones, the relics of useful implements—pottery, knives, jewellery—brought forth and held in the light of modern science, assume their former relations and repeat the story of their owners many centuries ago.

---

[*] Campbell, Journey through North Corea. Proceedings of the Royal Geographical Society, London, 1892, vol. xiv, p. 145. Also Leclerc, Rev. Scient., Paris, 1893, vol. li, p. 72.

The fourth to take the stand is commonly called Folk-lore. This witness can recall all the superstitious beliefs and practices among the poor and ignorant about rocks and plants and trees; about goblins and witches and medical charms; about magic and divination. She is familiar with old-time customs in seasons of festivity, or in the ceremonies of birth and coming of age, of marriage and burial. The games of the young and of grown-up folks, as well as the peculiarities attaching to any region, are at her tongue's end. She can talk to children by the hundred, telling them nursery tales and fables, or gather the adults around her to listen to more serious myths, or traditions, or legends. On occasion she can sing a song or ballad, or lullaby, or repeat riddles and proverbs by the hour. All these contain precious bits of history necessary to the comparative study of culture.

The last witness to come forward will be one now living, a member of any tribe accessible in every continent, belonging to a people that have stood still during all the ages. By visiting enough of these it may be possible to re-edify the structure of very ancient history. At least, this witness will inform us as to what her sisters have been doing in this present century that resembles the primitive woman's work in the past.

By piecing together what they all have to say, the narrative of woman's earliest history will be known. From this it will be possible to reckon what the present owes to her and what should be her lines of progress to success in the future. Clio, Glossa, Archaiologia, Paradosis, and Ethnologia are they whose friendly offices we humbly crave in perfecting this historic study.

We may close this introductory chapter with the significant words of Plutarch : * "Concerning the virtues of

---

* Plutarch, Concerning the Virtues of Women. Morals, Boston. 1870, Little, Brown & Co., vol. i, pp. 340, 341.

women, O Cleanthes, I am not of the same mind with Thucydides. For he would prove that she is the best woman concerning whom there is the least discourse made by people abroad, either to her praise or dispraise; judging that, as the person, so the very name of a good woman ought to be retired and not gad abroad. But to us Gorgius seems more accurate, who requires that not only the face but the fame of a woman should be known to many. For the Roman law seems exceeding good, which permits due praises to be given publicly both to men and to women after death.

"Neither can a man truly any way better learn the resemblance and difference between feminine and virile virtue than by comparing together lives with lives, exploits with exploits, as the product of some great art; duly considering whether the magnanimity of Semiramis carries with it the same character and impression with that of Sesostris, or the cunning of Tanaquil the same with that of King Servius, or the discretion of Porcia the same with that of Brutus, or that of Pelopidas with Timoclea, regarding that quality of these virtues wherein lie their chiefest point and force."

CHAPTER II.

THE FOOD BRINGER.

To cook the dinner, to name the dishes, and to serve the repast is indeed a burdensome task in these days; but the primitive aristologist was more grievously puzzled, though she had not so many courses in her dinner nor so much crockery to worry about.

The division of labour at present requires the whole earth to be ransacked that one may entertain his friends. In early times, on the contrary, a chief might dine his neighbour chief in grandest fashion, and a little coterie of women, styled his wives, would make the whole preparation. In this chapter we are to note the multiplicity of industries set agoing by woman in prehistoric times for the supply of aliment to mankind, in which she brings food and drink, and even medicine, to the use of her family.

To feed the flock under her immediate care, woman had to become an inventor, and it is in this activity of her mind that she is specially interesting here. The hen scratches for her chicks all day long, because Nature has fastened her hoes and rakes and cutting apparatus upon her body. But here stands a creature on the edge of Time who had to create the implements of such industry. It is true that all the ages and all experiences and examples of the zoölogical world were around her. So had they been around other creatures. But the power to associate new ideas constantly and independently were to be for the first time her peculiar endowment as a bringer of food.

Upon three kingdoms of Nature she made requisition to furnish aliment for her species. Each one of these supplied her with food substances, with the means of manipulating them, and with the possibility of serving and storing them. Her ingenious mind accepted the problem and solved it.

In each of these kingdoms, when the light of history rose upon her, the work was nearly done. She had explored them and selected in each the best for her purposes.

In her exploitation of the vegetable world woman first appears as taking from the hands of Nature those fruits and other parts of the plant that are ready for consumption without further preparation. On the next journey she ventured a step further. With digging stick and carrying basket she went to search out roots and such other parts of plants as might be prepared for consumption by roasting or perhaps by boiling with hot stones. On her third journey she gathered seeds of all kinds, but especially the seeds of grasses, which at her hand were to undergo a multitude of transformations. Wherever tribes of mankind have gone women have found out by and by that great staple productions were to be their chief reliance. In Polynesia it is taro and bread fruit. In Africa it is the palm and tapioca, the millet and yams. In Asia it is rice, in Europe the cereals, and in America corn and potatoes, and acorns or piñons in some places. The whole industrial life of woman is built up around these staples. From the first journey on foot to procure the raw material until the food is served and eaten there is a line of trades that are continuous and that are born of the environment. The occupations necessarily grouped around any vegetal industry are the gathering of the plant or parts to be utilized, the transportation of the harvest from the field to the place of storage, the activities necessary to change a raw foodstuff into an elaborated product, and, lastly, the cooking and serving of the meal. It may be stated with much certitude, though there are noteworthy exceptions, that all of these processes in savagery were the function of woman, and in their performance she includes within herself a multitude of callings, some of which now belong largely to men.

In the myth of the aged Navajo and his family, told by Matthews, we read: "Every day while the sons were gone the old man busied himself cutting down saplings with his stone ax and building a house, and the daughters gathered seeds, which constituted the only food of the family."* The Navajos belong to the Athapascan family of the northwestern part of Canada, where the women are very industrious in other matters. They learned the seed industry after they moved to the southwestern portions of the Union in a manner now to be explained.

The Panamint woman, of Death Valley, California, of Shoshonean stock, in harvesting the sand-grass seed (*Oryzopsis membranacea*) carries in one hand a small funnel-shaped basket and in the other a paddle made of wicker-work, resembling a tennis racket. With this she beats the grass panicles over the rim of the basket, causing the seeds to fall inside. When the basket becomes filled she takes it on her back, holding it in place with her two hands brought over her shoulders, or by means of a soft band of buckskin across her forehead.† This woman's ancestors taught the daughters of the aged Navajo in the myth to gather seeds and feed their family.

The thousand and one manipulations at the hands of women formerly practiced on vegetal substances preparatory to consumption were all anticipatory of methods

---

* Matthews's Mountain Chant, Fifth An. Rep. Bur. Ethnol., p. 386.

† F. V. Coville, American Anthropologist, Washington, 1892, vol. v. p. 351.

now in operation on a grander scale. They were the predecessors of harvesters, waggons and freight trains, granaries and elevators, mills and bakeries. The little wicker basket, holding about a barrel, set up in some northern California hut to preserve acorns, the larger granaries in

FIG. 5.—BEAN GRANARY, MOJAVE INDIANS, SOUTHERN CALIFORNIA. (After Henshaw.)

the Mojave country, the pretty structures conspicuous in the pictures of African villages, are all familiar now on the farm and in the great grain elevators.

One has only to glance at the many illustrations of granaries in such a work as Schweinfurth's Artes Africanæ * to learn the origin of Mohammedan domes. The author just named says: "The receptacles for corn in these curi-

---

* Artes Africanæ, Leipsic, 1875, Brockhaus, pl. xx. Also in other places. Holub, Führer durch das Museum, etc., Prag, 1892, Otta., p. 27.

ous structures, formed of unburnt clay taken from the mushroom-shaped structures of the termites, are very artistically connected on the top of the pile by means of a basketlike scaffolding, and in a most regular manner ornamented by several mouldings. Equally protected from moisture and from the teeth of termites and rats, these storehouses for corn, always situated near to the dwelling huts, are also through their height more difficult of access to thieves."

In this rôle of inventing the granary and protecting food from vermin the world has to thank woman for the domestication of the cat. There may be some dispute as to who has the honour of subduing the dog and the milk- and fleece-yielding animals. But woman tamed the wild-cat for the protection of her granaries. Of the time when this heartless beast laid down its arms and enlisted in her service no one knoweth. Already at the dawn of written history in Egypt the cat was sacred to Sekhet, or Pasht, daughter of Ra and wife of Ptah. Then as now the cat and the goddess had among their other qualifications the faculty of seeing in the dark. Her method of domestication was to secure the young wild-cats and rear them about her household as playthings for her children, and to gratify them in their instincts of prowling and seizing.

There is abundant proof among the three typical divisions of humanity still living in savagery—the American Indian, the negroid races, and the Malayo-Polynesians—that women were the builders and owners of the first caches, granaries, and storehouses of provisions. A stroll through any market house will be convincing that they still keep up the very ancient custom of guarding bread.

When the time came to grind her seeds the woman discovered two implements, one of which is now exalted to the service of the apothecary, and may be seen any day over his door covered with gold leaf; the other holds its own as the implement of the miller.

Mortars are common enough in savagery, occurring in the forms of stone with stone pestles, of wood with wooden pestles, of wood with stone pestles, but stone mortars with wooden pestles are rare. For the fabrication of these woman was entirely competent.

The arctic women grind nothing for food, but, the moment one passes Mount St. Elias, coming southward, mortars occur in abundance for pulverising dried fish.

There is then a stretch of country devoid of this apparatus until the acorn and piñon region of California is reached, when the mortar and pestle again make their appearance. In northern California the inventor has produced a unique device—a stone mortar, very shallow, around the outer border of which she glues a hopper of finely woven basketry, her own handiwork. In the absence of cement, she holds the hopper down so firmly with her limbs, while she pounds with the pestle held in her hands, that only the fine meal escapes between the hopper and the stone, and falls on the mat or skin upon which the stone sits. Just across in Nevada the Shoshone squaw selects from the mountain stream a smooth, spheroidal, water-worn boulder of trap, granite, or lava, of convenient size to carry from one camp to another. Constant pounding upon the side most convenient gives a start, and further use deepens the cavity. Wherever such material was scarce or hard wood was plentiful in the land of maize the wooden mortar was in constant use, either with the wooden or the stone pestle. The people of the Pacific and the Indian Ocean had little need for mortars and pestles. But on the Asiatic continent, for hulling rice and for bruising food, they were in daily employ.

Africa also south of the Sahara is noted for this method of grinding wherever the women can procure the necessary materials, and this has been their plan from time immemorial. In tropical Africa,* and among all heathen negro tribes, without exception, the work of grinding grains devolves upon the women. It begins with bruising the winnowed corn by means of wooden pestles in a wooden mortar, and subsequently grinding it finer on a large stone by aid of a smaller one. Sifting and winnowing effect the rest.

In the old plantation days in the United States every farm was equipped with a mortar and pestle of wood for hominy crushing.

"The Panamint people have learned to cultivate a little patch by irrigation, but in their primitive condition they ate the nut of the pine (*Pinus monophylla*). In early autumn the women beat the cones from the trees, gathered them in baskets, and spread them out to dry. As soon as the cones had cracked, the primitive harvester beat out the nuts, raked off the cones, and gathered her crop, which she carried on her back to a dry place among the rocks, where she made a cache of her spoils.† When she was ready to serve them she put them into a shallow basket with some coals, and shook the mass around until the nuts were roasted. Thus prepared, she and her lord and her little family either shelled and munched them without further preparation, or she ground them in a wooden mortar with a stone pestle, to be eaten dry or made into soup. Every other edible seed this practical botanist gathered and roasted in the same way, but some of them were so hard that she had to grind them between two hard, flat stones, after the manner of the Mexicans." The method of winnowing here described was practiced every-

---

* Schweinfurth, Artes Africanæ, London, 1875, pl. vi.

† Coville, American Anthropologist, Washington, 1892, vol. v, pp. 351-360.

where in North America where seed food was eaten. The illustration here cited from the Panamint represents a common scene among tribes of the Shoshonean, Athapascan, Yuman, Zuñian, Tañoan, and Keresan stocks in the Southwestern States of the Union. Here is a veritable Toeoia, whose sieve is not only seed proof but absolutely waterproof. Her problem is to burn up the chaff, roast the seed, and to gather her harvest on the blanket at her feet.

Of the California Indian women Mr. J. F. Snyder says: "I have seen them gathering acorns in huge conical baskets, confined to the back by a band around the forehead, and then have watched them constructing the acorn cribs in the mountains for winter storage. I have seen them pounding the acorns in stone mortars which their own hands had quarried, leaching the meal in a sand filter to take out the bitter taste, and cooking the mush in water-tight baskets with hot stones. Along many of the streams there are bare flat ledges of rock in which the squaws have worked numerous holes, eight to ten inches deep, which they use as acorn mortars, pounding them with long stone pestles." Here we have in one woman harvester, builder, carrier, miller, and stone worker.

The second class of implements for grinding seeds were in the nature of mills—and women grinding at a mill have passed into a proverb.

If a great stone cylinder be suspended on a shaft revolving on a pivot and over a similar stone which is stationary, that is the form of mill which has been in vogue latterly up to the invention of the roller process, which is a return to the more primitive crusher.

The same type of apparatus small enough for women to turn is the affair of which Biblical and other ancient writers tell us. But simpler than the pivoted Irish quern are the metates and mullers of tropical portions of Ameries. Whoever has seen a woman with tub and washboard cleansing clothes will have no difficulty in imagining the tub to be a box of stone, the washboard to be a slab of hard, porous rock, and the piece of clothing to be a small slab of the same hard material. By the selfsame free motion of the woman's body the slab is rubbed up and down

FIG. 6.—THE PRIMITIVE MILLER. CALIFORNIA INDIAN WOMAN USING METATE AND MULLER.

and sidewise upon the nether stone, while the kneeling miller constantly brings a small quantity of the corn between the surfaces. The amount of fineness depends upon the time bestowed upon the work. The rectilinear motion of the muller becomes often curvilinear in the hand of the grinder. The metate and muller, therefore, are older than the quern. Just how the latter is related to the metate or to the mortar is not known. Thomson gives the following account of the hand mill in the Holy Land:

"From this on southward through Philistia there are no mill streams, and we shall not cease to hear the hum of the hand mill at every village and Arab camp morning and evening. When at work two women sit at the mill facing each other; both have hold of the handle by which the upper is turned round upon the nether millstone. The one whose hand is disengaged throws in the grain through the hole in the upper stone. It is not correct to say that one pushes it half round and then the other seizes the handle. Both retain their hold. I can not recall an instance in which men were grinding at a hand mill.*

It is again the woman, ransacking the vegetal kingdom, who learns to know the drinks that Nature yields.

"It is a singular sight to see a Quissama woman, in Angola, barelegged, climb up the gigantic palm trees, with a calabash of immense size around her neck. As soon as the top branch is reached and she succeeds in tapping the tree with a piece of rough iron, and finds that it gives vent, the woman then suspends the calabash in order that the liquid may flow into it. She then descends the tree, and in the course of about twelve hours again climbs up, this time to take down the calabash, which is full of palm beer."†

In the chapter on woman as a beast of burden, and in what follows concerning her mineral industries, will be explained more fully the mission of women as the guar-

---

* Thomson, The Land and the Book, New York, 1880, vol. i, p. 108. Figure on page 107.

† Price, J. Anthrop. Inst., London, 1872, vol. i, p. 190. For the middle American drink preparations, see Im Thurn, Indians of British Guiana, London, 1883, p. 310; also numerous authors on Polynesian Kava.

dian and patron of springs and wells and devices leading up to our more convenient water supply and hydrotechny.

There are in many lands plants which in the natural state are poisonous or extremely acrid or pungent. The women of these lands have all discovered independently that boiling or heating drives off the poisonous or disagreeable element. The Indians of southern California gather the leaves and stems of several cruciferous plants, throw them into hot water, then rinse them out in cold water five or six times, then dry them and use them as boiled cabbage. This washing removes the bitter taste and certain substances which are likely to produce nausea and diarrhœa.* The removal of poisonous matter from tapioca by means of hot water is the discovery of savage women.

The common reed of the Southwest (*Phragmites vulgaris*) furnishes a kind of sugar. In early summer, when the plants have attained nearly their full size, the women cut them and dry them in the sun, after which they grind them and separate the finer portion by sifting. They mould the moist, sticky flour thus obtained into a thick, gumlike mass, set it over a fire and roast it until it swells and browns slightly, and in this taffylike state it is eaten.†

Honey is largely an animal product, and all the primitive folk had to do was to climb for it. But many sweet fruits were cooked with flour, and meat, and fish to make savory dishes.

Up to this point our study is with the very lowest grades of food-getting from vegetables. But long before the days of discoverers and explorers who wrote about them, women in America, Africa, and the Indo-Pacific were

---

* Coville, *op. cit.*, p. 354. † Ibid., p. 355.

farmers, and had learned to use the digging stick, the hoe, and even a rude plough. Livingstone figures a double-handled hoe that was dragged through the ground by women.* The evolution of primitive agriculture was first from seeking after vegetables to moving near them, weeding them out, sowing the seed, cultivating them by hand, and finally the use of farm animals.

The exploitation of the mineral kingdom by women in savagery was chiefly in the search and care for water. Their habitations were erected near to springs or streams, and from these to the domestic hearth an uninterrupted caravan has marched since the uses of fire. In the discussion of other employments will appear the multitudinous inventions for carrying, storing, and using water. The effect of environment in deciding whether the vessel shall be of skin, or bark, or wood, or pottery is worthy of attention.

In speaking of the Malays, Wallace says: "Thin, long-jointed bamboos form the Dyaks' only water vessels, and a dozen of them stand in the corner of every house. They are clean, light, and easily carried, and are in many ways superior to earthen vessels for the same purpose. Water is also brought to the houses by little aqueducts formed of large bamboo split in half and supported on cross sticks of various heights so as to give it a regular fall."†

The scooping out of a spring deeper and deeper forms a well, and the lengthening of a conducting pipe converts it into an aqueduct or a conduit. Both of these industries had very humble origins at the hands of women.

Whether women invented the suction pump may remain in doubt, but the Bakalahari dames, when they wish to draw water, provide twenty or thirty ostrich eggshells

---

* Travels, etc., in South Africa, New York, 1858, p. 442.
† Wallace, Malay Archipelago, New York, 1890, 00.

and place them in a net. They tie a bunch of grass to one end of a short reed for a strainer and insert the apparatus in a hole as deep as the arm will reach, then ram down the wet sand firmly round it. Applying the mouth to the free end of the reed, they draw the water upward by sucking, and discharge it into an ostrich shell, guiding the stream by means of a straw. The whole stock of water passes through the woman's mouth as a pump. The shells are taken home and buried in wet sand for future use.*

The first article one notices on entering a modern kitchen is a knife. It may be in Japan, it may be in Aryan countries. No cook, purveyor, or commissary can do without a knife. Most of these articles are stamped "Sheffield," which I take to be a synonym for all peaceful knife-makers in the world. If in Sheffield men make swords and bayonets and daggers and spears and battle axes, that does not appear. They are cutlers, and that leads to the question, Who were the first cutlers, the real founders of Sheffield? When a Roman soldier was armed with a knife he was called *cultellarius*, which is not very good Latin. *Cultellurius* was a little knife; *cultellus*, a small knife; and *culter*, a ploughshare, also a vintner's knife, a butcher knife, a cooking knife, a knife in general. As woman was the leading character in the first rendition of all these homely dramas, it matters not which definition we use as a test—she was the primitive cutler.

The men of those early times made weapons and all the paraphernalia of their daily use, and so did their female companions chip off the spall or flake of flinty rock to make their knives withal. They each carried at their sides a hard bit of bone, answering in every respect to the

---

* Livingstone, Travels and Researches in South Africa. New York, 1858, p. 53.

butcher's steel, and gave therewith from time to time new edge to their homely cutlery.

And while we are looking at this rude implement we may follow the owner through a series of employments involving its use. The husband has slain the deer, the elk, the moose, the musk ox, the bear, the buffalo, and there his share of the operation ends. The woman must now go out to the game equipped to transport the slain victim home, or she must—on her sledge or on her back—get it near her door. Her rôle of pack animal will be noticed later on. She removes the skin and rolls it up,* and then divides the carcass for immediate consumption or to be dried. In these she is a butcher, and the whole earth are her shambles. This meat she then proceeds to apportion according to the rules of her tribe and her clan.†

The Eskimo women have a knife precisely like the mincing choppers in every kitchen, which they use at present for all sorts of work. But is it not interesting to find dainty little women almost at the jumping-off place of the globe holding on to the primeval form of an implement as well as its use whose modern representative does service both in our kitchens and our saddler shops? The saddler and his wife now divide between them an implement which many thousands of years ago would have been hers alone, and he would have been defiled to touch it. With it, in that early day, she made harness for dogs and for herself to wear, besides cutting out clothing and tents, skinning animals, and mincing food.

This same butcher and cook, in one, invented another industry in this connection and fabricated another stone implement. There are seasons on the plains of the great

---

* For her treatment of the hide see Chapter VII.
† Cf. Dodge. Our Wild Indians, Hartford, 1883, p. 206. Compare Dorsey, Third An. Rep. Bur. Ethnol., 263.

West—on the borders of desert regions everywhere, for that matter—where the aridity of the atmosphere is sufficient to cure meat and fish without the aid of salt. The Indian women would in the aboriginal days cut buffalo and other meat into thin strips, hung it out to dry in the sun, and then take a stick or flail and beat it until it was perfectly fine. What a curious thrashing floor was that!

Fig. 7.— ... Pemmican Maker pounding Cracklins and Dried Meat—Sioux Indians, Dakota. (After Jungling.)

With a stone maul—their own handiwork—made by pecking a groove in a boulder of the proper shape, fastening a hickory handle about this groove, and incasing handle and head in wet rawhide until it shrunk and bound all fast and strong, they crushed the bones of the animals slain and extracted the marrow.

The pulverized meat was then sewed up in sacks of buffalo rawhide and the melted marrow and other choice fat poured over it, exactly as the country housewife to this very day imbeds sausages in jars of hog's lard to keep them over for future seasons of scarcity. When this became solid it was called pemmican, and the cleverly made mulls may be seen in any ethnological museum.

This pemmican was used by the Indians as an article of barter. In old times it was eaten by United States troops for rations, and is said to have been extremely nutritious, though malodorous.

This same mull served the good women other purposes. With it they broke the dry wood of the forest for faggots, drove down the tent pins, and, on occasion, gave the *coup de grace* to their enemies.

It is a little difficult to sum up the operations in this daily act of drudgery, each of which would demand a separate manufactory, such as stone cutter, wood worker, rawhide manufacturer, meat curer, inventor of a mechanism of exchange, all in addition to the fundamental business of feeding her clan.

The bone-breaking mulls are most widely distributed. Captain Ray brought from Point Barrow choice specimens in the jade of that region, made in shape of cylinders, having handles of reindeer antler lashed on with thongs of walrus rawhide.

In many parts of the world broken bones have been found in shell heaps, etc., among the *débris* of feasts, and the apparatus for breaking them could also have been discovered; but the ancient cook, I fear, has been usually voted a stupid thing, who would extract marrow as monkeys open cocoanuts—namely, with the first rock they could pick up.

The butcher's cleaver is also a grandchild of the woman's bone-breaking mall of stone.

The cooking of vegetal substances in savagery underwent an evolution something like the following: 1, parching, as we do popcorn and peanuts; 2, roasting or baking in pits with hot stones; 3, in the form of mush or gruel; 4, as griddle cakes, often very thin; 5, as hominy, rice, potatoes, etc., boiled in a pot, either on the fire or with hot stones. Bread, except as thick griddle cakes, is unknown in savagery. The Scotch oatcakes and bannocks of pea or barley meal, the scones of the East Indies, the Passover cakes of the Israelites, the dampers of Australia, the hoe cake in the United States, are all of a kind—flour mixed with water and heated; which makes the starch more soluble. An excellent example of parching has been given in Mr. Coville's account of the Panamint woman. In addition to his account of roasting in pits with stones, it will be curious to note this custom in Polynesia. Indeed, this is a matter of such importance that professional men cooks supersede the women in the preparation of food pits.*

"'If there be any one discovery owing to chance, it is that of leaven. The world was indebted to the economy of some person or other for this happy discovery, who, in order to save a little dough, mixed it with the new. They would, no doubt, be surprised to find that this old dough, so sour and distasteful itself, rendered the new bread so much lighter, more savoury, and easy of digestion.'† More probably leaven arose in hot countries, in the preference shown for the acid flavour of stale porridge (compare the practice of adding curds to fresh milk in order to turn it sour for immediate consumption), as in the caffa or porridge ball of Guinea, which is considered insipid while fresh (Lander)."‡

The most primitive of all meat or fish cooking was the roast or the toast—that is, the bit of meat or the fish was

---

* Consult Payne, History of America, New York, 1892, vol. 1, p. 334.

† Goguet, Origin of Laws, vol. 1, p. 105.

‡ Payne, loc. cit.

hung on a stick in front of the fire or wrapped in harmless leaves and buried in the ashes. There did not seem

FIG. 6.—TURKISH VILLAGERS—CARRYING ON THE HEAD, THE SHOULDERS, AND THE HIPS.

to be any demand for patent attorneys in that. The processes have been invented over and over again, and the fireplace could scarcely be dignified with the name of hearth.

Out-of-door ovens, pits lined with stones on which fires had been kindled and coals accumulated, were known by very primitive tribes, and some of the patterns will be described; but our concern is with cooking devices. And this brings the aristologist to the cooking pot. Frying pans were of much later origin.

Now the savage *cuisinière* had her choice from the beginning to bring her pot to the fire or to bring her fire to the pot. In the latter case she found a mortar-shaped rock, or made a water-tight basket, or hollowed out with stone tools and fire brands a log of wood, or dug a hole in the ground and lined it with rawhide or woven stuff. Into this she put her meat or mush, and also clean hot stones, which kept the pot a-boiling. In the former case she had to become a stone worker or a potter in order to put the cooking vessel on the fire.

In the chapter on the weaver the method of manufacturing the basketry cooking pot will be set forth, and in the chapter on the potter attention will be paid to the origin of cooking-dishes. Here the boiling trough and the "olla," or cooking pot of stone, will be described.

Whether women actually felled trees with stone axes it is a little difficult to ascertain. Certain it is that they helped in the work by the dexterous use of fire. As soon as the tree was felled, or taking advantage of the wind giant's sport, they burned and hacked off a convenient length of the trunk; then, gathering from the forests a supply of fat pine knots, they burned out the cavity of the future boiler. They carefully watched the progress of the fire, and when it threatened to spread laterally, they checked its course in that direction by means of strips of green bark or mud or water. As soon as the ashes and charred wood prevented the further action of the fire, this marvellous Gill-at-all-trades removed the fire and brushed out the *débris* with an improvised broom * of grass. Then, by means of a scraper of flint which she had made, she dug away the charcoal until she had exposed a clean surface of wood. The firing and scraping were repeated until the "dugout" assumed the desired form. The trough completed, it was ready to do the boiling for the family as soon as the meat could be prepared and the stones heated. This apprenticeship of fire in woodworking calls for woman's help in more industries than one not strictly her own.

Every savage knows that stones heated and brought in contact with water are fractured hopelessly. But there is no exception to this rule in the class of rocks usually called soapstone, steatite, potstone. The aboriginal mineralogist, after scouring the earth, discovered this fact. All over Eskimo land both lamps and cooking pots are made of this material. In one locality, where it seems to be absent, mud from the tundra is wrought into a rude pottery for the same purpose. Quarries of soapstone, anciently worked, have been found in eastern North America, and in them not only fragments of broken pots, but the quartzite tools with which the quarrying and the scraping out were done. The fragments lately discovered reveal the fact that the shallow, open, tray-shaped vessel of the Algonquin resembled that of the Eskimo. But one must go to southern California, among the graves of the extinct tribes of the Santa Barbara Islands and the mainland opposite, to get acquainted with a very dainty stone-working woman. The steatite pots of that region are almost globular, the mouths are only a few inches in diameter, and the walls are in many examples less than an inch in thickness. Many are capable of holding several gallons,

---

* The early occurrence of the broom is quite significant in this connection, admitted on all sides to be to our day one of the industrial perquisites of the sex.

and numbers of them show long-continued exposure to fire. The etymologists of our language seem to be in doubt whether the word "seethe" meant originally to burn as a sacrifice or to boil. At any rate, long before Jacob sold pottage for his father there were abundance of seething pots all over the world, made of wood, or grass, or stone, or clay, as Nature furnished the material, and good women invented the art and apparatus for boiling food.

The elaboration of the dinner pot was a work of the ages. The traders who first visited the North American Indians could have offered no better boon to the women than the brass kettles and the faithful iron pot. At the same time they placed in the hands of the men the gun, the pistol, the iron arrowhead. What the latter did has been written; the former has scarcely been mentioned.

These kettles received by the Indian women were the acme of a long series of inventions beginning with a bit of soapstone that would not crack in the fire.

The earliest pots had no legs, but were propped up by loose stones against the base, serving the twofold purpose of preventing the tipping of the vessel and of lifting it up to allow the air to circulate thereunder and to create a draught.

One sunny day a company of savage women were alternately chatting and chipping in a soapstone quarry, when it occurred to one of them to leave a bit of the stone projecting here and there for legs. Happy thought! No sooner said than done. And after that all soapstone pots had legs.

Whether it was the stimulating sunshine that brightened the woman's wits, or the purely accidental leaving of an ugly hump or two that proved to be blessings in disguise, or seeing the birds hopping around on legs, that suggested the leaving the bits of stone on the pot, no one knows. It was much safer and easier than propping up a round-bottomed pot, and so it went into use.

There are, indeed, among ethnologists opposing schools of interpreting this simple act, some minimizing the poor woman's share therein, others giving her all the praise and Nature none.

Before dismissing the patient creature who all this time has been practicing for our instruction a multiplicity of arts it may not be amiss to ask her what is done with the fish and flesh that is not immediately to be cooked. To this she would reply, "This portion will be smoked, another will be sun-dried and ground and packed in marrow, as explained in describing the pemmican malt." If she were asked why she did not cure it with salt, she would say no savage woman ever thought of that. Salted food is a product of civilization."*

These same people dried clams, oysters, fish, and meat.

Mrs. Allison, in her account of the Simalkameen Indians, of Canada, produces a bill of fare provided by the women so diversified and elaborate that I beg leave to copy it: " Formerly their food consisted of venison, fresh and dried game of all kinds, beaver tails and bears' paws being esteemed as dainties. The seeds of the sunflower pounded furnished a sort of flour that was made into cakes. The root of the *spultum* was dug in the spring, and eaten either boiled with the bark of the service berry or dried. The cactus was roasted and eaten with meat. The *skilome* (a sort of wild potato), growing abundantly in wet land, was gathered in its season. Various edible fungi in the earth or in the woods were much used. The long black lichens on which the deer fed were gathered and soaked a long time in the river; a pit was then dug and

---

* Lord, Mackenzie, Poole, Vancouver, Dunn, Mofras, Pemberton, Parker, quoted in Bancroft, Native Races, vol. i.

lined first with a layer of hot stones; over these a layer of green branches was placed; the wet lichens were then put in the pit and covered with another layer of green branches, and more stones and weeds; the whole was then earthed over. When the pit was opened some days later the lichen was found to have run into a substance resembling India rubber in taste and tenacity. This was cut into cakes, but it is not much wonder that the delicacy has been given up. The berry of the milshettleman (or nic-a-nuc) was called *ike*, and when dried and pounded was used as sweetening. The nic-a-nuc, or kinnikinic, is an evergreen creeping plant with a brilliant red berry. The leaves are still dried and smoked when tobacco is scarce. The wild onions are still dug and cooked in pits in the manner of cooking lichens. There are numerous edible roots; the bulb of the tiger lily and a yellow snowdrop are much used, also a kind of celery. Lehine is made from the soap berry, which is beaten with the hand in water till it forms a stiff froth resembling soapsuds. There is a tea, said to possess many virtues, which the Hudson's Bay Company tried to introduce into England under the name of Labrador tea. The service berry was a staple with the Simalkameens. When the berries were ripe mats were laid under the bushes, and the berries beaten off them on to the mats and dried in the sun. A portion was then reserved for home consumption; the rest were put in sacks made of rushes strung together by threads of wild hemp, and traded with either the Hope or Okanagan Indians for dried salmon or water-tight baskets, in the manufacture of which the Hope Indians excelled."[*]

The Nutka women of Vancouver Island had four styles of serving food, says Bancroft:

---

[*] Mrs. S. S. Allison, J. Anthrop. Inst., London, 1892, vol. xxi, p. 308.

1. Boiled—the mode *par excellence* applicable to every kind of food, and effected by hot stones in wooden vessels, carved out of the giant cedar wood with great skill.
2. Steamed—of rarer use—by pouring water over the food laid on a bed of hot stones, and covered over tightly with mats.
3. Roasted—rarely practiced, except with smaller fish and clams.
4. Raw, as in the case of fish spawn, and, indeed, any other kind of food when conveniences were not at hand.*

Among the ancient Mexicans the preparation of food was most elaborate. Maize, when in the milk, was eaten boiled; when dry it was parched or roasted; but the commonest form of serving dry corn was in the form of tortillas, the standard bread, then as now, in all Latin America. The women boiled the corn in limewater. When the hulls would come off freely the mass was crushed on a metate with a muller or roller, and was then kneaded by the hands of the woman into thin, round cakes, and baked on earthen or stone griddles. Sometimes they were flavored with plants or flowers. There were many kinds of this tortilla bread, varying with the kinds of corn, the degree of fineness of the flour, and the recipe for preparation. *Atolli* was a kind of thick gruel. The mashed corn was mixed with water and boiled down, variously sweetened and seasoned, and eaten both hot and cold. Beans (*frijoles*) were eaten green or dry or ground into flour.

Chili or pepper was likewise treated. A sauce was also made from it, forming their only spice. Fish, flesh,

---

* Bancroft, Native Races, New York, 1874–'76, vol. i, p. 167. See references under "Women," vol. v, p. 727. Upon Indian bills of fare also consult Morgan, N. A. Rev., 1869 and 1870, on the Food Preparations of the Columbia Region; and Matthews, Navajo Mountain Chant, Fifth An. Rep. Bur. Ethnol., p. 430.

and fowl, salted and fresh, were stewed, boiled, and roasted in every conceivable proportion, the product taking a different name with every change of ingredients.*

Next to chili, says Bancroft, salt or *iztatl* was the condiment most used by the ancient Mexicans, and most of the supply came from the valley of Mexico. The best was made by boiling the water from the salt lake in large pots, and was preserved in white cakes or balls. It was oftener, however, led by trenches into shallow pools and evaporated by the sun. The work would seem to have been done by women, since Sahagun speaks of the women and girls employed in this industry as dancing at the feast in honour of the goddess of salt in the month of Tecuilhuitontli.†

The Indian women of Guiana are excellent purveyors. They have but one way of cooking meat or fish, and that is by boiling it down into a sort of thick soup, with peppers and cassareep, or the juice of strained cassava boiled down to a sirup. The cassareep reduces all meat to one common flavour—its own—and has antiseptic qualities which keep meat boiled in it good for a long time. The result is the far-famed pepper pot, which all settlers in the West Indies have learned to make and to like.

The staple vegetable food is afforded by the roots of cassava (*Manihot utilissima*), which are made into bread.

No scene is more characteristic of Indian life than that of women preparing cassava. One woman, squatting on her hams and armed with a big knife, peels off the skin of the root and washes it. Another woman, grasping one of the roots with both hands, scrapes it up and down an oblong board or grater studded with small frag-

---

* The whole subject of Nahua cuisine is well worked out in Bancroft, Native Races, New York, 1874-'76, vol. ii, pp. 851-857, with references to many ancient authorities.

† Bancroft, Native Races, New York, 1874-'76, vol. ii, p. 362.

ments of stone like a nutmeg grater. One end of the grater stands in a trough, the other rests on the woman's knees. It is violent exercise. As the woman scrapes, her body swings down and up again from the hips. The rhythmic "swish" caused by the scraping is the chief sound in the house, for the labour is too heavy to permit talking. The grated cassava is placed into a long sieve or matapie so woven that a weight on the bottom will compress and open the sides, and we have press and strainer in one. The cassava, saturated with its poisonous juices, is forced into this matapie and suspended from one of the beams of the house. Through a loop in the bottom of the matapie a heavy pole is passed, one end of which rests on the ground. A woman now sits on the pole, and her weight stretches the strainer and forces the poisonous juice, which is caught in a vessel below. This is afterward boiled, and becomes cassareep. The cassava is taken from the matapie, broken, sifted, and baked into griddle cakes, which are dried in the sun. The cooking is done after the following fashion: A large flat slab of stone is placed over a fire, and on this griddle a thin layer of meal is spread. A woman, fan in hand, sits by the fire watching. With her fan she smoothes the upper surface of the cake and makes its edges round. In a few minutes one side is done, and when the cake is turned it is done in two minutes more. They are next thrown on the roof to dry, and I have often vainly tried to imitate the skill with which an Indian woman "quoits" up one of these large and thin cakes on to the roof, often high above her head. When thoroughly dried the bread is hard and crisp.

Of the starchy matter remaining in the wickerwork matapie, called *smov*, the Carib women make a cake which is half gelatinous and has a pleasant subacid flavour.[*]

---

[*] Im Thurn, Indians of British Guiana, London, 1883, pp. 260–265.

This rather extended account of pepper pot and cassava is introduced to show how diversified may be the industries of a savage woman. By reading again the description, the Carib woman will be seen in the rôle of potter, butcher, cook, beast of burden, fire maker and tender, miller, stonecutter (stone-griddle maker), most delicate and ingenious weaver, engineer (devising a mechanical press and sieve in one woven bag and using a lever of the third kind), baker, and preserver of food. Add to this her function of brewer, and you have no mean collection of primitive industries performed by one little body, all of which underlie occupations which in our day involve the outlay of millions of dollars and the co-operation of thousands of men.

CHAPTER III.

THE WEAVER.

THERE is no work of woman's fingers that furnishes a better opportunity for the study of techno-geography, or the relationship existing between an industry and the region where it may have been developed, than the textile art. Suppose a certain kind of raw material to abound in any area or country; you may be sure that savage women searched it out and developed it in their crude way. Furthermore, the peculiar qualities and idiosyncrasies of each substance suggest and demand a certain treatment. Women of the lowest grades of culture have not been slow in discovering this; so that between them and the natural product there has been a kind of understanding or co-operation leading to local styles. If these women were moved far away, they carried oftentimes these processes with them and plied the old trade upon such strange materials as they discovered in the new home. The negro women, transported formerly as slaves from Africa to tropical America, found palm trees growing in the Western Hemisphere. They continued to make here the type of coiled basketry they had made in Africa. It is not surprising, therefore, to come upon this art in two hemispheres. In some cases where Indian men have married negro women the mothers have taught the daughters their own arts, and these have come, after a few generations, to consider the arts as indigenous.

It is customary to divide woman's textile industry in

savagery into basket work and weaving. The former art employs more rigid materials, has some stitches of its own, and the products of its operations are vessels made complete in the working.

Weaving, *par excellence*, is the production of a flat textile. It employs usually softer material, its meshes or stitches are plainer, and its products are mats, bags, sails, garments, and the like. The distinction between basketry and weaving, at first, is not well defined, and it will be profitable to consider them together under forms or types of meshes or stitches.

Subsidiary to these chief divisions of the textile art as practiced by women in savagery are spinning, netting, looping, braiding, sewing, and embroidery. Bark-cloth beating, described further on, though Nature does the weaving in this case, is practiced by females in the tropics all round the world.

Each and all of these require tools which the workwomen must fashion for themselves. And, though the earth had the raw materials in abundance, it did not yield them without a search which would do honour to the manufacturers of our day.

Basketry in its coarsest form is the making of crates, winding brush in and out to keep the wind or the sun from the wretched habitation, wattling rods and twigs into fish weirs and game drives. There are no savages on earth so rude that they have no form of basketry. The birds and beasts are basket-makers, and some fishes construct for themselves little retreats where they may hide. Long before the fire maker, the potter, or even the cook, came the mothers of the Fates, spinning threads, drawing them out, and cutting them off. Coarse basketry or matting is found charred in very ancient sepulchres. With few exceptions, women, the wide world over, are the basket-makers, netters, and weavers. The tools of the basket-maker are of the simplest character—those necessary to the harvesting of the material and those used in manufacture. As baskets are made of wood in one place, of bark in another, and of grass, bast, skins, roots, and so forth, according to locality, the tools for harvesting and preparing the material must vary from tribe to tribe. But the one tool that is never absent is the bone awl or stiletto,

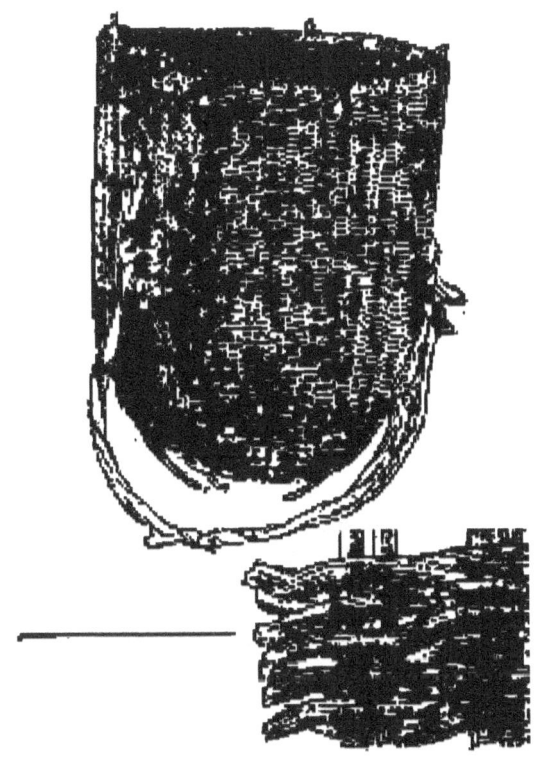

Fig. 4.—Moki Fruit Picker's Basket, Arizona. (After Mason.)

which is useful with every type of manufacture, and is ever present in the graves of primitive women.

In civilization we are somewhat puzzled in our conception of the word "basket," thinking it always to be something like the homely objects displayed about our market houses, manufactured by a weaving of pliable splints over a rigid warp. Here and there, even in this coarse modern ware, a diaper effect is secured by the method of crossing the weft and warp, and a fanciful curl will be seen around the borders now and then; but the general plan of weaving is the same. Most of these examples were made by men.

On the contrary, aboriginal woman's basketry excites the admiration of all lovers of fine work. It is difficult to say which receives the most praise—the forms, the colouring, the patterns, or the delicacy of manipulation.

Primarily, her basketry divides itself into two sorts or types—the *woven* and the *sewed*, the former built up on a warp, the latter produced by the continuous stitching of a coil. Of these two main classes there are many subclasses, which have been necessitated by the nature of the material which the fabricator has at her hands and by the uses to which the products have to be put.

Woven basketry occurs in the form of plain weaving, wickerwork, and twined weaving. A diaper effect is possible in each. Plain or chequer weaving is effected when warp and weft are made of fillets having the same thickness and flexibility. The effect is that of the commonest bagging or cotton cloth. The bottoms of our common splint hampers are chiefly made thus.

Now, when the pristine artist desired to vary this chequer type, she had several possible methods from which to choose.

Among the Algonquin tribes of North America the women had learned that birch and other woods grow in layers. They also discovered that by beating a log or stick of this wood at the proper time of the year the annual rings or layers could be made to peel off. This gave them thick shavings of tough wood, of uniform thickness, which they could cut into ribbons and weave into chequer-

work basketry. The bottom of a Polynesian basket and of an Algonquian basket look precisely alike, though of quite diverse material. In the tribes along the Pacific coast of Washington and British Columbia women treat the tough cedar bark in the same way, and, following the Algonquian method, a great many civilised basket-makers manufacture coarse market hampers in the checker pattern.

One step upward from this plain work was secured when the weaver bethought herself to let each strip overlap two or more instead of one warp strip. This would secure on the surface, still flat, a diaper or diagonal effect, the same as in fine linen weaving. Examine a fish wallet from the Clallams, of the State of Washington, or, much finer, the black and brown ware from Guiana, and it will be seen that the tasteful effect was secured by the simple counting of one, two, three, over and under, from beginning to end.

Further ornamentation of chequer basketry is effected, either in plain or diaper varieties, by dyeing the strips of different colours and working them with proper alternation, producing geometric designs of great beauty.

Finally, these ingenious savages had not failed to discover that the thin strips used not be all of the same width. This was a very happy thought, enabling the weavers to achieve such effects as we should get by manufacturing cloth from ribbons of varying widths and colours. The Samoan Islanders were very happy in this style, using only black and white strips of palm leaf.

Imagine, now, that the savage woman in her wandering has come to the country of twigs, of osiers, of rattan, of reeds, and has got somewhat out of the track of palmleaf, or cedar-bark, or hard-wood splints. Her effort to produce plain, flat chequer weaving would not succeed. Just as likely as not women learned their first lesson on twigs and wattling; in that case, by reducing the size of her material, she arrived at the door of the modern basket-maker. Her ware became wickerwork by an understanding between her and her material. The philosophy of the texture is that the warp splints or sticks remain practi-

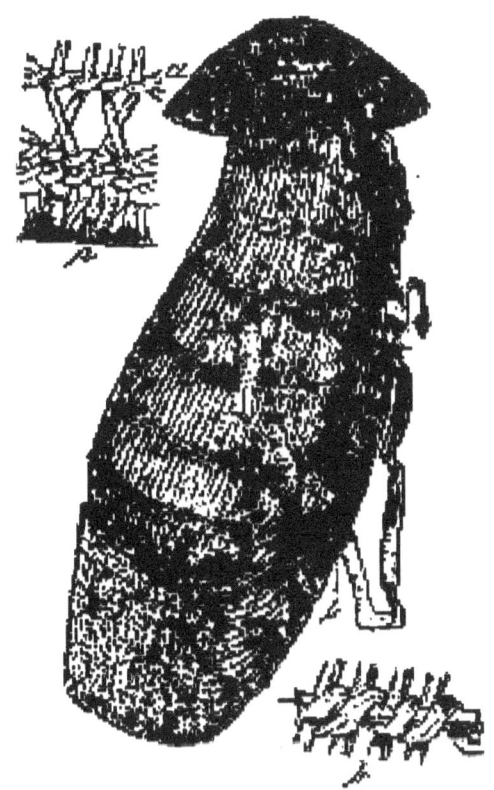

FIG. 11.—TWINED WEAVING BY HUPA WOMAN, NORTHERN CALIFORNIA. (After Mason.)

cally rigid, and the weft pieces bend out and in, over and under the warp pieces, in alternate rows. This gives to the surface of all such work a ridged or wavy appearance.

Still keeping within the notion of weaving, we now come to a type of basketry which must have been in use before womankind separated over the earth at all. I have elsewhere called it the "twined pattern," because the weft is a genuine two-ply twine. It can be easily learned, and its possibilities are endless. In one country it will be made of the root of the spruce, in the next of bark, in the next of twigs, and before we shall have gone the round we shall find twisted threads of the finest material wrought therein.

The warp of this kind of ware is rigid, and is designed to be entirely concealed. The woof is double. That is, the basket-maker takes two weft strands around at a time and gives them a half twist or half twine between each pair of warp strands, pushing her twine down close upon the preceding as she goes on. This last step is not necessary, however, as many open-work pieces are to be seen.

If the reader will think a moment, or drive a few pins in a row along a soft board, and with a coloured and a white cord make a row or two of twined weaving backward and forward, what I am about to explain will be better understood.

In the first place, the twines can be driven so close together as to make the vessel water-tight. Many of the pots in which the aborigines boiled their food by means of heated stones are made after this fashion.

Again, if the root or grass be homogeneous in size throughout, the effect will be uniform and extremely pleasing. Furthermore, by using two colours in the twine each row will be spotted and the spots of adjacent rows up and down may match or alternate so as to give rise to an endless variety of geometric effects. Once this style was mastered by any tribe, its capabilities were illimitable. Many thousands of specimens of pottery are found in the Eastern United States marked on the surface with this very twined weaving, showing that women before the advent of the whites were familiar with it.

So primitive is the twined style of basketry that specinieve from East Africa resemble almost undistinguishably others from Alaska. The wattling is so simple as to suggest itself again and again to various peoples. Yet this very twined or wattled style is capable of the most delicate finish on the surface. In the first place, both elementary strands of each twine or either one may be plain or dyed. And the combination may be changed at each round or at any time. This fact alone gives to the basket woman the greatest possible scope of decoration. But, as at each half turn of twine she has a double stitch, half inside and half outside her basket, it is possible to embroider any figure she likes entirely on the outside without going more than half through the texture. The figure will be on the outside and not appear on the inside at all. Furthermore, there is nothing to prevent her twisting her strands across two or more warp twigs, which, indeed, she does, producing a diaper effect all over the surface. The most beautiful specimens of this twined ware embroidered on the outside are wrought by the women of southeastern Alaska; but the Shoshone and Apache women weave a coarser variety and dip it into hot pitch to make indestructible water bottles. These far excel goatskins, or pottery, or metal canteens for durability and lightness.

The African women practice the twined stitch chiefly on flexible sacks. In the mound and surface pottery left by the ancient Americans, frequent marks of this twined or string weaving are deeply imbedded, leaving the conviction that nets or baskets were used by the ancient potters.

The second class of basketry is the coiled or sewed variety. The most simple as well as the most beautiful types come from Siam and the other lands of the bamboo. The basket-maker provides herself with a number of small rods and a quantity of split bamboo of uniform thickness. The rods are coiled like a watch spring, and united firmly by wrapping a splint of bamboo around two rods continuously from the centre of the bottom of the basket on to the last stitch on the border. As the work goes on the splint passes between two stitches of the preceding round and over the fundamental rod.

Ware quite as beautiful as that of the far East may be seen in the spruce country of North America, where the fine roots furnish a tough and uniform fiber when split.

Now, suppose that the woman in sewing her coil introduced a thin splint or some tough grass between her rods in going around; that would furnish a kind of packing or caulking, which would render the work water-tight. And that is the case with the Indians of British Columbia and Washington in making the baskets in which they boil their food by means of hot stones.

Going further south, the fundamental rod becomes a bunch of coarse grass or the split stems of palm or other tropical plant. The sewing in such cases is done with stripped yucca or finely split and dressed splints of osier or rhus, or stems of grass, so nicely and homogeneously dressed as to enable the maker to produce a basket with hundreds of thousands of stitches over the surface which do not show the slightest variation in size.

Great variety is secured in this ware by the material, by the use of coloured stitches, and by the introduction of birds' feathers, beads, and other decorative objects into the texture.

In the arctic regions spruce root is the material with which the coil is sewed. In California it is split osier and rhus. In the Moki Pueblos it is extremely finely divided yucca fibre, while the stems serve for the body of the coil. The tropical regions of both hemispheres abound with palms of many varieties whose leaves when split supply the very best material for the coiled ware.

In Tierra del Fuego, as well as in Japan, the basket-maker produces an attractive variety in the coiled stitch by passing once around the standing part of the sewing splint, then between the coil rods, down, through, back, and over, to repeat the process for each stitch. Of all the varieties there are many subtypes too intricate to mention here. We have all the generic forms.

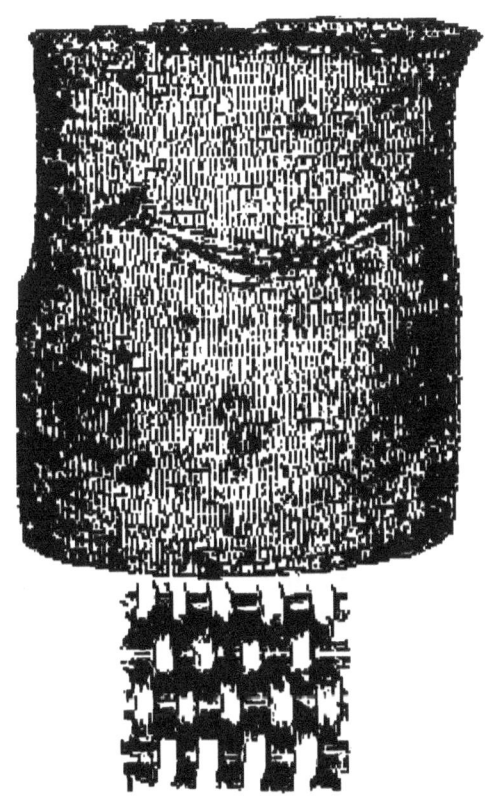

FIG. 12.—COILED WEAVING BY UTE WOMAN, UTAH. (After Mason.)

Mr. F. V. Coville says that the Panamint Indian women, of Death Valley, California, make their baskets of the year-old shoots of tough willow (*Salix lasiandra*), the year-old shoots of aromatic sumac (*Rhus trilobata*), the long black horns on the pods of the unicorn plant (*Martynia probos-*

cidea), and the long red roots of the tree yucca (*Yucca baccatifolia*). The first two named give the light wood colours, the third the black colour, and the fourth the red. The women prepare the willow and the sumac in the same way. The bark is removed from the fresh shoots by biting it loose at the end and tearing it off. The woody portion is scraped to remove bad protuberances and allowed to dry. As these Indians make coiled basketry, the rods just described form the basis of the work. The splints for sewing are prepared as follows: A squaw selects a fresh shoot, breaks off the too slender upper portion, and bites one end so that it starts to split into three nearly equal parts. Holding one of these parts in her teeth and one in either hand, she pulls them apart, guiding the splits with her hand so dexterously that the whole shoot is divided into three nearly even portions. Taking one of these, by a similar process she splits off the pith and the adjacent less flexible tissue from the inner face and the bark from the outer, leaving a pliant, strong, flat strip of young willow or sumac wood. This serves as a fillet in sewing or whipping the coils of the basket together, or in twined basketry two of them become the weft or filling. The coiled basketry is most carefully made. In the olden times a stout, horny cactus spine from the devil's pincushion (*Echinocactus polycephalus*), set in a head of hard pitch, furnished the needle. When grass stems are carried around inside the coil with the shoot of willow or *rhus* they form a water-tight packing for the pot baskets. Patterns in red and black are wrought in by means of fillets from the *martynia* or fern root.*

In Matthews's Mountain Chant it is asserted that the Navajo, before they learned to weave blankets, made mats of grass to lie on and to hang in the doorway and fine

---

* Coville, Am. Anthropologist, vol. v, p. 355.

cedar mats to cover themselves with. The soles of the moccasins were made of hay and the uppers of yucca fibre.* I have elsewhere alluded to the delightful confusion of time and place in this myth. When we recall that the ancestors of the Navajo journeyed to Arizona from Alaska by way of the Pacific coast we are not surprised to find mats of grass and shredded cedar bark and yucca fibre in the same sentence.

A careful study of all woman's work in basketry, as well as in weaving and embroidery, reveals the fact that both in the woven and in the sewed or coil ware each stitch takes up the very same area of surface. When women invented basketry, therefore, they made art possible. Along with this fact, that each stitch on the same basket made of uniform material occupies the same number of square millimetres, goes another fact—that most savage women can count ten at least. The production of geometric figures on the surface of a basket or a blanket, therefore, is a matter of counting. If the enumeration is correct each time the figures will be uniform.

Now, many of the figures on savage basketry contain intricate series of numbers, to remember which cost much mental effort and use of numerals. This constant, every day and hour use of numerals developed a facility in them, and, coupled with form in ornament, made geometry possible. The Polynesian and Melanesian club carver transferred this style of decoration to his woodwork, but the ever-present geometrician of savagery is the woman basket-maker. She knew lines, triangles, squares, polygons of all sorts, meanders and a set of cycloidal curves.

In the chapter on pottery it will be shown how the plasticity of the material rounds off the corners of this rectilinear, and makes the beginning of curvilinear geom-

---

* Matthews, Fifth An. Rep. Bur. Ethnol., p. 368.

etry. Many savage basket-makers, on the other hand, in trying to represent birds and clouds and the human form on their geometric material, conventionalized them, and then abridged these conventionalities, until they produced forms that might be the envy of Chinese rug weavers.

These ancient forms are nowadays copied by pattern drawers for all sorts of work, and the needlewoman and lace-maker of our day follow the lead of their primitive sisters without being aware of it.

Akin to basket and mat making art is hand weaving, or the making of fabrics with the hands, without any frame or machinery whatever. The Mexican and Panama hats are thus produced, and travellers in Africa tell of negro women who sit on the ground with a bundle of split palm leaf by their side and work most delicate matting and other articles with the fingers alone.

The New Zealand and other Polynesian women manufacture mat robes with long pile after the same fashion.*

The fillets from which all of these kinds of hand weaving are done are not twisted, but are either straws or leaves, or bast split finely and evenly. The woman commences in one corner of the piece, and works diagonally toward the opposite corner or end. Instead of carrying each fillet its whole length through a series of warp threads, as in loom weaving, she makes a loop in each fillet as she progresses two or three inches from a starting point, runs this short loop in and out through a dozen or more strands of the series of warp fillets at right angles, and then draws the long end of her fillet through. In the same manner she treats this whole set of fillets, and then takes up the warp set, crossing these in the same manner through the weft. By doubling her strands and making short excursions she

---

* See Ellis. Polynesian Researches, vol. i, p. 180. Compare Turner, Samoa, London. 1884, p. 120.

keeps all her work along parallel, and avoids tangling. She believes in the tailor's method of short threads for quick work. To weave a mat with long pile, it is only necessary not to use up a few inches of each end of her fillets, but to let them remain as fringe and pile. Some of the New Zealand mats woven after this fashion are three feet wide and nine feet long.

Another kind of textile, if we might use the term in this connection, is the result of beating out the bast or inner bark of certain trees. In Mexico, all over Central America, in the South American states certainly as far south as the tropic of Capricorn, throughout equatorial Africa, in Oceanica, both among the brown and the black peoples thereof, culminating in Hawaii, is to be seen a lace-like fabric with fibres intertwining like paper or felt, or in coarser fashion. Some pieces thus made are of immense size. There is one in the National Museum in Washington forty feet long and over ten feet wide. In the Australasian area the stuff is never cut into garments, but is made up into long bolts, as we make calico, and stamped with patterns, some of which are exceedingly attractive. In America men as well as women manufacture the cloth. Indeed, it is said that the India-rubber gatherers, when an old tunic becomes too much soiled and infested, have a knack of beating a clean shirt out of a single cylinder of bark. All of the costume of the Andean tribes, decorated with shells, teeth, seeds, and feathers, has the bark cloth for foundation.

In Hawaii the manufacture of bark cloth was the work of women exclusively, and the female chief took pride in the sheets of paper-like cloth she had formed by her own skill and toil. A log of hard wood, smooth on top, a variety of hand clubs, and calabashes, to hold water or mucilaginous fluids, were all the instruments necessary in the manufacture of *kapa* or *tapa* ("the beaten"). The sound of the beater upon the log was quite musical, and the women are said to have signalled to one another thus from settlement to settlement.*

The bast of the cottonwood, the willow, the linden, the cedar, will not make *tapa* or bark cloth, but the good woman of the forest many centuries ago discovered that it will fray or fringe or shred under proper treatment, and so she applied her ingenious mind to this operation. Introductorily to this art, as into all other arts, fingers preceded tools. So she set to work fraying long pieces into fringes, out of which she made petticoats or divided skirts.

But farther north, from Columbia River to the Fraser mouth, to heckle the fibrous cedar bark, she drove two short stakes into the ground, fastened a cross piece to their tops, and then, with a dull chopping or breaking knife of bone, separated the filaments until they resembled silk.

The Indian hemp (*Apocynum cannabinum*), common over the United States and Canada, was treated as modern spinners treat flax to remove the tough fibre, and in South America cotton was gathered and picked from the seed by hand. These simple processes were repeated in Africa and in Polynesia, in Mexico and Central America, in each case upon pita fibre or palm leaf or cocoa bark, as the region suggested.

Among these rude inventors of thread-making the woman who worked in sinew is not to be forgotten. She removed the tough tendon from the back or leg of the deer and other mammals, dried it in the sun, and then scraped and shredded it as long as fibres would separate. Owing to the toughness of the material and the long "staple," this process of separation could be carried to any degree of tenuity. Some of the thread of the Eskimo

---

* Brigham, Bishop Mus. Catalogue, Honolulu, 1892, p. 23. Ellis, Polynes. Res., vol. iv, pp. 109, 172, 184.

women is quite fine enough for our smallest sewing needles.

Twining, twisting, spinning, yarn-making, antecedent to netting, looping, braiding, or weaving, were begun in

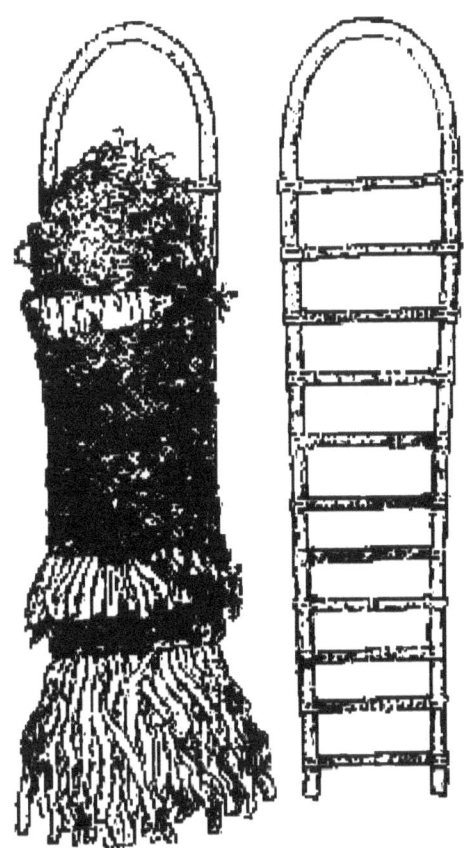

FIG. 12.—MOHAVE CRADLE FRAME, SHOWING THE SHREDDED BARK BED, THE FRAMEWORK, AND THE GEOMETRIC PATTERNS IN WEAVING.

savagery by rolling a small bundle of fibres or a narrow strip of bast between the palm of the hand and the thigh, after the fashion in which the cobbler untwists his thread to break it.

Among some tribes a twisting device consists of two

pieces of wood, bone, or ivory, as the case may be, one revolving on the other, as in a watchman's rattle. The fibres are attached to the revolving part, and made to twist by its revolutions. The Eskimo and the Zuñi women both use this process, especially in heavy work.

The same fly-wheel arrangement used by the Eskimo women in making sinew thread is applicable to the twisting of twine from two or more spindles; indeed, the apparatus is better adapted to the production of stout cord and lines, the motion being slower, while the momentum is greater. The tool, therefore, is more suggestive of the ropewalk and the devices connected therewith than of the spindle. I have found the apparatus in use among the Eskimo for making rawhide lines, and among the Pueblo peoples for twisting stout twine and rope. African women have a still simpler process of manufacturing excellent twine, which is also to be seen among Sicilian women. The whole process of twisting the filaments and the twine is carried on by one person, who takes four rushes or a double set of bast or other filaments between the thumb and forefinger of the left hand, twirls one set four or five times quickly about the forefinger of the right hand, passes them under to be held between the fingers and palm of the left hand, and deftly seizes the other set at the same time to give them a twirl. This process is repeated with the strands alternately, the finished twine being drawn along simultaneously. The Alaskan Indian women also know this process of making twine just as our boys twist whip crackers, twisting and twining with both hands at the same time. The finished part is fastened to some object or held by another person.*

But the world-wide method of twisting yarn from the

---

* See Kalm, Travels, London, 1771, vol. ii. p. 101.

most primitive times and among very uncultured peoples has been with the spindle. The distaff at first was absent. The workwoman held a bunch of prepared fibres in her left hand and spun with her right.

The rudest spindles were merely straight sticks, with no hook at the upper end, but the fly wheel or spindle whorl is as old as the hills. To imitate the originator of the spinning jenny, take a bunch of flax or wool in the left hand, and with the right draw out the fibres a foot or two in a homogeneous thickness, and fasten the ends securely to the top of the spindle shaft. At first it is better to sit on the ground and let the lower end rest in a little cavity of a rock or in a bowl. Twirl the spindle and twist the yarn as much as you desire, then wind the part twisted on the spindle shaft, draw out another bunch of fibre, and give another twirl. The process, in effect, is precisely the same as that followed by our grandmothers, only the spinning wheel reduced greatly the time of the operation. In Roman and Grecian and Egyptian sculptures and paintings the spinner is standing and twirls the spindle in the air, but the shaft in such cases must have a hook at the top. The spindle is used by the spinning and weaving Indians of North America throughout the entire operation of twining. It reduces the wool to yarn, and then serves as a spool for it. It subsequently twists the yarn for two- or three-ply twine. It is an interesting sight to watch an Indian woman's dexterity as she twirls the spindle on her bare thigh and drops the end into a vase or bowl while the yarn is wound. It has scarcely ceased its rapid revolution before her right hand is ready to pick it up, carry it to the top of the thigh again, and give it another impulse. The motion is practically continuous.*

---

* Bancroft, Native Races, New York, 1874, vol. i, p. 695.

Thomson noticed a very primitive type of spinning at Bakah, in Palestine. "Some of the women were spinning thick strands of goat's hair, with which coarse sacks, bags, carpets, and tent covers are woven. They use no spindle, but merely fasten the strands to a stone, which they twirl round until the yarn is sufficiently twisted, when it is wound upon the stone and the process repeated over and over."* "They can weave without any loom. The threads of the warp are stretched upon the ground and made fast at either end to a stout stick. The threads of the woof are passed through with the hand, and pressed back by a rude wooden comb.†

> To save their plaiding coats some bred
> Upo' the hurdsh a bonnet braid,
> Or an auld wecht or kalriding skin
> To rub and gar the spindle rin
> Down to the ground wi' twirlin' speed,
> And twine upo' the floor the thread.

Old Scotch ballad. Chambers's Encyclopædia, 1862, s. v. "Spinning."

In the art of braiding sennit from cocoa fibre the Polynesians excelled, and men as well as women engaged in making it, because it was of use to men quite as much in their arts as it was to women, taking the place of nails and screws in housebuilding and boat-making.

But savage women in other parts of the world could braid or platt also. In America they were most skillful in giving a plaited effect to borders of baskets and wallets in the use of a single strand by the continuous loop. The modern straw hat is a survival from savagery. Indeed, the braids of them are still made either by savages or by white women who live in a very primitive state.

Weaving is the climax of the textile industry. The

---

* Thomson, The Land and the Book, New York, 1880, vol. i, p. 50.
† Ibid., p. 105.

very simplest form of loom, out of which might have grown the most intricate of modern patents, is to be seen in use among the savage women of British Guiana in making their *queyus* or embroidered aprons. The frame consists of two rods, one flexible and bent in a semicircle, the other straight and having its ends tied to the ends of the former. In form it resembles the letter D. The warp threads pass from one stick to the other, widening apart slightly on the bent one, and giving to the finished apron the form of a right trapezoid.

The ancestral form of the heddle or heald in a hand loom was, in the earliest looms, a rod laid across the warp and attached to the hinder or under series of warp threads by a continuous thread, which passed around the heald rod and around those hinder warp threads all the way across the warp. The weaver crossed her warp for the shuttle by simply pulling this heald rod forward, passing the shuttle through, and then letting go for the next passage of the weft, the warp readjusting itself by its own tension. Her shuttle was nothing more than a slender stick upon which a quantity of yarn was wound, and this was guided between the two sets of warp threads slowly by the fingers as in darning. This thread was pressed into place by means of a baton made in shape of a sword blade. Sailors use a similar but clumsier device in making sword mats. The warp threads were crossed by pulling or releasing the heald and the tedious shuttle was worked across and back, occupying a minute with each excursion.

In later times any number of these heald rods could be employed to give a diaper effect, but in the beginning this was produced by counting warp threads and carrying the right number in the mind, a surprising phenomenon to one who has patiently watched a Zuñi belt weaver. While the modern processes are of immense advantage in rapidity, the savage weaver could interrupt her darning process at any point and introduce fresh colour, working in each independently, just as tapestry is built up.*

Among all the types of modern savagery—American, negroid, and Malayo-Polynesian—intricate processes of weaving were in vogue before they were approached by the white race.

In American and European factories cotton and wool are sorted, carded, and spun by machinery tended by women. The goods are then made into bales, shipped, sold by wholesale, and delivered to retailers by men. They pass out of the hands and sight of women until they reach the retailer or the manufacturer of garments, where

Fig 14.—The Primitive Loom Weaver—Navajo Woman, Arizona. (After Matthews.)

they are again in the hands of their original owners, to be made up, as any one will testify who has looked into a retailer's shop or a tailoring establishment.

In the last operation of using up these goods the aborigines of America, Africa, Polynesia, and Australia have a share. The looms of Europe and of the United States have to cater to the demands of the savage women of these areas. This is especially true in Africa, where the traders' goods must be *au fait* or the women will not have them.

In comparison with this complex and world-embracing activity of modern weaving and commerce, how simple

---

* Minutely described by Matthews. Third Annual Report of the Bureau of Ethnology. Washington, 1881–'82.

the process in savagery! The women there go to the fields or to the animals for the fibre, or hair, or wool. They transport the material on their backs, in carrying frames and apparatus that they themselves have made, and prepare it, as we shall see further on, to be woven or sewed or embroidered. They make up the bag, or mat, or garment, or sail of a whole piece, and wear it out in use—the same woman in each case following the material from the cradle to the grave.

In lower savagery, indeed, this same woman has to be adept in many other crafts beside, but in upper savagery the skilled weaver is pensioned or allowed to do that work only. When she arrived thus far on her upward journey, she was prepared to hand the art over to the male sex and to machinery, in whose workings she will still bear a part.* The finer kinds of cloth in Mexico were made of cotton, of rabbit hair, of the two mixed, or of cotton mixed with feathers. The rabbit-hair fabrics were pronounced equal in finish and texture to silk, and cotton cloths were also fine and white. The cloth in the manufacture of which feathers were employed often served for carpets, tapestry, and bed coverings. Maguey fibre and that of coarse palm leaf—*ixcotl* and *izhuatl*—were woven into coarse cloths, the maguey cloth being known as *nequen*. This *nequen* and the coarser kinds of cotton were the materials with which the poorer classes clothed themselves. All the work of spinning and weaving was performed by women.†

At the Chicago Exposition were immense collections from the cliff dwellings, containing, among many other relics of woman's handiwork, feather cloaks used as

---

* Adair, History of the North American Indians, London, 1776. Dilly, p. 423.
† Bancroft, Native Races, New York, 1874–'76, vol. ii, p. 484.

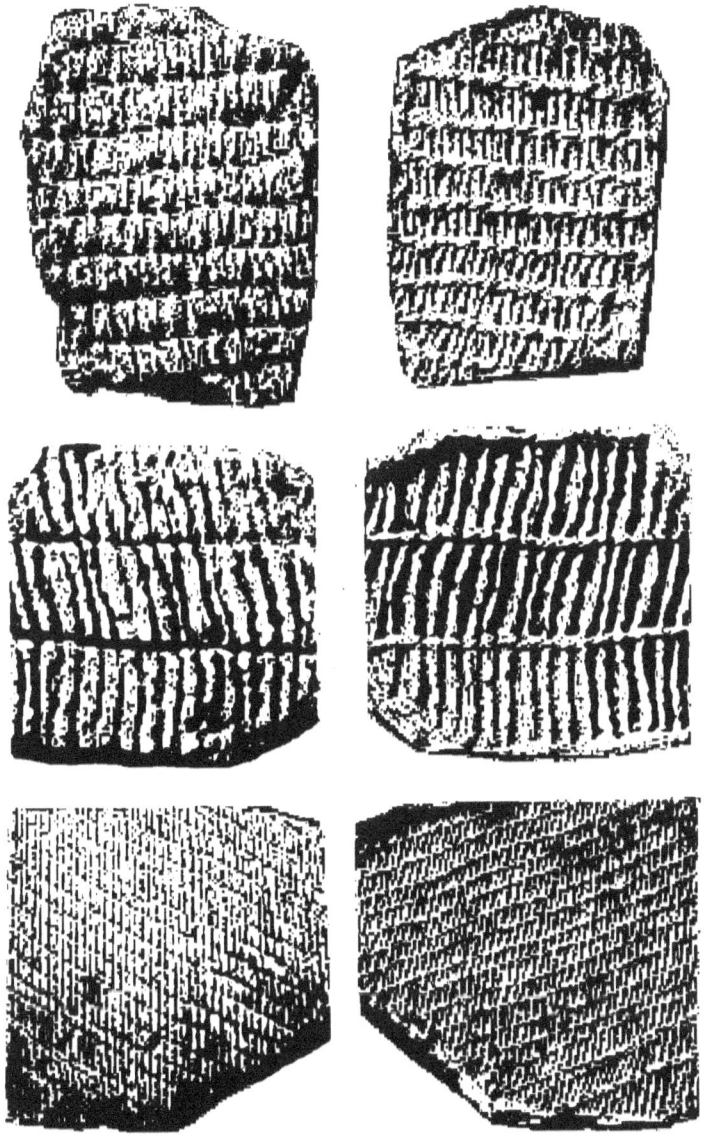

shrouds or wrapping of mummies. These cloaks were made in "twined weaving" of cords wrapped with the downy feathers of the turkey or rabbit skin. The skin of the rabbits and of the birds after the quill feathers had been plucked was cut in strips and wound around the warp and the weft cords, as in the rabbit-skin robes of the Pueblo peoples. In some examples the soft quill feathers had been split and wrapped around the cords.

The process of weaving is thus described by Wafer: "The Women make a Roller of Wood, about three Foot long, turning easily about between two Posts. About this they place Strings of Cotton of three or four yards long, at most, but oftener less, according to the use the Cloth is to be put to, whether for a Hammock, or to tie about their Waists, or for Gowns, or for Blankets to cover them in their hammocks, as they lie in their Houses, which are all the uses they have for cloth. And they never weave a piece of Cotton with a design to cut it, but of a size that shall just serve for the particular use. The threads thus coming from the Roller are the Warp; and for the woof, they twist Cotton yarn about a small piece of *Macaw* wood notched at each end. And taking up every other Thread of the Warp with the Fingers of one Hand, they put the Woof through with the other hand and receive it out on the other side; and to make the Threads of the Woof lie close in the Cloth they strike them at every turn with a long and thin piece of *Macaw* wood like a Ruler, which lies across between the Threads of the Warp for that purpose."*

Another example of a textile art involving a multiplicity of occupations is to be found in the Carib tribes of South America. They have got far enough along to have

---

* Luet, Nov. Orb., p. 343, quoted by Bancroft, Native Races, 1874, vol. I, p. 708.

plantations of a primitive sort. So the women plant the cotton seed and cultivate the crop. They pick the cotton, remove the seeds, and card it into long, loose bands. Winding one of these about her right wrist, the spinner then fastens one end of the band to a spindle, which she twirls with her left hand, drawing out the band evenly meanwhile with both hands and taking up the thread on the shaft of her spindle. When she has completed a number of these she by the same process combines two threads or three into a twine, and now she is ready to become a weaver. Four pieces of wood are set up, for all the world after the manner of an old-fashioned quilting frame, around which she winds in a continuous coil enough string to form the warp of her hammock and adjust the distances to a nicety. Across this warp she weaves bands of three-ply plaits at equal distances so as to hold the warp firmly in place and give air through the texture. The men apply the ropes or "scale lines." *

Nothing in handicraft has ever exceeded in beauty featherwork. The feather plumes and canopies of the Incas, the shields and mosaic work of the Mexicans and Central Americans, the war bonnets and other regalia of eagles' feathers among the Northern tribes, have not failed to evoke unbounded admiration from the conquerors.

In India travellers admire the fans and screens made from the plumage of pheasants and peacocks. The old Assyrian kings were attended by servants holding immense umbrellas of feathers. In New Guinea it is the bird of paradise and the cassowary that provide the gaudy material for head ornaments, while the Australians went to the emu and the lyre bird for supplies.

Throughout Polynesia, as elsewhere, feather currency was in vogue, but the Hawaiians, after all, seem to have

---

* Cf. Im Thurn, Indians of British Guiana, London, 1883, p. 365.

excelled in the art of weaving with feathers. Helmets, cloaks, standards, and necklaces were most elaborately wrought on network of the *olona* fibre (*Touchardia latifolia*). The arrangement of the feathers is said to have been the work of noble women.*

Colours in textiles are produced first by the happy mixture of natural materials of different tints. Often the two sides of a leaf will give distinct colours, as in the case of the yuccas (out of which the Moki women of Arizona make the pretty and substantial meal trays), or the palm leaves abounding in the tropics. The California women get a black effect with *martynia* pods, a deep brown with the stem of the maidenhair fern, and a bright red in the use of the roots of a yucca. These added to the wood colour of different plants produce a pleasing variety. The women of our Pacific coast have found out that burying spruce root and other woody fibres in certain springs or muds produces a chocolate colour, and natural dyeing may be found elsewhere. But our primitive folk also know how to make dyes from mineral and vegetal substances and how to fix colours by means of mordants. Until the discovery of the coal-tar dyes—a plague upon them!—the most commonly used colours were those borrowed from the hands of savage women.

The Navajo woman since the introduction of sheep into Arizona by the Spaniards has dyed wool in a good variety of colours, partly with her native dyes and partly with new materials. Ingenuity of no trifling order is shown in this combination. The wool itself occurs in three natural colours—white, rusty black, and grey. The native dyes are black, yellow, and reddish. Black is produced by boiling the leaves and stems of *Rhus aromatica* (sumac) and mixing the decoction with baked yellow ochre

---

* Consult Brigham, Cat. Bishop Mus., Honolulu. 1892, p. 10.

and piñon gum (*Pinus edulis*). Though the Navajo woman is not skilled in modern chemical terms, the tannic acid of the sumac combines for her with the sesquioxide of iron in the roasted ochre to form a rich blue-black ink whose colour is deepened by the carbon of the gum.

For yellow, the flowering tops of *Bigelovia graveolens* are boiled and the decoction mixed with almogen or native alum, and this gives her for use a lemon tint. Or, for "old gold" she grinds on her metate of stone a root of which our science is ignorant, and for a mordant mixes therewith the native alum.

Her reddish dye is extracted from the bark of the *Alnus incana* and the root of *Cercocarpus parvifolius*, the mordant being fine ashes of the juniper. On buckskin this produces a brilliant tan colour, but a paler shade in wool.

Dr. Matthews thinks they formerly had a blue dye of their own, which they abandoned for indigo. The native blue with native yellow would have given them green; at any rate, they now mix indigo with their native yellow.

The brilliant red threads in their best modern blankets were procured by unravelling *bayeta*, a bright scarlet cloth with a long nap, much finer than the strouding which is so dear to the heart of the Indian women of the North.[*]

In Hawaii, roots, leaves, and bark of various plants yielded dye-stuffs, the chief colours being yellow, red, green, various shades of browns, and the greys, produced by an admixture of charcoal. It was customary to prepare a kapa intensely imbued with colour, and keep this for use as solid pigment to be beaten into white kapa. For producing figures, pigments were ground in oil in a stone mortar and applied (1) by cords dipped in the liquid and

---

[*] Matthews, Navajo Weavers, Third An. Rep. Bur. Ethnol., Wash., 1884, p. 370.

snapped as a quilter's starch line; (2) by pens of bamboo; (3) by brushes; (4) by natural objects used as dies; (5) by stamps cut on bamboo strips. In some islands elaborate stamps were made several feet square."

The subsidiary textile arts are of great importance in savagery, and they are of great antiquity, remains having been found in very old deposits. Sewing and embroidery will be noted further on in the study of the skin-working art, but in this place it is important to observe the net. The "reef knot" and the "weaver's knot" were both known to savage women, but there are simpler forms conducting up to these. Imagine a row of trees leading to a pitfall. If a stout vine were carried along this row, being wrapped once around each tree in passing, it would form an excellent "wing" to the trap. Three or more would furnish a good fence, and the whole suggests a very simple form of net. The Mojave Indian women living about the mouth of the Colorado River construct a carrying basket in this very way. A number of upright strings connect the hoop at the top with the bottom of the basket. The meshes are formed by wrapping a stout string around and around the four upright frame sticks, taking a single turn about each upright thread in passing.

Now and then the archæologist finds an impression on pottery showing the same type of weaving. It is not widely diffused, and must have been limited in its application on account of the slipping of the warp on the weft.

A more widely dispersed style of net is the running loop, or simplest form of crochet. It is a continuous spiral hooked into itself from round to round, and is an exceedingly varied and pretty stitch in the hands of aboriginal women in both continents. The Pima Indian

---

* Brigham, Cat. Bishop Mus., Honolulu, 1892, p. 23.

women of California construct their burden baskets of such network, and, by omitting stitches regularly or taking turns about the coiled part, give to the surface the appearance of lacework.*

But in the true net the cord is knotted at the intersections of the meshes, which are kept at a uniform size by what is called in museums a spacer. The natives of New Guinea, and, indeed, aborigines in other lands, were perfectly familiar with our square knot or reef knot, and the Ute Indians in the great interior basin of the United States employed the weaver's knot in making their carrying nets from the fibre of the native hemp. The very same type reappears in the netting of the ancient cliff dwellers, who had many resemblances in art with the Ute or Shoshonean tribes.

In Samoa it is the work of the women to make nets chiefly from the bark of the hibiscus. After the rough outer surface has been scraped off with a shell on a board, the remaining fibres are twisted with the palm of the hand across the bare thigh. As the good lady's cord lengthens, she fills her netting needle and works it into her net.†

We may pause long enough to note that the Samoans are also among the most skillful makers of tapa or bark cloth from the same material. The example of one of the Samoan women twisting, without the aid of a spindle, strips of this same bark into cord is as near to the invention of spinning as we may hope to come.

We have followed the savage woman through the manipulations of the textile art, and shown that up to the introduction of machinery it was her own. There

---

* Both styles figured in the Rep. U. S. N. Museum, 1887, pp. 264, 265, Figs. 7-9.
† Turner, Samoa, London, 1884, p. 767.

are certain decorations of textile consisting of overlaying, omitting, variation of stitch and colour, which will be more properly described in a chapter on her share in the origin of æsthetic products and processes. This art remains yet peculiarly the property of those who originated it, a fact that should not be overlooked by those who seek the good of women.

CHAPTER IV.

THE SKIN DRESSER.

PAUSE for one moment to consider all the modern industries included within the one word "leather." It involves everything done to the hides of animals from the moment they are taken off by the butcher until the products are ready to be used up by the consumer. The hides of cattle, sheep, goats, horses, dogs, and other domestic animals, the skins of all wild beasts that are of any use, are gathered up in a sort of bloody harvest by butchers, hunters, and trappers and sent to the tanners or to the manipulators answering to their trade, most of whom are men. Here commences a diversity of treatment ending in the preparation of the hide with the hair remaining by the furrier, in the production of soft leather by a process called tawing, or in the manufacture of true leather by the use of tannin in some form, these also being now man's work. The products of these establishments are prepared for consumption by harness-makers, shoemakers, glove-makers, clothiers, satchel-makers, embossers, bookbinders, carriage-makers, armourers, machinists, musical-instrument makers, taxidermists, and twice as many more to be passed on by the great Briareus of commerce to those who will wear out these products by using them.

It would be interesting to inquire in how many of these activities especially devoted to the manufacture and use of skin products modern women take part, how many women work on hides, and how many of these trades and industries are kept going in order to satisfy their needs and wants. This inquiry would be the climax of a study of which we are tracing only the first steps.

Strictly speaking, savage women were not tanners; they were the mothers of tanners, and they practiced a variety of arts on the skins of animals. In a former chapter, for the sake of orienting the woman as purveyor, a slain deer was laid before her door to see what she would do with it. But, in reality, there is scarcely a family of mammals in existence whose hides women have not reduced to some good use. On the American continent alone women skin dressers know how to cure and manufacture hides of cats, wolves, foxes, all the numerous skunk family, bears, coons, seals, walrus, buffalo, musk ox, goat, sheep, antelope, moose, deer, elk, all kinds of whales, squirrels of thirty species, beaver, gopher, muskrat, porcupine, hares, opossum, crocodile, tortoise, birds innumerable, and fishes and reptiles.

If aught in the heavens above, or on the earth beneath, or in the waters wore a skin, savage women were found on examination to have had a name for it, and to have succeeded in turning it into its primitive use for human clothing, and to have invented new uses undreamed of by its original owner. The operations through which they put the skins were tempered to the skins themselves and to the object in view. As any taxidermist, or farmer's boy, for that matter, knows, there are hosts of birds and fish and small mammals whose hides need only to be drawn off and dried wrong side out in the sun to be completely cured. The furrier has his way of keeping out the destructive insects, and the taxidermist knows the virtues of arsenical soap; but away on the boundaries of time or civilization the harmonies of Nature had not been so much disturbed, hence there was not such trouble with insect pests. Furthermore, the garment or what not was in daily use until it was worn out, so there was poor chance for moths or dermestes.

The hides and hair of these thin-skinned creatures were used chiefly in decoration and in weaving after being cut into narrow strips and wound around a stout twine. The Eskimo women made a most comfortable inner blouse or parka from the skins of birds sewed together, the feathers being worn next the person. We are told by those who have seen the operation that the only tanning or tawing through which the bird skins passed was a thorough chewing on the wrong side by the women and girls. These skins were sewed together by means of sinew thread by whipping the edges, after the manner of the carpet sewer, and when the seam was stretched and the garment was straightened out, no one could say where one skin left off and another began.

In the very same manner the hides of squirrels and the smaller mammals—indeed, of foxes and other fur-bearing animals—were cured and cut and sewed into garments of great beauty.

This might be called the drying process, and is doubtless the earliest of all, surviving on to our day—an art that has been familiar to man in all his history. The next process to this in simplicity, and thoroughly familiar to aborigines everywhere on continental areas, is the curing of the hides of larger mammals with the hair on for the purpose of making pliant robes or for clothing. A reference in any good dictionary to the words "skin," "dermis," "epidermis," etc., will show just what the savage woman had in mind in this operation though she did not comprehend anatomy.

Her problem was to remove the dermis from the seal skin, or from the hide of the moose, elk, musk ox, bear, buffalo, and the like, and leave the hair adhering to the epidermis, with only a thin portion of the true skin. Furthermore, if she were a woman of taste and pride and did not wish her good man to be laughed at, or, more properly speaking, if she wished not to get herself laughed at over his shoulders, this great surface, frequently more than thirty square feet in extent, had to be uniform in thickness throughout and she should not cut through the epidermis once. The whole must be as pliable, too, as a woollen blanket. The problem was to reduce a hide of varying

Fig. 14.—Eskimo "Scraper" made to fit the Woman's Hand. (After Mason.)

thickness and twice too thick everywhere to a robe of uniform thickness throughout without once cutting through the outer part of the skin. Her tools for this work varied with locality. The Eskimo women scrape off the fat with a special tool made of walrus ivory or horn and plane down the dermis with a stone scraper. But the Indian women cut off the bits of meat and fat and remove the dermis with a hoe or adze.

In the good old days of savagery the Eskimo woman made her fat scraper of walrus ivory or antler; her skin scraper was of flinty stone set in a handle of ivory, wood, or horn, whichever material was easiest to procure. But later on, it may be, the whalers helped her out with steel tools.

The Indian woman had three tools—to wit, the stone

knife for cutting away the flesh, the hoe-shaped scraper for splitting the skin, and the grainer, a hoe or chisel-like tool with serrated edge to roughen up the inner side of the robe and give it flexibility. Besides these, both Eskimo and Indians had hands and feet and teeth for pulling and pounding and breaking the grain.* They had

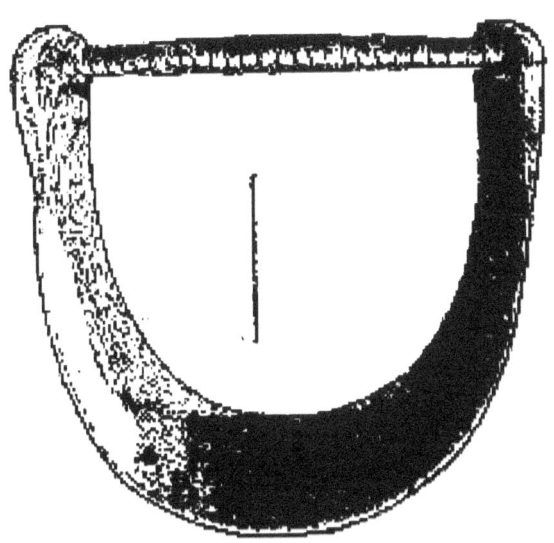

FIG. 17.—ESKIMO FAT SCRAPER OF REINDEER ANTLER AND RAWHIDE. (After Mason.)

also a wonderful supply of pride in their work and love of applause, which kept them up to the mark of doing the very best that could be done with their resources.

The universal plan, with local and tribal variations, upon the great hides for robes and clothing was to stretch them either on a stout frame or on a smooth, level place, and let them dry. They could at the same time be treated with the brains of the animal to render them more easily worked. As soon as the hide was well dried the

---

* Consult Dorsey, Omaha Sociology, Third An. Rep. Bur. Ethnol., Wash., 1884, pp. 310, 311.

process of hoeing or scraping commenced, a most exhausting operation, as all who have witnessed the task agree. In the days of plentiful buffalo Sioux women were no idlers in keeping the market stocked with robes.* Another industrial material in savage life, indispensable to both

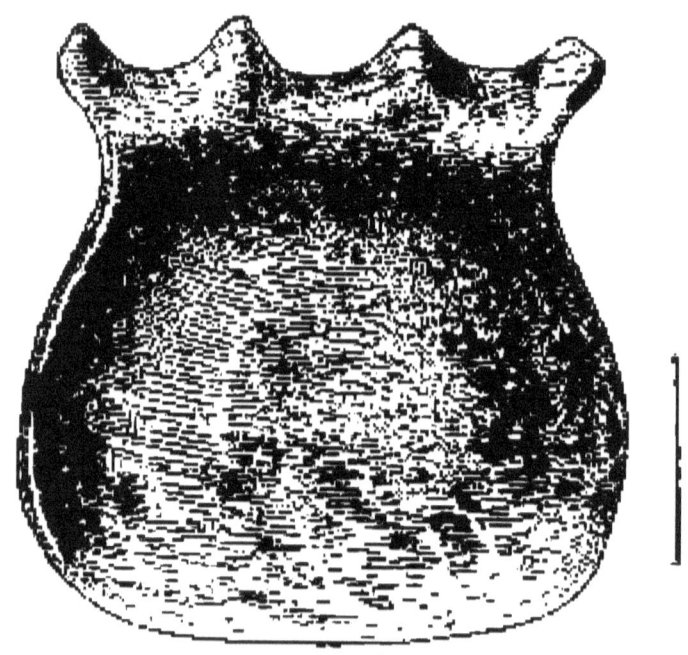

FIG. 18.—ESKIMO FAT SCRAPER OF WALRUS IVORY, MADE TO FIT THE FINGERS. (After Mason.)

men and women, was rawhide. This was procured with the aborigines precisely as it is with us—namely, by simply drying the skin and then cutting off the hair with a knife or adze. The lines used for ten thousand purposes in the cold north land, where nails and screws break like glass and where no textile plants are to be gathered, were made

---

* For an excellent picture of a supple Eskimo woman without the suggestion of a lacknebe or weakness of the spine, see Murdoch, Ninth An. Rep. Bur. Ethnol., Wash., Fig. 5.

of rawhide, and varied in thickness from that of a fine thread to half an inch. The Eskimo man covers his beautiful skin boat with the rawhides of seals, deprived of the hair, stretched, and oiled by women.

The most difficult method of treating hides is that which comes nearest to shamoying, the process formerly applied to the preparation of the skins of the Alpine chamois as well as to other deerskins. Buckskin and the chamois skin of commerce are our nearest representatives. The Eskimo do not treat hides in this way; the region is too cold; but the Indians adjoining them and all their kindred southward to the tropics were masters of the art, the work being chiefly done by women. Dr. R. W. Shufeldt, U. S. Army, at the request of the writer, observed carefully the whole operation of preparing a hide in this way, though the performer was a man. Others have carefully recorded the same in other tribes, as done by women, so that this savage art is tolerably well understood.*

The first thing to do is to remove the hair, a process performed in old-fashioned tanneries either by means of quicklime or by sweating the skins—that is, heating them, until putrefactive fermentation has gone on far enough to loosen the hair but not to injure the texture. The savage woman also comprehends the latter process. The writer has heard Lieutenant Emmons say that the Chilkat women of Alaska procure the hair of the Rocky Mountain goat for the sacred blankets by rolling up the hide until it sweats and the pores are open. A woman then sits on the ground, lays the skin on her lap, and with her hands scrapes off the hair in great flakes without the use of an unhairing tool of any kind.

To soak the skin thoroughly in a mixture of brains

---

* Mason, Aboriginal Skin Dressing, Rep. U. S. N. M, 1888–89.

and water, to pull and haul it and twist it while drying, exhausted every energy of the body.*

These stone scrapers, universal in present savagery, were once the favorite implement with our grandmothers many times removed. The Aryan peoples, both in Asia and in Europe, once clothed themselves in the same fashion as the American aborigines of to-day. If you were to visit their camp sites you would pick up among the implements of flint, scrapers in abundance.† In the pile dwellings of Switzerland and Italy fragments of leather have been found, and the Britons were clad in skins in the days of Julius Cæsar.

One of the most interesting testimonials to the peculiar adaptiveness of women to further the progress of civilization is furnished by this very apparatus, so often referred to by all voyagers in connection with the art of skin dressing. Imagine an Eskimo, or an Indian, or an African woman on her knees engaged in perhaps the most filthy work to be seen anywhere—namely, anticipating the unhairing department of a modern tannery. Her implement consists of a blade of stone set in a handle of antler or of wood, or the leg bone of a large mammal scraped to an edge. The better culture comes along and says, "My good woman, let me see that tool," and quietly slips out the poor blade of stone and substitutes one of steel. As her work is renewed she feels that a blessing has fallen from the skies upon her. She is not degraded by being made to take up occupations against which the prejudices of centuries revolt. A better implement does better work of the same sort, and so her mind and heart and habits are strengthened.

---

* Mason, Aboriginal Skin Dressing, Rep. U. S. Nat. Museum, 1888–89, pp. 553–589, pl. lxi–xciii. All the processes are described and figured.

† Cf. Taylor, The Origin of the Aryans, Lond., 1892, Scott, p. 171.

The deer and buffalo disappear. But when the cattle come and take the place of the wild creatures, the woman continues upon her knees, with the modified scraper triumphant, converting the hides of black cattle into white robes, upon which her husband paints himself pursuing his enemies and the ghosts of elk and buffalo, none of which will ever return.

The scraper is the oldest implement of any craft in the world. The Indian women of Montana still receive their trade from their mothers, and they, in turn, were taught by theirs, in unbroken succession, since the birth of the human species.

Crantz, in his History of Greenland (page 107), describes faithfully the Eskimo woman's processes of hide dressing:

"For their *kapitek*, or hairy seal-skin clothes, they scrape the seal skin thin, lay it twenty-four hours in the *korbik* or urine tub, to extract the fat or oil, and then distend it for drying with pegs on a green place. Afterward, when they work the skin, it is sprinkled with urine, rubbed with pumice stone, and suppled by rubbing between the hands.

"(2) The sole leather is soaked two or three days in a urine tub; then they pull off the loosened hair with a knife or with their teeth, lay it three days in fresh water, and so stretch it for drying.

"(3) In the same manner they prepare the *erersak* leather that they use for the legs of boots and the over-leather of shoes, only that it is scraped very thin to make it pliable. Of this leather they also make the sea coats which the men draw over their other clothes to keep out the wet when they go to sea. It is true it grows as soft and wet as a dishcloth by the salt water and rain, but it keeps the wet from the under-garments.

"(4) In the same manner they dress the *erogak*, of

which they make their smooth black pelts to wear on shore, only in working it they rub it between their hands; therefore it is not so stiff as the foregoing, but loses the property of holding out water and is not fit for boots and sea coats.

"(5) The boat skins are selected out of the stoutest seal hides, from which the fat is not quite taken off. They roll them up and sit on them and let them lie in the sun covered with grass several weeks till the hair will come off. Then they lay them in the salt water for some days, to soften them again. They draw the borders of the skins tight with their teeth, sew them together, and smear the seams and stitches with old seal blubber instead of pitch, that the water may not penetrate. But they must take care not to impair the grain, for if they do the corroding sea water will easily eat through the leather.

"(6) The remnants of this and the other sorts they shave thin, lay them upon the snow or hang them in the air to bleach them white, and if they intend to dye it red chew the leather with some bark of the roots of pine, which they gather up out of the sea, working it in with their teeth.

"(7) They soften the skin of the fowls about the head, and then draw it off whole over the body."

The processes of tanning, Hall says, are first to scrape the skin by an instrument called *sek-koon* (by the Frobisher Bay Innuit, *tey-se-koon*).

This instrument is about six inches long, including the handle, and is made of a peculiar kind of whet or oil stone, or else of musk-ox or reindeer bone or of sheet iron. The second step is to dry the skins thoroughly; the third, to scrape again with the *sek-koon*, taking off every bit of the flesh; the fourth, to wet the flesh side and wrap it up for thirty minutes, and then again scrape with the *sek-koon*, which last operation is followed by chewing the skin all over, and again scraping and cross scraping with the instrument. These laborious processes Hall describes as resulting "in the breaking of the skin, making the stiff hide soft, finished like the chamois skin." The whole work is often completed within an hour.*

"In Cumberland Sound," says Kmulien, "when a seal skin is about to be prepared for drying, the blubber is first removed somewhat roughly, the skin then laid on a board, and with the woman's knife the membrane underneath the blubber is separated from the skin. The knife must be very sharp to do this successfully. The operators always push the knife from them. It takes considerable experience to do the job well. When all the blubber is removed, which will take three or four hours of faithful work, the skin is taken outside, and by means of the feet is rolled and rubbed around in the snow for some time, and by this process they succeed in removing every trace of grease from the hair. When thoroughly washed the skin is put upon the stretchers, if it be winter, to dry; these stretchers are merely four poles, which are lashed together at the corners, like a quilt frame, the proper distance apart to suit the size of the skin. The skin is secured in place by seal-skin thongs passed through little slits along its edges and made fast to the poles.

"When the skin is properly stretched upon the frame it is put above the lamps inside the snow hut to dry. As the sun gets higher and begins to have some effect, the skins are stretched flesh side up, on the southern slopes of snow banks, and are secured by means of wooden or bone pegs about a foot in length."

Among the Central Eskimo, says Dr. Franz Boas, the latest authority, the skin of the seal (*Phoca fœtida*) is

---

* Narrative of the Second Expedition made by C. F. Hall, pp. 91, 92.

dressed in different ways according to the purpose for which it is intended. In skinning the animal a longitudinal cut is made across the belly with a common butcher's knife or one of ancient pattern. The skin, with the blubber, is cut from the flesh with the same knife. The flippers are cut off at the points, and thus the whole skin is drawn off in a single piece. The woman's knife, *ulo*, is used to clean and prepare the skins, in which operation the women spread the skin over a piece of whalebone (*usimentang*), a small board or flat stone, and sit down before it, resting on their knees, the feet bent under the thighs. They hold the skin by the nearest edge, and pushing the *ulo* forward, remove the blubber and deposit it in a small tub, which stands near the board. As they proceed to the opposite end of the skin the finished part is rolled up and held in the left hand.

If the skin is to be used with the hair on it, the tough membrane (*mumi*) which covers the inner side is removed in the same way as the blubber, and after it has been carefully patched and the holes have been cut all round the edge, it is stretched over a gravelly place or on snow by means of long pegs (*pualton*), which hold it a few inches above the ground, thus allowing the air to circulate underneath it. The skin itself is washed and rubbed with gravel, snow, or ice, and every hole made by the bullet or by the spear or in preparing it is sewed up. It very seldom happens that the women in preparing it damage the skin or even the thin *mumi*. It is particularly difficult to split the skin near a hole. First, they finish the work all around it, and then carefully sever the membrane at its edge. The skin is dried in the same way as the membrane. In the early part of spring, though it may still be very cold, a few choice young seal skins are dried on snow walls which face the south. In order thoroughly to dry a seal skin, one fine warm spring day is needed. If the Eskimo are greatly in need of skins they dry them in winter over the lamps. A frame is made of four poles, lashed together, according to the size of the skin. A thong passes through the slits along its edge and around the frame, keeping the skin well stretched. Thus it is placed over the lamps or near the roof of the hut. However, it is disagreeable work to dry the skins inside the huts, and as they are much inferior to those which are dried on the ground, the Eskimo avoid it if they can. When so prepared, the seal skins are only fit for covering tents, making bags, etc.; they are too hard to be used for clothing, for which purpose the skin of yearlings is almost exclusively employed.*

But the Indian woman's hardest work, Dodge tells us, was at the time of the fall hunt. If the buffalo were moving, success depended upon the rapidity with which she performed her work on a batch of dead buffalo. These animals spoiled very rapidly, and the men did not, therefore, wish to kill in any one day more than the squaws could skin and cut up. No sooner were the buffalo dead than the squaws were at work, and the skin was removed with marvellous celerity. The meat cut from the bones was tied up in the skin and packed to camp. The entrails formed the principal food during the hunt. Marrow bones and hump ribs roasted on the coals served for most delicious suppers after the day's work. All these were prepared by the women and brought to camp. The skins were spread, flesh side upward, on the ground, slits

---

* Consult the author's work Aboriginal Skin Dressing, Rep. U. S. Nat. Museum, 1888-'89, 553-560. Also Franz Boas on the Central Eskimo in Sixth An. Rep. Bur. Ethnol., Washington, 1884. Murdoch. The Point Barrow Eskimo, Ninth An. Rep. Bur. Ethnol., 294-302, Figs. 289-303. The last-named author is especially clear on the manufacture of clothing from skins, pp. 109-139, and draws attention to the strength and pliability of the Eskimo woman's body.

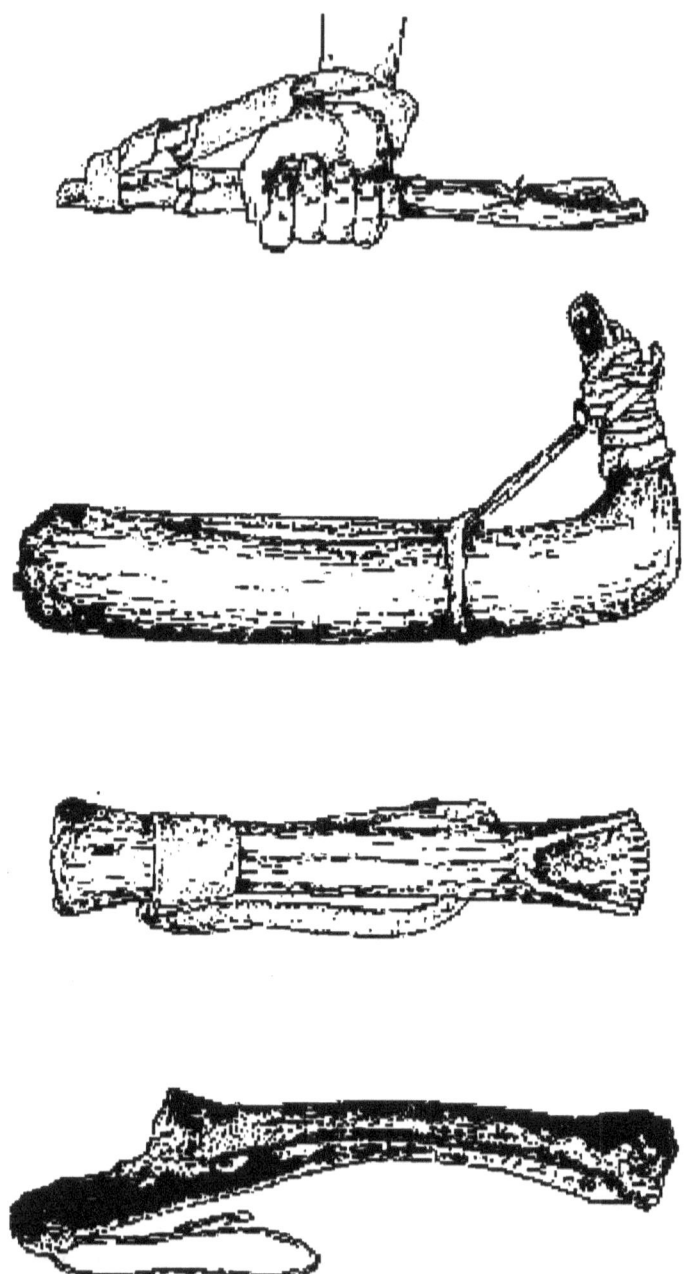

FIGS. 19, 20, 21, 22.—TOOLS OF THE PRIMITIVE TANNER—IMPLEMENTS OF BONE, ANTLER, AND IRON USED BY SIOUX WOMEN IN DRESSING HIDES.

cut in the edges, and each stretched and fastened down by pegs driven through the slits. There were four processes in the treatment of the skins. The thickest hides were selected for shields, meat cases [*parflèches*], etc. The hair was taken off by soaking the skins in water in which was mixed wood ashes or some natural alkali. The skin was cut into the required form while green. When it became dry it retained its shape, and was almost as hard as iron.

Making a robe was a much more difficult process. When the stretched skin had become dry and hard from the action of the sun, the woman went to work upon it with a small instrument shaped like a carpenter's adze, having a handle of elk horn or wood, to which the blade was tied with rawhide. With this she chipped at the hard skin, cutting off a thin shaving at each blow, so as to remove the superfluous inner skin and leave a perfectly smooth inner surface. To render the skin soft and pliable, every little while the woman smeared the surface with fat and brains of buffalo, thoroughly rubbed in with a smooth stone.

Hides for making lodges had the hair taken off, were reduced in thickness, and were made pliable. Deer, antelope, and other thin skins were beautifully prepared by a tawing process.*

"The Patagonian women, besides discharging all the household duties and fetching wood and water, dress the furs and manufacture the mantles of the young guanaco, fox, skunk, and ostrich skins, using, instead of needles and thread, sharp bodkins and sinew from the back of the adult guanaco. Some of the women also weave garters and fillets for the head, and occasionally work in silver. They also manufacture, pitch, and strike the *toldos* or tents, as well as load the poles and hides upon the horses. These

---

* Dodge, The Plains of the Great West, New York, 1885, p. 357.

tents consist of rows of forked sticks driven into the ground with ridgepoles overlaid with a covering made from forty to fifty guanaco skins sewed together and smeared with grease and ochre."*

The dried skin, the fur robe, the tawed skin, are now ready to be turned over to half a dozen other industries all belonging to women. The tent-maker, the shoemaker, the tailor, the hatter, the upholsterer, the trunk-maker, all need the skin dresser's wares. To deliver the prepared skins to so many crafts in our day would involve much labour and traffic and transportation. But in the undifferentiated period of savagery much of this getting about and handling is saved, for one little group of women will take the whole contract. They will prepare the hides of moose, deer, or buffalo, cut them into proper shape, sew them together with sinew thread, go to the swamp and cut down the poles, set them, stretch the new cover over them, and erect the house with their unaided hands. Having finished this, they will make the door, the cowl, the interior hangings in good proportion, and the ropes of rawhide to hold all firm.

In the Omaha tribal circle, says Dorsey, "though they did not measure the distances, each woman knew where to pitch her tent. Thus, a Kansa woman who saw a Wejinchte tent set up, knew that her tent must be pitched at a certain distance from that part of the circle, and at or near the opposite end of the road or diameter of the circle. When two tents were pitched too far apart one woman said to the other, 'Pitch the tent a little closer'; or, if they were too close, she said, 'Pitch the tent farther away.' In the former case there was danger from attack; in the latter the women had not enough room to work." †

---

* Musters, J. Anthrop. Inst., London, 1872, vol. I, p. 197.

† Dorsey, Omaha Sociology, Third An. Rep. Bur. Ethnol., pp. 219, 220.

As soon as the tents were erected each woman put up her drying frame, of which there were two or three for each tent. These were used for curing fresh meat, and each was made by sticking into the ground two forked sticks that were about four feet high, six or eight feet apart, and placing poles across them. The pieces of meat were hung across the transverse poles.*

These frames are universal in the domiciles of savages. Wherever skin garments are worn the frame serves as a convenient place for drying clothing that has been saturated with rain.

The tailoring of savage women, especially that of the North American women, is most interesting. While the weavers in the South were making blankets and *serapes* in the whole piece, never cutting their goods, the tailors north of the Mexican border were excellent cutters. For scissors they used the woman's knife, called *ulu* by the Eskimos, a blade of chert or other rock, crescent shaped on the outer edge, and a most excellent device for cutting skin without marring the hair. Scissors would be worse than useless in this connection, for they would shear the hair as well as the hide and make an ugly seam. In the fitting of garments these primitive tailors anticipated the long list of terms, such as puckering, gathering, inserting gores, and the like. For tucks in their more beautiful dresses they inserted band after band of the skins of different animals, bits from different parts of the same hide, and strips of bare hide ornamented by quillwork. Tufts of feathers or long hair, pendants of shell, hoof, teeth, or bone—in short, all objects of comely shape and pretty colour and proper size—were gathered into the costumes of men and children as well as into their own.

With soles of rawhide and uppers of skin beautifully

---

* Dorsey, Third An. Rep. Bur. Ethnol., pp. 245, 246.

embroidered or adorned they shod the good man and their children, and perhaps themselves. But the proverb often held in their case, that the shoemaker has no time to care for her own sole, and she went barefooted. In the history of journeyings this shoeing of human feet is to be studied by the side of the shoeing of horses or putting tires on wheels. The woman who invented sandals or moccasins should have a statue by the side of that of Watt. Savage women carry a part of their tool chests in their mouths. The Eskimo woman is a bootmaker, but has no clamps for stretching leather, so she puckers the upper and sole all around the edge where they come together, and uses her teeth for the purpose. In every other part of the world savage women utilize their teeth to clamp and cut and hold on.

Murdoch has worked out with the greatest care the variety and cut of the Eskimo suits for men and for women in winter and summer. The man's dress at Point Barrow consists of the hooded frock, without opening except at the neck and wrists. This reaches just over the hips, rarely about to mid-thigh, where it is cut off square, and is usually confined by a girdle at the waist. Under this garment is worn a similar one, usually of lighter skin, and sometimes without a hood. The thighs are clad in one or two pairs of tight-fitting knee breeches, confined round the hips by a girdle and usually secured by a drawstring below the knee, which ties over the tops of the boots. On the legs and feet are worn, first, a pair of long deerskin stockings with the hair inside; then, slippers of tanned seal skin, in the bottom of which is spread a layer of whalebone shavings; and outside a pair of close-fitting boots, usually reaching above the knee. The boots are of reindeer skin with white seal-skin soles for winter and dry weather, but in summer waterproof boots of black seal skin with soles of white whale skin are worn. Overshoes are sometimes worn over the winter boots. When travelling on snowshoes or in soft dry snow the boots are replaced by stockings of the same shape as the under ones, but made of very thick winter deerskins with the flesh side out. Over the usual dress is worn in very cold weather a circular mantle of deerskin, and in rainy weather both sexes wear a hooded rain frock of seal intestine.

The dress of the women consists of two frocks, which differ from those of the men in being continued from the waist in two rather full rounded skirts at the front and back, reaching to or below the knee. A woman's frock is always distinguished by a sort of rounded bulge or pocket at the nape of the neck, which is intended to receive the infant when carried in the jacket. On her lower limbs a woman wears a pair of tight-fitting deerskin pantaloons with the hair next the skin, and outside of these a similar pair made of the skins of deer legs with the hair out, and having soles of seal skin. Those who are well to do own several complete suits of clothes.

Mr. Murdoch, after enumerating the articles in the wardrobe of an Eskimo, describes minutely the manner in which each garment is cut out and the pieces fitted together, with the double purpose always to make it fit the wearer and to adorn the prominent parts, such as the bosom, shoulders, wrists, and borders, with pretty coloured fur and long, delicate fringes of hair alternating with inserted bands of varied material. It must not be forgotten that the creation of these wardrobes is the work of the women, that it takes a deal of patience and skill and artistic education to make a comely suit of clothing for an Eskimo gentleman, and Mr. Murdoch informs us that some of them are quite exacting in this particular.[*]

---

[*] Murdoch, The Point Barrow Eskimo, Ninth An. Rep. Bur. Ethnol., Washington, 1892, pp. 100-106. Figs. 51-86.

Hearne relates of the Indian women west of Hudson's Bay: "We had no sooner joined the women, on our return from the expedition, than there seemed to be a universal spirit of emulation among them, vying who should first make a suit of ornaments for their husbands, which consisted of bracelets for the wrists and a band for the forehead, composed of porcupine quills and moose hair, curiously wrought on leather."* The Indian women visited by Hearne belong to the great Athabascan stock, and all their work on costumes is beautifully done. The buckskin is as soft as silk, the clothes are neatly fitted, and the ornaments are put on with much taste.

The modiste, the hatter, the milliner, were practically one, but more than half the time all members of the tribes went bare-headed. The war bonnets and such toggery for the great ceremonies were made by men, though it must be admitted that they borrowed much of the material from the good housewife. There is a beautiful war bonnet of eagle feathers in the United States National Museum, all the sewing on which was done with a sewing machine. It was the regalia of a celebrated chief whose daughter had been educated at Carlisle School.

The reticule, the tobacco bag, the travelling case, the bandbox, the packing trunk, all exist among savages, and in North America were made by women, chiefly from the hides of animals. For the first two, skins of pretty little rodents and "such small deer" sufficed. For the "fire bag," as it is called, to hold the pipe and tobacco, the yellow buckskin was the thing, covered at the bottom with embroidery and finished out with a long fringe of the body material. The bandboxes and trunks were of rawhide, as stiff as a board and painted in green and red stripes.

As an offset to the tasteful needlework of the Eskimo

---

* Hearne, Journey, etc., London, 1795, Strahan, p. 305.

tailors it is entertaining to read of the German women in Tacitus's day. "These make choice of particular skins, which they variegate with spots and with strips of the furs of marine animals, the produce of the exterior ocean [northern ocean] and of seas unknown to us. The dress of the women does not differ from that of the men."* Compare with the spotting of fur clothing the modern practice of decorating ermine with black lamb's wool and the universal practice of adding to costly fur capes and cloaks borders of otter and other skins of various colours.

Following the course pursued in other chapters of this book, we ought to inquire what has become of all the hard labor and varied skill of primitive women involved in the skin-working industry. It is true that in the "Great Lone Land" much of it is going on still. But the buffalo and caribou and elk and deer are practically gone. Furthermore, the ancestors of most Europeans were once clad in skins. Houses of wood and brick and stone cover the very spots where stood the tents of hide, but women do not build them. The beds and packing boxes and furniture that used to be of skins are now made of wood and iron, but men are the fabricators of the hard parts, while women manufacture the soft parts. Clothing is fashioned out of wool and cotton and linen. For the most part women do the weaving and cutting and sewing. In the conservation of their energy the force that disappears with the feral animals reappears in the manipulation of the silkworm and the fleece and hair of domesticated creatures. But leather has taken the place of the prepared skins. It enters into industries without number. No kind of skin is despised. Glove-makers and shoe-makers are still largely women. At present, men have ceased to wear furs, but by the inevitable law of survival

---

* Tacitus, Germania, chap. 17; also Pliny, xix, 1.

and conservatism women use up nearly all the harvest of wild skins that are obtained. At this moment, while the author is penning these lines, the two foremost nations of the world have invoked the good offices of arbitration rather than go to war over the fur-bearing seals, whose hides are needed to clothe the backs of fine ladies. The skins of all the beautiful birds in the world are being mercilessly hunted for the plumage to deck the heads of women. The sea otter, the beaver, and the other producers of elegant furs have been nearly extinguished on their behalf.

CHAPTER V.

THE POTTER.

WOMEN were the first ceramic artisans and developed all the technique, the forms, and the uses of pottery. The inventions concerned in this industrial progress are far-reaching in their own extent, in the influence which they have had in the refinement and development of women, and in the rewards of happiness which they brought to the races and tribes favoured by their presence. As has been previously shown, pottery or earlier substitutes therefor had no place in the kitchen until the mush-making or meat-seething stage of cookery had arrived.

It is a piece of good fortune that this industry may still be seen in America in its pristine simplicity in two areas widely separated and serving entirely different purposes.

The first is among the Eskimo, who use the pottery for the stove or fireplace and not for the cooking vessel to set on the stove. These hyperboreans have neither coal nor wood to burn, so they generally fashion their combination stove-lamps of soapstone. These lamps are shallow dishes or pans, straight on one border and curved on the other, in outline like a "turnover" pie.

In Greenland, Labrador, all about Hudson's Bay, along the Arctic and Alaskan coast, wherever the material can be found, these lamps are hung up or set up in the underground home. Over the lamp is suspended a small cooking pot of the same material and a frame for drying clothing. Considerable warmth is imparted to the chamber by this apparatus, and the blaze affords light enough for the needs of the inmates. Now, in the Bristol Bay region of Alaska the soapstone seems to have failed the maker of lamps and cooking pots, for in that area these utensils are formed out of clay, mixed, it is said, with dog's hair and blood. The soapstone lamp is copied in the softer material, but the form is changed owing to the demands of technical economy. The Bristol Bay woman's lamps are made, therefore, in form of bowls or saucers, though she never saw one of these. Murdoch also figures rude fragments of pottery from the vicinity of Point Barrow.*

With her lamp-stove of clay and wick of moss or other vegetable fibre abundant in that region, and with the fat or blubber scraped from the inner side of the seal skin in the process of curing and dressing it, this primeval vestal still keeps her vigils. In all essential particulars the Eskimo woman's lamps at Bristol Bay are similar to the ones tended long ago in the Prytaneum at Athens and in the temple of Vesta at Rome, and many hundreds of extremely rude examples are now in use all about the lands bordering on the Mediterranean.

For the other ceramic artist, still holding and using the earliest letters patent, we must go to the arid regions of New Mexico and Arizona. She could also be found in South America, in Africa, and in New Guinea, but not in Polynesia. In the Southwestern States of our Union women have, from time immemorial, practiced the art of the potter with the greatest success. There is no reason to believe that their present methods and tools and products are different at all from what they were a thousand years ago. See what a multiplicity of occupations is in-

---

* Ninth An. Rep. Bur. Ethnol., Fig. 28.

volved in the production of one of those fragile vases with
which we love to adorn our houses!

The women go forth to the mesa where the proper
layers of clay are exposed, and quarry out the raw material. To do this, one would say they ought to be good
mineralogists and skillful engineers. They also gather
from the sediment of the streams most excellent clay for
their paste. "After the passage of a storm and the rapid
disappearance of the transient flood, the pools of the arroyos would retain a sediment of clay two or three inches
thick, having a consistence perfectly suited to the hands
of the potter." †

This is one of those interesting occurrences in which
Nature, asserting her true motherhood over our race,
prepares beforehand the materials of industries and announces what they are to be. In a certain sense, therefore,
the fine pottery of the Pueblos may be said to have been
created by the floods in the cañons.

If the potter is not fortunate enough to find this excellent paste, she gathers and carries home on her back
the clay quarried from the mesa. In this act the quarry
woman assumes the rôle of pack woman. In the absence
of the grinding apparatus of the world-renowned potteries and of the sieves and bolting cloths, she washes the
clay, lets the gravel and worthless material sink or float,
decants the liquid, and allows the fine aluminous earth
to settle. Though the term "specific gravity" was not
known to her, she seems to have seized upon this principle
in order to gather out the elements desired.

This fine paste will not make pottery; it will crack
badly in drying and baking. But our ceramic worker is
equal to the occasion, and long ago had discovered, as
every archæologist knows, that sand or some other tem-

---

† Holmes, Fourth An. Rep. Bur. Ethnol., p. 267.

pering material must be added. The oldest fragments yet discovered reveal in their texture grains of sand, put there by Nature or by the potter, bits of pulverized shells, or the remains of old pots ground fine and worked over into new vessels. The exact way in which these little foreign bodies prevent cracking in the clay does not seem to be known. That the mere haphazard combination of unlike materials will suffice is disproved by the crumbling of such ware on exposure. Indeed, there is more professional knowledge involved than the uninitiated realize. Recently the Smithsonian Institution employed some Pamunkey Indian women to prepare a collection of their ware for the Chicago Exposition. They failed in half the pieces because they calcined the shells in burning the pottery. As soon as the pieces were exposed to moisture they slaked like quicklime.

In the process of washing and mixing her clay both the ancient Pueblo woman and her modern representative assorted it for different kinds of ware—coarser material for her ruder ware, and finer material for more artistic productions. In this she was cultivating the delicacy of feeling, the keen sense of colour, and exercising her judgment. The potter was being developed in the exercise of her craft. This process can not be too frequently alluded to in the growth of any industry.

In making up her clay into ware she followed three processes, but all without the faintest semblance of the potter's wheel or other machinery. The age of machinery had not arrived in the Colorado basin, but she had a substitute for the symmetrical operation of machinery in her true eye and her steady hand. There are those who hold that the sense of beauty is more gratified in contemplating such hand work than the monotonous products of machinery.

The simplest process pursued by these potters in the

Colorado basin was that of children playing with mud, or Eskimo women in forming up their lamps, or the cook in making a pie, not neglecting even the pinching of the edges in a precisely similar manner. This free-hand work leads more directly to sculpture than to the ceramic art. It were better, perhaps, to regard it as the ancestral type out of which the others were differentiated. The Pueblo women of our day not only occasionally model whole pieces at a time, but they constantly finish out and decorate ware made after other methods by this free-hand operation. The Pueblo woman is severely plain in her tastes, but her kinsfolk, who dwelt in the Mississippi valley and in tropical America long ago, were more venturesome, and modelled rude little figures of men and beasts and conventional designs and luted them to their vessels with fresh clay.

If we had been able to look into the workshops of the ancient Mexicans, or of the Central Americans, or of the most skilful tribes of South America, we should be surprised at the barbaric extravagance in modelled extraneous ornament. It comes to pass in our day that men do this modelling in pottery most cleverly, especially in Mexico; but I shall not say that it was so from the beginning. The modern ware is made for sale and not for use, and everybody knows that the demands of commerce first drove men to doing woman's work. I have found an interesting allusion to this barter in pottery in New Guinea.[*]

The second process of the potter is that of moulding the soft clay around or within some object to give it shape. This process may be employed in the one next to

---

[*] Thomson, British New Guinea, London, 1892, Philip, p. 76; two figures on p. 77, one olla-shaped, the other a shallow bowl, both with puckered ornament about the rims.

96   WOMAN'S SHARE IN PRIMITIVE CULTURE.

be described, but it was also practiced by itself. Abundant evidence exists that the primitive potter shaped masses of prepared clay on the outside and on the inside of gourds, baskets, nets, and other shapely objects. This is shown not only by the forms of the vessels themselves, but by the markings left on their surfaces by the texture of the

FIG. 21.—MODELLED VASE, WITH RATTLES IN THE LEGS. (After Holmes.)

mould. There is no doubt that this style of ware is woman's work. The cuneiform inscriptions left by the ancient kings of Mesopotamia are not so legible. In the last chapter the various stitches employed by savage women in hand plaiting and weaving were carefully described. They are the same that reappear on the surfaces of potsherds made hundreds of years ago, whether in Swiss lake dwellings, in Africa, or in the United States. The two arts, lovely and beautiful in their lives, in their death they were not divided.

As a far greater number of ancient fragments in the United States bear textile markings than are found with impressions of purely natural objects, such as gourds, it is fair to infer that basketry was invented or made here before pottery. Again, as every basketry stitch or pattern known to savages is found impressed on pottery fragments, the textile art was considerably advanced before it was applied to ceramics. And, finally, as the impressions found on fragments in each region conform to the peculiar patterns of basketry practiced by modern savages when first visited by the whites, we have an argument for the continuity of the same arts in the same areas, even though the peoples practicing them may have changed.

The elements abraded the surfaces of the fragments, but at the same time filled the twisted furrows with earth.

No more effectually has the dust of ages sealed up and preserved the Egyptian textile. The archæologist with a soft brush removes the foreign matter and takes the impression of the furrows with some plastic material. The very style of the spinner, the weaver, the netmaker, is revealed, and in some cases the material. Plain weaving, diaper weaving, twined weaving, coiled weaving, then as now, and with scarcely a change.*

The third style of procedure in ancient pottery-making is the most interesting of all, it is so ingenious and so widespread. In certain areas the archæologist finds small shards, indicating that the vessels were molded in basketry. Now we are to study the making of pottery like basketry.

---

* See Holmes, Third An. Rep. Bur. Ethnol., pp. 300-425. Profusely illustrated.

Prompted, it may be, by the very act of making a coiled basket, the ancient potter rolled out a fillet or slender cylinder of prepared paste about the thickness, say, of a chalk crayon. Every one who reads these lines has more than once seen children playing with putty, rolling it out into fillets and then coiling it. The cook also makes little cakes after the same process, and the tidy housewife supplies herself thus with mats for her tables.

The ancient potter also coiled her fillet of soft clay around and around in an orderly manner, pinching as she went. As hinted at in the description of the second process, this work is done occasionally on the outside of a basket, bowl, or another vase. But the work is more fre-

FIG. 54.—MARING COILED WARE IN BASKET BOWL. (After Cushing.)

quently built up by the hands, guided chiefly by the eye, until the vessel is finished. Luckily for the student, many vessels are left in the corrugated condition produced by the pinching and coiling.* These examples not only show the process here referred to, but they evidence a marvellous

---

* For the great variety in the imbrication and pinching of the coils consult Holmes, Fourth An. Rep. Bur. Ethnol., pp. 278–297, Figs. 210–250.

variety of finger-nail and finger-tip work. There would be no greater mistake than to suppose that all these pinched surfaces are alike. In most cases, however, with this kind of ware as well as with the modelled and the moulded, every trace of the finger marks is carefully obliterated, either with soft tools of hide or gourd very much like those used by the stone-ware-maker or with bits of gourd while the pot is soft. After the surface is dry it is rubbed down and thoroughly polished with very smooth stones. It is difficult then to detect the fact that the vessel was built up by coiling, and yet most of the pottery north of Mexico, ancient and modern, was so constructed.

The Zuñi woman often stands while forming a piece of pottery and leans over her work. She centres it under her eye. In turning it around in the base upon which she builds it up she includes all the elements of the potter's wheel. But there is no better example of the difference between hand work and machine work. The latter would make the vessel to be round if the potter were to shut his eyes; in the former, it is the knack of the eye that gives rotundity to the vase.

The ingenious Pueblo woman and her Papuan sister workwoman know how to combine the three processes just explained upon the same vessel. The bottom of the vessel may start with a coiled fillet of clay laid on the bottom of a symmetrical basket, or even of a gourd or of a mould made for the purpose. Or this same starting point may be moulded over an object for some distance before the coiling begins. In all these cases, the symmetry of form once secured, there is no difficulty in perpetuating it.

But even these poorly taught children of Nature displayed considerable originality by using an old bowl in which to set up a new one, and the constant revolution of the whole as on a pivot enabled the artisan to correct her mistakes of symmetry.* The wheat stacker, unloading his sheaves upon different sides of his structure, and the dressmaker rely upon the judgment of the eye in the same manner, looking at the work constantly from every point of view.

FIG. 25.—BASKET BOWL AS BASE MOULD FOR LARGE VESSEL, SHOWING ALSO THE SMOOTHING PROCESS AFTER COILING. (After Cushing.)

Nothing has yet been said concerning the evolution of form in this Pueblo ware. Not to proceed by guesswork, as some have done, it is necessary to take as our guide Mr. Cushing, who spent several years of his life among these people for the sole purpose of study. The Havasupai Indian women of Shoshonean stock, dwelling in Cataract Cañon, Arizona, still adhere to the good old ways of life

---

* This natural primitive potter's wheel is also observed among the New Caledonians by J. J. Atkinson, J. Anthrop. Inst., xxiii, p. 00.

in all their simplicity. Among their employments is the gathering of seeds and crickets and roasting them with bits of meat in a flat tray of basketry by means of hot stones or live coals. Several specimens of these in the United States National Museum have been seriously charred in this operation. And the happening of this misfortune doubtless led the Havasupai to lining the inside of this roasting tray with a thin wash of clay mingled with sand, which in time was turned by the hot stones into a veritable flat plate, to be used in its turn as a rude primitive brasier. Mr. Cushing tells us that the Zuñi Indians actually call the earthenware pot in which they parch food by a compound name which, interpreted, means a roasting tray of twigs.

The deepening of the flat dish becomes in pottery a bowl, just as the deepening of a basket tray becomes a basket bowl. But these poor Havasupai have two other devices worthy of notice in this connection. They make basket pots for boiling food by means of hot stones, and basket bottles with narrow mouths for carrying water.

It is easy enough to imagine how dishes become bowls and bowls pots, but the conversion of the latter into carafes or bottles, large and small, is worthy of a little further study. So long as a vessel is wider at the top than at the middle it can be lifted from any mould, but the narrowing process requires skill. Again, the women of savagery are exceedingly proud of their work. In the saints' calendar above all others stands the names of skilful women. There is a generous rivalry that keeps the best at their best. Now, in pottery, tenuity, smallness, and length of neck and flatness of the shoulder are the points that count.

In effecting these the necks would become so small that the hand of the operator could no longer be thrust inside to sustain the shoulder and finish the upper parts. Says Mr. Cushing: "The effect of the pressure exerted in smoothing them on the outside, therefore, naturally caused the upper parts to sink down, generating the spheroidal shape of the jar. Without any instruction from me beyond a statement of my wishes, a Zuñi woman sprinkled the inside of a basket bowl with sand, mounging the clay upward by spiral building, making the shoulders high. When she had finished the rim, she easily caused the shoulders to sink with a wet scraper of gourd until she had exactly reproduced the form of my drawing. She then set the vessel aside in the basket. Within two days it shrunk about one inch in twelve, leaving the basket far too large."* It could then be removed.

We may turn aside one moment from this detailed account of technique to inquire into the number of occupations, the variety of thought, and the ingenuity involved in an operation of this character.

Quarrying, carrying, washing, assorting, mixing, tempering, modelling, moulding, coiling, smoothing, polishing, shaping—all with humble enough tools, but with artistic instinct, a marvellous knack, and an educated eye that a modern builder might envy—the savage potter finishes her vessel. It is now less than one eighth of an inch in thickness. These processes have not been repeated thousands of times, but millions of times, as any area will testify where such work went on. They were the daily occupation of Indian women.

The good housewife of nowadays has her last thought of the evening as well as her first waking thought upon those associations with crockery that have become a second nature to her, and they frequently monopolize her dreams.

---

*Cushing. Fourth An. Rep. Bur. Ethnol., p. 500. Consult the whole chapter, pp. 467-521, Figs. 490-564.

THE POTTER 103

If we only knew how many imaginings and volitions and studies the Pueblo woman experiences in a day over her ceramic work, there would be little wonder that she does it so well.

For the delicate glazes with which pottery would be surfaced in our modern factories savagery has a poor substitute. The primitive workwoman used a wash or "slip" made of the finest clay she could procure by her simple processes. Among the Pueblo people "this wash took the place of the enamels used by more accomplished potters, and, being usually white, it gave a beautiful surface on which to execute designs in color."*

Aboriginal American potters were ignorant of vitreous glaze, even of the common use of salt, as in making stoneware or drainpipe. Now and then a piece is found whose surface is true glaze, and many other pieces have a lustrous

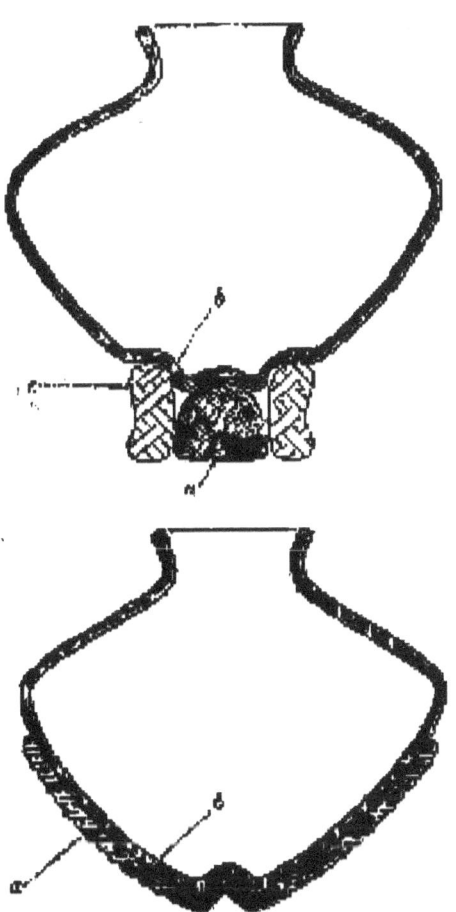

FIG. 26.—THE PROCESSES OF BUILDING UP THE MOST FINISHED TYPE OF JAR. (After Cushing.)

* Holmes, Fourth An. Rep. Bur. Ethnol., p. 268.

coating due to the polishing before burning. This is due to the accidental presence of alkaline matter in the water used. In the arid regions of the Southwest the husbanding of drinking water is necessary, and at other times even the drinking water becomes sufficiently alkaline to incrust pottery made with it.

Perhaps the reader is impatient for the furnace; but a word must be previously said about ornamentation—that is, the mechanical methods of effecting the decoration of pottery. Variety in color of Pueblo earthenware is produced in the simplest fashion by the ingredients of the native clay. Indeed, savage women in many lands understand this, but none of them are far enough advanced in their studies to mix oxides of iron with clay to vary the color of the burnt vessels. However, the variety which Dame Nature gives in color to vessels through the clays found in different regions was not slow in being apprehended by her ready pupils.

In addition to these varied body colors, the resources of decoration on the surface of the ware were, first, colored clays and mineral and vegetal paints laid on with brushes made of the shredded fibre of tough plants. These colors would be oxidized or carbonized in the burning. The further surface ornamentations were parts of the corrugated surface, intentionally left there in the smoothing, indentations and reliefs produced by the fingers when the clay was soft, tool markings, impressions laid in with cord, or nets, or basket work, or stamps, and, finally, modelled ornaments made up separately and glued or luted on with soft clay. In speaking particularly of the Pueblo potters we are really describing those of all parts of the world.

Mr. James Mooney collected a number of potters' stamps for the United States National Museum from the Cherokee Indians. They look like the old-fashioned butter paddles, with geometric designs cut on the surfaces.

One hundred and fifty years ago Dumont wrote thus graphically of the Choctaw women in Mississippi: "Moreover, the industry of these girls and women is admirable. I have already alluded to the skill with which, by means of the fingers only, and without a wheel, "that great perverter of the plastic tendencies of clay," they make pieces of pottery. The following is their method of work: After having collected a proper quantity of the proper kind of earth, and having cleaned it thoroughly, they take shells, which they break up and reduce to a very fine, loose powder; they mix this fine dust with the earth which they have collected, and, moistening the whole with a little water, work it with their hands and feet into a paste, from which they make rolls six or seven feet long and as thick as they may desire. If they wish to make a dish or a vase they take one of these rolls by the end, and, marking on this lump with the thumb of the left hand the centre of the vessel, they turn the roll around this centre with admirable rapidity and dexterity, describing a spiral. From time to time they dip their fingers into the water, which they are always careful to have near them, and with the right hand they flatten the inside and outside of the vase, which without this would be uneven. In this way they make all kinds of earthen utensils, dishes, plates, bowls, pots, and jugs, some of which hold as much as forty, or even fifty, pints. This pottery does not require much preparation for baking. After having dried it in the shade they make a large fire, and as soon as they think they have enough embers they clean a place in the middle, and, arranging the pieces of pottery, cover them with charcoal. It is thus that the pieces are given the necessary heating, after which they are as strong as our pottery. There is no doubt but that we must attribute their strength to the mixture which these women make of powdered shells with the earth which they employ.*

As hinted by Dumont, the burning of the vessels was a very simple affair. Upon fires made of charcoal, or in the desert country of chopped straw and dried dung, were the savage woman's kilns. There is little wonder that the pieces are not uniform in shade, and often show stains and burned spaces. Colonel Stevenson, who knew much of our Southwestern country, told the writer that a very attractive black ware was produced by secondary burning. When the fire of chopped grass and dung was at white heat, the burning mass was raked off and fresh fuel applied. A smudge was produced which seems to have been inhaled by the cooling vessel, dyeing it a permanent black almost through and through.

The Nicobarese are a rude of savages whose reputation has rested upon their piracy. But the women are excellent potters, and their mode of procedure is a good example of the question frequently discussed by ethnologists, whether the same art has arisen independently in widely separated areas or is an evidence of contact.

They prepare and cleanse the clay precisely as the Pueblo women do, kneading it with fine sand. The operator seats herself on the ground and places before her a piece of board on which she lays a ring of cocoanut leaves neatly bound together. Upon this ring she sets a shallow dish lined with a circular piece of plantain leaf. With a lump of clay the bottom of the vessel to be constructed is moulded in the dish. Upon this basis, by means of rolls of clay, the work is built up, the operator meanwhile turn-

---

* Butel-Dumont, Mém. sur la Louisiane, Paris, 1753, vol. ii. pp. 271-273. On the Indians of South America, C. F. Hartt, American Naturalist, February, 1879, pp. 83-89. Also, E. A. Barber and Captain Moss, the Ute Indians. All quoted by Holmes, Fourth An. Rep. Bur. Ethnol., p. 270.

ing the pot round and round, shaping it with her eye and hand. The vessel is set aside on a platform under the hut for a day or two to dry; only the smallest kind can be got ready for the kiln in one day.

The dried pot is taken from the platform and scraped with a shell, after which it is reversed and all excess of material externally removed by means of a fine strip of bamboo, moistened with water, as also are the fingers of the potter, and gently passed over the inner and outer surfaces of the vessel in order to smooth them. The pot is then replaced on the platform for ten days.

The kiln is prepared by sticking bits of broken pottery in the ground a few inches apart, and on these the pots are set upside down. In the space under the pot a layer of fine wood ash and a quantity of coconut shells and scraps of firewood are heaped. A wheel-like object, larger than the circumference of the pot, is laid on its upturned base, and against this the firewood is stood on end. The fuel is kindled, two or three women fan the flame, and they also with pokers of wood prop up and replace the fuel. When a vessel is baked, it is removed with the same implement and laid in dry sand. The stripes are laid on by means of strips of unripe coconut husk placed against the vessel while hot. The acid juice turns black the moment it touches the heated surface. Finally a handful of moist strips of husk are passed over the inner and the outer surface, imparting a light copper color to the parts not stained by the deeper dye. The vessels are stored for a year or so to season.[*]

The technical materials and processes having been considered, attention may now be given to what Aristotle would denominate the formal cause of aboriginal ceramic,

---

[*] E. H. Man, Journal of the Anthropological Institute, London, 1893, vol. xxiii, pp. 21-27, with plate.

the thoughts that were in every savage woman's mind whenever she laid her hands upon a mass of accommodating clay. It must not be forgotten that the vessel was always the result of the thought, and not vice versa. There is no doubt, also, that the making of the vessel was the occasion of much thought; but invention, in the last resort, is always a subjective process.

For holding, carrying, storing, cooking, serving food and drink, vessels have existed among all peoples. Of what they shall be made Nature has a deal to say, but in what shape they must appear the Mother of Invention will dictate in that matter. But the whole cause of the form is a little further to seek. For instance, our Bristol Bay Eskimo woman makes her rude lamps to burn blubber, but she continues to make them partly like the soapstone lamps and partly after her own fashion. So one might truly say that the absence of soapstone, the presence and docility of the clay, the need of a lamp-stove that will burn blubber with a moss wick, the patterns of the soapstone lamps, the stimulus of necessity, the ingenuity of the woman—that one and all of these were causes of the clay lamp and gave it its form. But the fundamental fact remains that the Eskimo woman was the true cause of the lamp of clay, and she was the inventor of it.

There is no doubt that all fictile artists primeval stumbled upon many forms, some of which were relegated to the company of rejected patents, and a limited number that have survived in the test of experience as the best for the purpose. Many of these forms they learned in Nature's art school, imitating here a gourd, there a shell, in other places more complicated vegetal and animal shapes.*

---

* Henry Balfour, The Evolution of Decorative Art, London, 1893, Percival; Holmes, Evolution of the Æsthetic, Proc. Am. Assoc., Salem, 1892, vol. xli, pp. 239-255.

This varied curriculum, this numerous corps of able instructors, have frequently been noticed in works on the origin of art forms. Here attention is drawn to the pedagogic limitations within which all pottery-making women have wrought. They rarely imitate canoes or other objects with which men have to deal. Their natural instigators were the things of daily experience. Moreover, when the potter's art passed largely out of the hands of women the shapes remained the same. This imitation of Nature is also supplemented by an imitation of woman's own art in other substances. Pottery is a laggard among the industries, and the ancestresses of the first potters had long been going to school in other materials. Mr. Holmes thinks that the potstone globular olla of California's southern coast could possibly have antedated the globular pottery; that the wooden tray is older than a similar form in clay, or the horn ladle than one in pottery. Even bark vessels and baskets for all purposes could have suggested forms in the softer paste. The same law of imitation could just as easily have worked the other way. That is not in question now. If it be granted that the soapstone olla was woman's creation and woman's implement which she invented, that is all that is asked. The wooden prototype would have been one that she dug out of a log, the birch-bark vessel of all uses, the basketry jar or carrying device or bottle, or what not—all were hers from first to last. Nowhere before the introduction of machinery and the potter's wheel does the stream of her activity in clay run into or come out of forms invented by men.

A pattern once acquired, there sets in with the priscan artists something akin to those linguistic softenings and abbreviations which Müller attributes to phonetic laziness. That is to say, a kind of plastic laziness, rounding of corners, inflating of sides, shortening of limbs, atrophying of parts nonessential or actually pernicious, until it requires a ceramist to reinstate the missing portions, to read backward the visible speech of generations of women who have kept the thought but varied the expression. A better name for this process would be "plastic economy," since most of the changes are wrought to save labour in the making or to render the thing made more serviceable.*

Not only is form borrowed from the things personally familiar to women, but the study of added features will show how little help she had from men.

The functional additions to pottery—the parts that are to serve some use—grow out of the experiences of women in the handling of the plain, round wares, in supporting or carrying them. The flaring out of the rim would admit of a string. The addition of handles, borrowed or original, are for the purpose of lifting. The little ring of fibre placed on the head to aid in carrying may be made in clay and stuck to the vessel in making. We have then the base, which may be secured also by punching up the bottom as in a bottle.

FIG. 27.—CLAY VESSEL MODELLED AFTER A SHELL VESSEL. (After Holmes.)

The structural element in the addition of ornament or of useful parts is extremely suggestive. The coil is ever present before the imagination of the potter in her own art, and so also is the great variety of indentations produced by her hands and finger tips. Seams, stitches, plaits, twists, knots, and the like are easily carried over from the textile art by moulding from them or by imitating them. And all these are ready in woman's special laboratory.

* See Holmes's analysis of ceramic ornament, Fourth An. Rep. Bur. Ethnol., p. 453.

The suggestions from accidents attending construction drop into receptive minds, whether made by the dainty fingers engaged, by the implements employed, or by the moulds in or upon which the material is wrought. The last class in Holmes's table is made up of those ornamental features which have no ideographic or pictorial significance to the artist, but which are derived from more intelligible forms that had real meanings, just as there are hundreds of derivative words in our language,

Fig. 26.—Vessel or Shell as Model for one in Clay. (After Holmes.)

used by us every day, of whose etymology few, if any, know aught. To declare that the stories and pictures hidden in all aboriginal designs on pottery of this class relate to woman's life and work and experiences alone would be going too far. Yet a review of the progress of the art of painting on pottery may reveal further woman's connection with the early nurture of designing. The colors employed were such as Nature furnished—white, black, and a great variety of reds. In following the patterns derived from other sources, the free hand produced creditable work, but when it left these leading strings and wandered into the imaginary or the descriptive area the operation is tentative and enigmatical. Still, an economy of effect was ever in mind. Those surfaces were chosen for painting that were most exposed; bowls received the ornament on the inside and on the outer rim. Jars with incurved rims were decorated on the outer, upturned border; bottles and ordinary jars were painted only on the exterior surfaces. The exposed surfaces were either covered with ornament in elaborate patterns, or the design was placed merely upon medallions, areas, or zones about the vessel. Where there is room for a multiplicity of designs these need not be related to one another, and the greatest liberty of grouping is allowed. The artist follows no special design, never traces in sand, or on skin, or any other surface the patterns she will produce. The formal cause of the decoration is in her mind; her working drawings are sketched on the walls of her imagination. It would consign a modern potter to retirement if his panels and pictures were not geometrically accurate. But the savage artist seems to relish asymmetry. She is not the least embarrassed if, with four repetitions of the same group in mind, she finds by and by that three of them have nearly exhausted her space. The quaint manner in which she compels the fourth to squeeze itself into the allotted area has been the delight of more than one civilized artist. The Pueblo woman seems to have passed through three well-marked stages of development in her pictorial, plastic art. In the first the forms of expression are mainly geometric. The elements are chiefly checkers, zigzags, chevrons, meanders, frotted figures, and scrolls, all developed out of woman's work in other technical fields. The second stage is the introduction of pictures, totemic emblems, mythic symbols and beings, and so forth, drawn out quite fully or in such half-abbreviated form as to contain still an intimation of the original. Compared with rhetoric, this stage is a species of trope in clay—ceramic metaphors, similes, and synecdoches. The third stage is that in which the pictorial, the synecdochical, the hieroglyphic art becomes still more abbreviated, syncopated, apocopated, until the relics of former ideograms become mere letters in an alphabet on the way to a higher language or, under the pressure of a higher civilization, degenerates into a jargon. At this point the savage woman stands *vis-à-vis* with two important roads forward

of which she does not seem to have taken either one.
The first leads to sculpture, to modelling, the creation in
the willing clay of new forms quite apart from her homely
work in surgery. The other leads to the potter's wheel,
the application of machinery to the production of symmetrical and exact work. The mere mention of machinery startled her. You must go to China for the simplest
form of this device, where you will see a man kicking the
spindle around with his naked feet without the aid of
wheels to multiply the speed. He is producing cylinders of
clay, which he will cut into two or three segments length-
wise for making tiles for roofs of houses. Other male
descendants of this primeval artist is the brickmaker, the
draintile maker, the village potter. But with them her
poor out-of-door fire is replaced by kilns and furnaces
capable of producing a vitreous glaze and organizing a
new art with which she has little to do.

This chapter would not be complete without a brief
reference to the functions of pottery. Long ago women
made pottery for themselves to wear out and only a little
for the convenience or delight of men. The very first
woman that made pottery, perhaps, set the vessel on her
head and went to the spring for water. A procession of
women have been walking about over the earth ever since
with jars on their heads. This first woman used another jar
to cook food and another to serve it, and another to keep
it clean and away from vermin and insects. Pray, what
are millions of her great-grandchildren doing this very
day but the selfsame things? It matters not who makes
pottery, they are making it for women. Their convenience alone is consulted in its form, its temper, and material. Its decorations are borrowed, and, though her
hands be no longer grimed with the paste, her wants and
her imagination preside over the wheel.

CHAPTER VI.

THE BEAST OF BURDEN.

ENDEAVOR to comprehend all that is involved in the word "transportation" or the "carrying industry." Take your stand as near as safety will allow to a passing freight train or a flying express, and drink in the excitement of civilization which it represents. Or, perchance, it may be your fortune from some commanding place to look upon a great harbor by day or by night and to reflect upon the time and money, the tons of freight, the miles of voyaging, the endless variety of things involved. Besides the train and the ship, there are innumerable occupations subsidiary to their management. Indeed, everything that is being moved would seem to be on its way to or from a car or a ship.

But these steel rails and steamships are of our century. There are men and women alive who remember when there were none of them. So we are not here concerned with the tedious operations by which the locomotive and its followers have been wrought out of the forest and the mine, nor of all the workshops that have co-operated in the making of a ship, but of something very much antedating these. Neglecting even all the wagon trains, mule trains, couriers, pack horses, dog trains and sleds, reindeer sleds, donkeys, elephants, camels, llamas, and other beasts of burden, we come at last to the common pack woman, for she was the first beast of burden on the earth.

From woman's back to the car and the stately ship is

the history of that greatest of all arts which first sent our race exploring and possessing the whole earth, and when they had acquired wealth and knowledge and refinement, brought these discrete civilizations together again for the purpose of developing humanity as a whole. I do not wonder that the ship carpenter carves the head of a woman on the prow of his vessel, nor that locomotives and railroad appliances should be addressed as she.

It might be denied that women were the first burden bearers, as there are innumerable examples of animals transporting materials to distant places to utilize them. The nest-building birds, the beavers, the lamprey eels, the bees, the ants, are all carriers. Many animals also modify natural objects and substances in using them. I shall not here inquire how much more industrious the females of all animals are, but the idea of modifying a natural object for the purpose of creating a carrying tool seems first to have occurred to the human female. She was primarily the only creature that transformed nature to produce an apparatus for the carrying of burdens. And this is in the line of our fundamental proposition.

There are two sets of motives in the harnessing of an engine or a draught animal and in the freighting of vessels and pack beasts. They may exist separately or combined in the same device, and they were as active in the mind of the earliest woman carriers as they have ever been. These two motives are *conveyance* and *freighting*, or the carrying of human beings and the carrying of things.

The former may, indeed, be older, for devices in which to carry infants may have been first in the order of invention. But in that early day the backs of women were palace car and freight car, and the woman herself supplied the energy.

Many other industries were created, stimulated, and

modified by this carrying trade. The member of pristine society who went to the fields to gather nuts and seeds and fruit must necessarily have brought them home. Hence the burden bearer must be a basket-maker, and the pack woman is patron of husbandry and of the textile art.

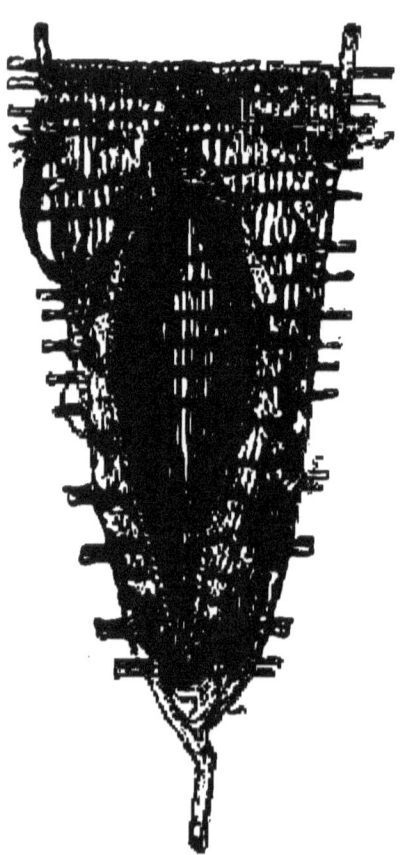

Fig. 31.—California Cradle Frame. (After Mason.)

Clay and fuel must be brought to make pottery, and pottery, in turn, has to be shaped to carry water and food, so the potter and the carrier are sisters.

In short, the burden bearer stands between each industry and its successor, passing the more or less changed material from one to the other.

It can not fail to be interesting to know how ingeniously those early passenger cars were constructed. It will be no disparagement to the vestibule train, so luxurious and so complete in all its appointments, to think of the savage woman, with papoose cradle strapped to her weary forehead, as the starting point of its elaboration.

When we consider how largely the comforts of the palace car minister to the ease of women, we may also think that the daughter is only reaping the harvest sowed by the mother. Though immensely less complicated, the earliest form has some points of interest that can not be neglected.

The primitive passenger coach builders were strictly scientific in their methods, as we shall see—that is, they ingeniously adapted structure to function and environment.

Fig. 20.—Eskimo Mothers. (After Cody.)

The Eskimo mother knows full well that her babe can not keep up the heat of its body when the temperature outside is forty below zero. To strap the little creature to a cradle board would insure its death at once.

So she makes a baby carriage of her hood, and her offspring, when she takes it abroad or when she is on a journey, is safely ensconced between the soft fur and the mother's warm neck. We need not stop to inquire how the modern parent would enjoy having a naked infant crawling about her equally naked shoulders all the day.

Between the land of the Eskimo on the north and the Tropic of Cancer on the south there dwelt in America many stocks of aborigines, speaking different languages, and having separate social organizations, but all characterised by the use of a papoose frame of some sort. The distinguishing marks of this apparatus were the back, the sides, the lashing, the bed, the pillow, the covering, the awning, the decoration. All of these were present in some form, but in each stock, and especially in each natural-history region, there were just such variations as were necessary and proper. In Canada the cradle was made of birch bark and the bed was of the finest fur. In the coast region of British Columbia and southward little arklike troughs were excavated as the boats were, and beds and pillows and wrappings of the finest shredded cedar bark took the place of furs.

Farther south still, as the climate became milder, the ark gave place to a little rack or gridiron of osier, sumac, or reed, and the face of the child was shaded from the sun by a delicate awning.

Across the Rocky Mountains, in the land of the buffalo, the papoose frame looks like a great shoe lashed to an inverted trellis or ladder, and nowadays the whole surface is covered with embroidered beadwork. It matters not where we travel within the limits assigned on the Western Continent, the primitive passenger car was exactly suited to the meteorological and other local conditions. A carriage made in Chicago would not suit the work to be done in California. Home products out of home ma-

torial, and made by home labour, were the rule. Upon the same isotherms in Asia children are borne as with us, but the peoples are far above savagery. In South America, outside the tropics, the conditions of North America exist.

When we come within the tropics, the papoose frame and all such inventions fail, and for a good reason. The preservation of the life of the infant is of greater importance than carrying it around. Hence the woman again must set her wits to work. Among savages in the tropics the head, shoulders, and limbs of the mother are usually unclothed, and the loins are in some way clothed, if only with a girdle and a sash or apron. Furthermore, the child is also unclothed. The only place for the passenger is on the locomotive. He has to straddle the mother's hips as best he can and hold on to the girdle. Where a *serape* or shawl of any kind is in use, the rider can crawl into that; and when the mother, in addition to being passenger car, has also freight to carry, the youngster rides on top of the freight.

It is interesting to note that among the animals most nearly resembling man in structure—the anthropoids—the mother travels always with the young holding on to her neck or riding on the hips. But there is no provision for the passenger in this case in the shape of a girdle or the shawl. The long hair of the mother bars her out from ever inventing anything of the kind.

In the division of labour, which in the progress of civilization enabled some adult persons to ride, the carrying of passengers fell to the lot of men. With this we have naught here to do. The *silleros* and *cargadores* and palanquin men and coolies have had enough to bear to command our respect and eulogy, but they are not now under examination.

In our later civilization the infant has come around

from the back to the left arm usually, but the curious train of baby carriers moves on from the beginning of human history, one of the few occupations that culture has not replaced.

In British New Guinea young infants are carried in small baskets over the mother's left shoulder. It is a common occurrence to see the mother carry on her back a basket of food, a large bundle of firewood—both being supported by a band extending round the forehead—and on top of all her little two-year-old baby. The women are habituated from early life to carrying enormous burdens.*

The top of the head and the forehead are almost universally used to help support a load resting on the back. But the Papuan mothers of Port Moresby, New Guinea, put their babies in a net sack, which is borne in front against the stomach and suspended by a line reaching over the bregma or crown of the head.†

If any one doubts that woman is a burden bearer by inheritance as well as by necessity let him take his stand near any market house or along a shopping street. There does not seem to be any bone in the body that is not in some way called on to bear its load. On the head it is toting. The Indian woman hangs a small weight on the very crown of her head, by means of a buckskin band, and lets it hang down her back. If the weight be increased, the strap is drawn to the forehead and the load falls more on the shoulder blades. But the Pueblo female has a more world-wide custom; she sets her water jar on her head, with or without the milkmaid's pad. The negress of the

---

* Thomson, British New Guinea, London, 1892, Philip, p. 121. Dodge says: "I have seen a Nez Percé woman playing a vigorous game of ball with a baby on her back." Our Wild Indians, Hartford, 1883, p. 190.

† Ibid., p. 80.

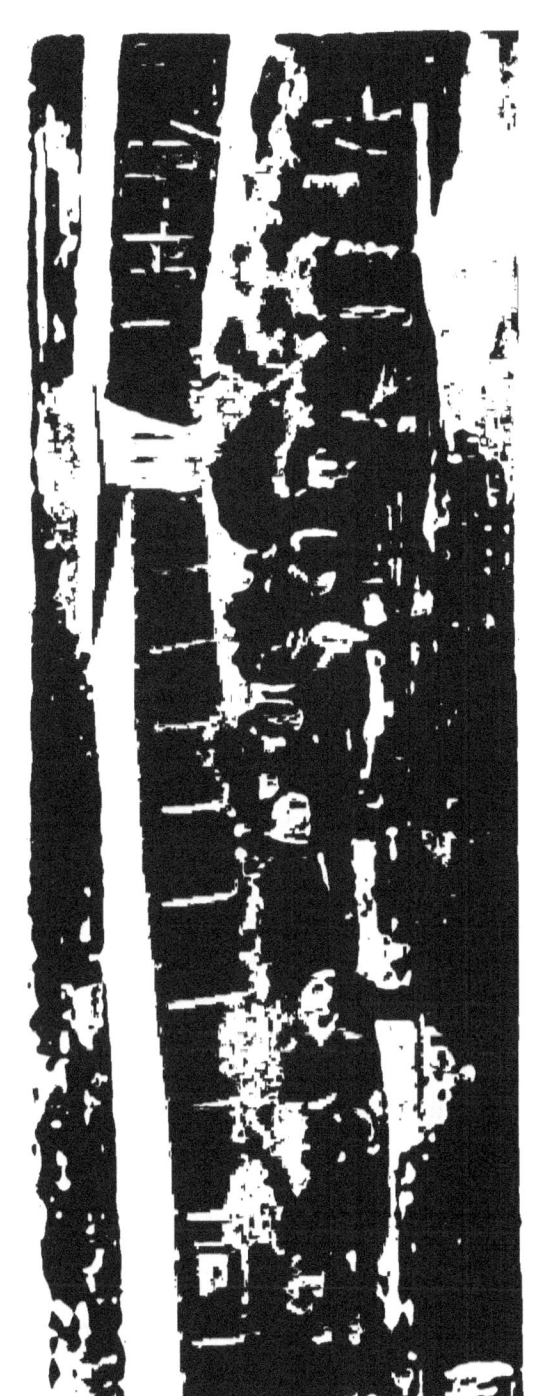

FIG. 22.—ESKIMO MEN AND WOMEN DELIVERING HAY TO THE GOVERNMENT.

Southern States brought with them the custom of toting, and the Irish as well as the Italian women are able to poise delicately almost any load on the calvarium. Descending to the neck, there is a fashion of hanging all sorts of fakir's merchandise on the nape by means of a broad strap supporting a miniature counter; but men are the fakirs in our country. The shoulder is also a great bearer of burdens, even for women, as the millions of travelling satchels will testify; but lower down than this interminable caravan of satcheled females are the true pack women, whom you may see by thousands in most Continental cities wearing knapsack fashion some sort of a device for bearing the impediments of life's struggle. By means of a Holland yoke the shoulders and the atlas are all brought into requisition, not to mention the hands and arms. No doubt many of my readers have seen a milkmaid bearing a pail of milk on her head and two more on her shoulders and arms by means of such a yoke.

The Chinese and other Oriental peoples use a yoke on one shoulder at a time, pointing the way the bearer is going. Away down in Arizona hay is delivered at the agency by Mojave Indian women, who go out and cut with common house knives the "grammar grass," put it up in immense sheaves, and bring it to the agency on their backs—on their shoulders rather, we should say, for they trudge along like Chinamen with poles resting on the shoulder and a sheaf of hay sticking on either end of the pole. What shall we call them? Mowers and rakers and common carriers all in one poor body. This hay is brought to the agency for the benefit of the beasts, and these poor creatures will undertake to deliver a ton of hay cheaper than it can be got in any other way.

From the shoulder we come to notice the back. Those who have no loads to carry complain of backache, but if all the serious loads resting on women's backs could be added up they would rival those of railroads and steamers.

As a beast of burden, whether in Germany or Mexico, or among the savage American tribes, woman in her carrying basket moves the food and household effects while her husband shoulders the gun or more primitive artillery.

I pass over the millions of tiny packages that are borne in the hands all day long and everywhere, amounting in the long run to a great deal and about Christmas time becoming quite burdensome. But we must not overlook the poor man's wife, who goes every day to the market and, after studying maxima and minima—that is, how to get the most provisions for the least money—to the extent of her ability and of the advice of her numerous confidantes, hangs from twenty-five to fifty pounds of eatables on her elbow and rests the basket on her hip. It would take a practised physiologist to tell how many bones and muscles and nerves and brain cells are in active operation during this fatiguing exercise.

We should be extremely ungrateful to the washerwomen and lose a most interesting scheme for hitching up a pack woman if we did not note them holding to the lugs or ears of a tub or boiler which they were supporting on the limbs just above the knees. A very heavy load may be carried in this way, the burden being shifted from one knee to the other as the woman steps along.

From this review it is very easy to see that a woman has more ways of being hitched up than any of the pack animals. At this point it is necessary to look more minutely at some of the appliances for sustaining loads upon the various parts of her body.

There is in the National Museum at Washington a series of rings of vegetable fibre. The various substances of which they are composed show that they are from lands wide apart. But all are labelled " carrying rings or

Fig. 23.—Ute Children Carrying Water in Basket Bottles. (After Powell.)

pads." They were made to fit on the tops of savage women's heads when they were bearing jars of water or other loads. When the jar of water or basket of seeds is lifted from the head the pad is set on the ground and the jar rested upright thereon. One day some clever savage woman bethought herself to make the bottom of her jar or basket concave a little bit by pushing the clay or frame splints upward. Presto! The carrying pad is antiquated. From that day to this every basket and bottle and tub has stood on its own bottom. It is wonderful how this method of freighting has stuck to women. The negresses of the South, not less than the dark-haired and dark-eyed Europeans practice toting everywhere. But the blue-eyed and blond-haired women take their loads on their backs.

Before dismissing the top of the woman's head as a place of attachment for loads attention may be recalled to the Apache and other tribes of Arizona, whose women carry water in jugs made of basketry and dipped in pitch. The maker ties two strong loops of horsehair to the bulging sides, to which are fastened the ends of a long buckskin strap. The middle of this hangs to the very top of the head and enables the carrier to walk tolerably upright because the load is not heavy.

There is an engineering device called "parbuckle," and the International Dictionary, if speaking in the language of this volume, would call it "a kind of purchase for hoisting upon a woman's back a bundle of fagots or other cylindrical load." The middle of a long rope (flat and soft) is made to pass aloft around the woman's forehead or brow and both parts are looped under the load behind her and brought back over her shoulders to her hands. The load is rolled up on to her back or let down by hauling up or paying out the ends. Such "burden straps" or ropes, are made of hide or textile stuffs, with a broad, flat, soft piece in the middle. In some tribes the women make a pad in shape of a diadem to keep from wounding the forehead. It would be curious to find out whether such a plain thing were the starting point of the regal decoration. The stitch and material of these objects must be studied under the substance of which they are composed. In form they are bags of leather or woven work, inverted cones of basketry or network with or without frames and even gourds sustained in netting. Each one of these with its load rests on the back of its bearer, and is kept from slipping down by the band of soft leather passing from the vessel to the forehead. Where the loads to carry are compact and heavy the baskets are small, but where the load is bulky and light the apparatus is so large as to conceal the carrier under the burden. It is in the manufacture of this peculiar class of carrying inventions that the reactions of trades upon trades may be studied advantageously. The basket-maker has a good customer in the carrier, and her wits are stirred to devise something light and strong for the purpose. Many of the forms of primitive basketry, and even some of its stitches, were devised exclusively for the burden bearers.

FIG. 34.—THE KRAPEACK IN WOMAN'S WORK.—GERMAN PEASANT WOMAN.

The knapsack, we say, belongs to soldiers and schoolboys. Let us not be too sure of that. If you will get up early some morning and walk around the busy portions of a German city you will see upon a box or table a cylindrical basket, holding half a bushel, more or less, with the sticks of the frame projecting an inch or two downward from the bottom, and two broad straps fastened at one end to the rim of the basket, and having eyelets or loops at the loose ends. Presently you will see a woman back up to the basket, draw the straps over her shoulders, and pass the ends backward around the projecting frame sticks below. She is now hitched up and may walk off with such load as the basket may contain. Perhaps this is older than the knapsack.

In the interesting lecture of Lieutenant Peary on his trip across Greenland he represents an Eskimo woman carrying a rough stone for the foundation of a house, and computed that it could not weigh less than three hundred pounds. The distance travelled was about twenty yards. The rock was slung in a walrus line and borne on the back. Murdoch says that the Eskimo women of Point Barrow have great flexibility of body, and show a power of carrying heavy loads superior to most white men.[*] Collinson says that among the Eskimo whom he visited all the drudgery falls upon the women; even the boys would transfer their loads to their sisters.[†]

This faithful creature, whose sturdy back sustained so many tons of the world's commerce at first until it had gained some momentum, was in those early times, as she is now in many places, among the toilers of the sea. The Eskimo, who occupy the entire arctic shore of America,

---

[*] Murdoch, Ninth An. Rep. Bur. Ethnol., Wash., 1892, p. 38. See also Cruise of the Corwin, Wash., 1885, p. 40; Petroff, Trans. Anthrop. Soc., Washington, vol. I, p. 33.

[†] Collinson, J. Roy. Geog. Soc., London, 1855, vol. xxv, p. 201.

have two kinds of boat—the *kaiak*, or man's boat, a sort of man-of-war, covered with sealskin all over instead of steel; and the *umiak*, or woman's boat, for freight and passengers. The skin of the ground seal (*Phoca barbata*) is prepared by the Eskimo women by removing the hair and the inner integuments and stretching it like a drumhead over the excellent frame, which her husband constructs out of driftwood. In the propulsion of this boat she uses often an oar and not a paddle, and her rowlocks are worthy of a patent, for each one consists of two loops of rawhide interlocked like the links of a chain and fastened to the gunwale at a proper distance. Between these loops the oar is thrust, and Boas tells us that three or four women work at each oar. There are no patent devices for steering, the oar serving also for that. Once in a while, with a fair wind, a sail is set, made of the intestines of the seal carefully sewed together. In these craft the women of the Eskimo are accustomed to move the family and their effects from place to place when the exigencies of hunting demand.

Mrs. Allison, in her account of the Similkameen Indians of British Columbia, reveals in a few lines an instructive mixture of trades and traffic involving much carrying. The service berry was a staple with the Similkameens. When the berries were ripe mats were laid under the bushes and the berries beaten off them and dried in the sun. A portion was then reserved for home consumption; the rest were put into sacks made of rushes strung together by threads of wild hemp, and traded with either the Hope or Okanagan Indians for dried salmon or water-tight baskets, in the manufacture of which the Hope Indians excelled. These baskets were used for boiling water or meat; they were filled with water and hot stones were thrown in till it boiled. To roast the meat it was transfixed with stakes which were driven into the ground in front of their fires. The Hope Indians wove mats of cedar bark, and these the Similkameen Indians greatly preferred to those they made themselves with tule or rushes threaded on twine, as they were stronger and did not harbour vermin. The summer dwellings were made of these mats thrown over a circular frame of poles. The winter houses were simply pits dug in the ground and roofed with poles and earth. A hole in the top afforded ingress and egress to the dwellers (a notched ladder serving as ladder or stairway); this orifice was also the sole chimney.*

In Hearne's delightful old narrative we read: "He attributed all our misfortunes to the misconduct of my guides; and the very plan we pursued, by the desire of the governor, in not taking any women with us on this journey, was, he said, the principal thing that occasioned all our wants; 'for,' said he, 'when all the men are heavy laden, they can neither hunt nor travel to any considerable distance; and in case they meet with success in hunting, who is to carry the produce of their labor?' 'Women,' added he, 'were made for labour; one of them can carry, or haul, as much as two men can do. They also pitch our tents, make and mend our clothing, keep us warm at night, and, in fact, there is no such thing as travelling any considerable distance, or any length of time, in this country without their assistance.' 'Women,' said he again, 'though they do everything, are maintained at a trifling expence; for, as they always stand cook, the very licking of their fingers in scarce times is sufficient for their subsistence.' This, however odd it may appear, is but too true a description of the situation of women in this country: it is at least so in appearance, for the women

---

* Mrs. S. S. Allison, J. Anthrop. Inst., London, 1892, vol. xxi, p. 308.

always carry the provisions, and it is more than probable they help themselves when the men are not present."[*]

The most primitive ferrywomen belonged to the Sioux tribes on the Missouri River, of whom Mr. Catlin relates that the old chief, having learned that he was to cross the river, gave directions to one of the women of his numerous household, who took upon her head a skin canoe, made of a buffalo's hide stretched on a frame of willow boughs, which she placed in the water. When Catlin and his two friends were seated in this wicker tub the woman stepped before the boat and, pulling it along, waded toward the deep water, where she turned her buckskin tunic over her head and, throwing it ashore, plunged forward, swimming and drawing the boat. In the middle of the stream they were surrounded by a dozen young girls from the opposite shore. They all swam in a bold and graceful manner, gathering around the boat with their long black hair floating about on the water. They had discharged meanwhile the conductress from the other shore, and were playing with the boat, whirling it around in midstream in hope of larger pay, which, indeed, they received in the form of bead necklaces which the distinguished traveller placed over their necks as they rose out of the water. The party were then towed ashore by the dusky mermaids much to their own delight. In the days of plentiful buffalo hundreds of these wicker-lined tubs of rawhide were made and navigated on the Missouri River by Sioux women.[†]

"A Dyak woman generally spends the whole day in the field, and carries home every night a heavy load of vegetables and firewood, often for several miles, over rough and hilly paths; and not unfrequently has to climb

---

[*] Hearne, Journey, etc., London, 1790, Strahan, p. 55.
[†] Cf. Catlin, Smithson. Rep., p. 400.

a rocky mountain by ladders, and over slippery stones, to an elevation of a thousand feet. Besides this she has an hour's work every evening to pound the rice with a heavy wooden stamper, which violently strains every part of the body. She begins this kind of labor when nine or ten years old, and it never ceases but with the extreme decrepitude of age." *

The Egyptian women of the laboring classes work very hard. They draw the household water supply from the river or from a neighboring canal, carrying it in large earthenware jars of native manufacture on their heads. In addition to household duties they also work in the fields among the crops, and one may frequently be observed leading out to water and to such scanty pasture as may be found the family gamoos or black-skinned buffalo (*Bos bubulus*), the native milch cow of Egypt.†

In Africa, Sir Samuel Baker "observed that women were constantly passing to and fro with baskets on their heads, carrying salt from Gondokoro, and each returning with a goat led by a string."‡

The Quissama women of Angola carry large baskets made of plaited grass slung upon their backs, supported by a band or strap which passes across the forehead. This band is generally ornamented with the teeth of animals they have killed themselves, such as the leopard, hyena, etc."ⁿ

Among the Bedouins, when the elders had "decided to emigrate in search of better pasture, the men set off with about eighty camels. Immediately after their departure the women in the camp broke out into bustling and noisy activity. As if by magic the tents fell to the

---

* Wallace, Malay Archipel., New York, 1869, p. 109.
† Robert Wallace, J. Soc. Arts, London, 1893, vol. xl, p. 599.
‡ Sir Samuel Baker, Ismailïa, New York, 1875, p. 135.
ⁿ Price, J. Anthrop. Inst., London, 1872, p. 189.

ground, were bundled up and placed on the few camels left for that purpose, and in an inconceivably short time the whole caravan passed up the river and disappeared. The women did the whole work, while those 'lords of creation,' their masters, sauntered off in utter unconcern." *

In the Holy Land, even in our day "the daughters of the men of the city come out to draw water" (Gen. xxiv, 13). Thomson says: "The only well is at least half a mile from the village, and women and girls, in many groups, were passing to and from it all day long, with tall black jars perched upon their heads." †

The loads borne by Kurdish women are thus graphically described: "Soon we came to a place where the road was washed away, and we were obliged to go around. We saw a woman there with a loaded donkey which could not pass with its load. The woman took the load on her back and carried it over and led the donkey over. She also carried a load of her own weighing at least one hundred pounds, and she had a spindle in her hands. Thus she went spinning and singing over the rugged way which I had passed with tears and pain. In the evening they spin and make sandals; when they lie down they place under their heads the ropes used in binding the heavy loads of grass and wood which they bring down the mountains. After midnight they go up to get loads. In the early morning I often saw the women, looking like loaded beasts, coming down the precipitous mountain path, one after another, spinning and singing as they came. I saw women with great paniers on their backs and babies on top of these or in their arms,

---

* Thomson, The Land and the Book, New York, 1880, vol. iii, p. 608.

† Ibid., vol. i, p. 90.

going four days over that fearful Ishtaxin pass, carrying grapes for sale and bringing back grain. Men said that women must suffer much more before God forgave Eve's sin. A few years ago a woman from Jeloo came to my home in Geoglapa. Her husband, who was almost a giant, sickened in Gawar, and she told me she had carried him on her back all the way, four days' journey. I did not believe her then; now I do, for my eyes have seen what loads these women carry." *

One of the interesting survivals of the old into the new time is shown in the report of Consul Dithmar concerning the working women in Silesia.†

The number of women engaged in hard manual labor in mines and furnaces is actually increasing. In zinc furnaces they are employed in removing the product and the refuse. In the morning the women must tend the ovens while the place is filled with dust and zinc vapors, and their severe physical labor is performed in an overheated atmosphere tempered only by dangerous drafts.

In the ore mines the women are employed mainly at the hoisting shafts and at pushing cars. At a depth of twenty-two yards the task of four girls is to hoist eighty tubs, containing from one to one and a half hundredweight of ore each, to the surface in a shift of eight hours. That workwomen prefer this severe labor to domestic service is owing to the restrictions placed on house servants and their long hours of labor.

In the foundries, steel works, and rolling mills women perform day laborer's services. But the condition of female laborers in mines, furnaces, and factories is not so

---

* Woman's Work for Women, November, 1889, p. 266.
† U. S. Consular Rep., 1889, March, No. 103, p. 481; also British blue book on the condition of woman's work.

11

deplorable as that of the women and girls who endeavor to earn a livelihood by hand labor in the cities.

One of the interesting sights of Copenhagen is the canal, where hundreds and hundreds of sturdy-looking women are engaged in the fisheries. There are men, of

FIG. 85. THE DANISH FISH WOMAN.

course, among the hardy folk, and they have their toils and their emoluments, but one never tires in leaning over the rail in looking at the women. They manage the boats, they transfer the fish from one craft to another, they sell them by wholesale and by retail, they deliver them. Furthermore, they prepare the fish in every way

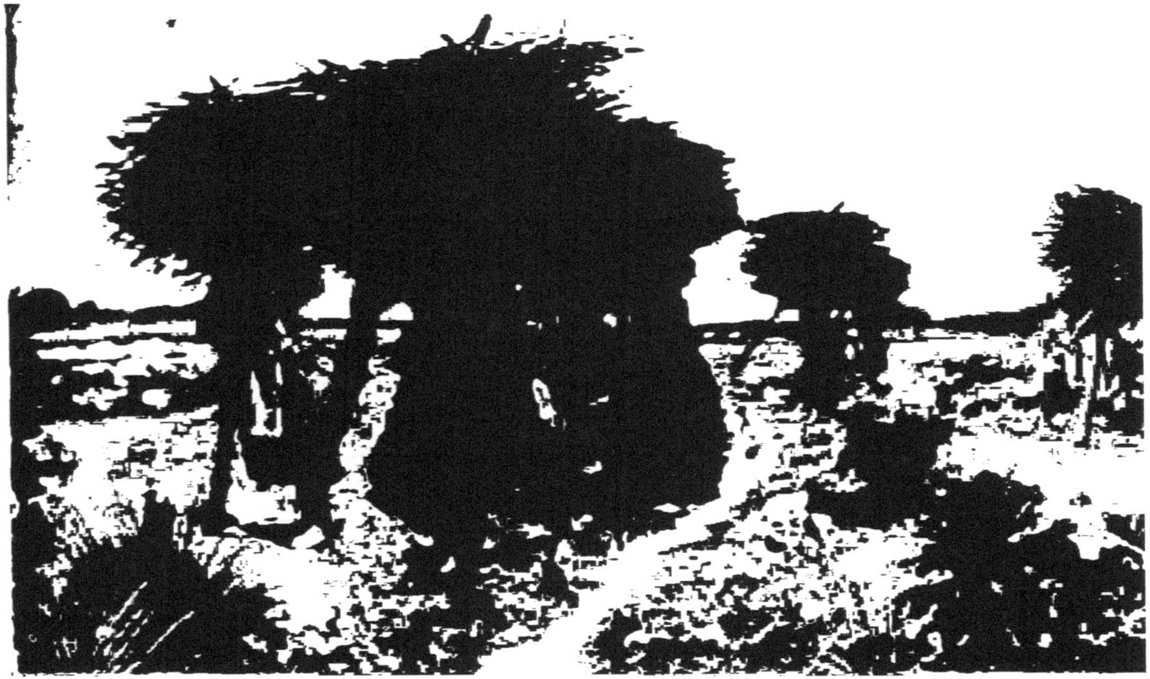

Fig. 24.—[illegible] Wood Gatherers. [illegible]

demanded by the tastes of the people. And one must visit the Scandinavians to find out how many ways there are of getting sea food ready for the table.

In this the women of Norway, Sweden, and Denmark are following in the footsteps of very ancient and very primitive sisters. Had they visited northern California only a few years ago they would have seen the Indian women gather the wild hemp, hackle it with their teeth, spin it with the hand on the thigh, manufacture out of it most excellent nets for eels and fish, and handle the creatures as skillfully as themselves. The Danish men and women have always been of hardy stock, and now the women are among the most industrious and laborious in the world.

The women in France who are successors of the primitive burden bearer are on the land what the Danish women are on the sea, chiefly concerned with harvesting. It is true that in Paris, the ideal capital of the world, one who is abroad early enough will see bread women and vegetable women hauling waggons about the street. But the peasantry are the true folk. They do not use the head band. European women are quite emancipated from that, and have adopted the shoulder strap, which is akin to the knapsack.

The soldier, with his back load of equipment and ammunition, and the peasant woman, with her back load of all sorts of industrial products, repeat the ancient story of civilization from the beginning. As long as the peace of Europe demands so much preparation for war the woman's back will continue to support the civil government.

At the Art Exposition at Venice in 1887, Gioli's picture of the wood carrier showed us that in sunny Italy, as in France, woman is the beast of burden.*

---

* Of Prof. Gioli's painting, Mrs. Zelia Nuttall, the distinguished anthropologist says: "It has fairly haunted me day and night. I

According to Mr. Kennan, the Russian women who take part in building or in moving heavy loads have the co-operative method of transportation, well known in the African carrying chair or the palanquin. In this case a frame resembling the top of a bier is borne by two women who together transport at least two hundred pounds. Besides this method of their own, the Russian women know every form of bowing the neck or the back to heavy burdens.

The German pack woman may be seen on any morning especially near the markets, and she is an interesting creature, because, if her face were brown and her hair coal black you could take her for an American sister before the discovery. There is this difference: that all American pack women wear the band across their foreheads, while the German type load the shoulders. A basket of willow or rattan, holding a bushel, flat at least on one side to fit the car-

Fig. 37. — German Bread Woman Supporting the Sinews of War.

rier's back, having a strap or rope fastened to either corner of the flat side at the upper edge, and looped at the lower end to pass easily over a projection at the bottom of the basket—that is the harness or furniture of this beast of burden. By this device—which works very much like a soldier's knapsack, only she gets out of it much easier—the German woman supports the throne of her emperor in time of peace. Her shoulders, and back, and

---

are yet aghast at the idea that hundreds of Italian women carry such immense loads of wool in our day and within a few miles from Florence."

groins, and hands, all take part in the exercise, and it is difficult to think of any more effective arrangement for getting work out of a human being. Really, in the light of this picture, Atlas should have been a woman, and if the originator of the myth or the designer of the picture had not been a man we should everywhere now behold an idealized female carrying the globe on her back in a basket.

FIG. 35.—GERMAN MARKET WOMEN.

Apropos to this wonderful survival of this ancient pack woman the following is taken from the New York World:*

"Work doesn't kill. If it did, the average German woman would die before she completed her girlhood. As it is, she is driven from the age of fourteen years until she reaches her second childhood.

---

* Sunday, August 7, 1899; cf. also Pit Girls in the Black District, vol. lix, p. 416.

"In the market place opposite the Frauenkirche, Nuremberg, there are two remarkable studies—'The Fountain of Beauty' and the little cherry woman. One has been there since 1361, and the other for the last sixteen years. She comes into town with a handcart as big as a bed; at one end is her brown baby, at the other her black cherries, and between them a garden of vegetables. This woman—mother, horse, and huckster—sits in the market from five o'clock in the morning until seven o'clock in the evening, with a pot of coffee and a loaf of bread for what she is pleased to call her 'second breakfast, dinner, and supper.' In the evening the cherry woman packs up the unsold greens, tucks the hay about her sleeping baby, puts herself in the traces, and drags her waggon home.

"But she doesn't go alone. The weary procession is a long one, and as varied as life itself. One truck has a cow and an old woman in harness; another, a dog and the farmer's wife; in a third, grandmother and grandchild make the team; and in the rear come the children, stunted in growth and rudely clad, with baskets bigger than their little selves strapped to their young shoulders.

"The life of the woman who picks up a living is not harder, though more uncertain. When she applies to the farmer for work she has no choice but to work. She fells trees, chops wood, hauls coal, cleans the cattle pens, gives the fattened hog a scrubbing when he needs it, oils the machinery, puts an edge on whatever tools she uses in the field, and performs the roughest kinds of stable work. In the city the woman who hires out by the day does, and is expected to do, anything and everything. She washes, scrubs, and irons; she hauls every drop of water that she uses from the fountain or neighboring pump, carrying it in a tin can from five to eight feet tall strapped on her back; she sweeps the stretch of cobblestone paving from the doorstep to the centre of the street.

THE BEAST OF BURDEN.   137

"Perhaps the most distressing figure in the rank and file of this involuntary servitude is a woman—wife and mother—of the last decade of the nineteenth century toiling up a plank to the top of a building in course of construction with a load of mortar on her back.

"One of the most picturesque of the eight gates of Nuremberg is the Ladies' Gate. It was designed by Albert Dürer in 1555. Early in the spring an appropriation was made by the city, and the work of restoring the old tower and the mediæval arches began at once. Assisting the staff of masons and mechanics are two female hod carriers, and it is not an exaggeration to say that they are harder worked than any day laborer on the force. They arrive at the tower at six o'clock in the morning, and at once begin their labors.

FIG. 55.—HOD CARRIERS IN NUREMBERG.

The tin in which the mortar is carried is perhaps eighteen inches in diameter at its greatest width, and three feet deep. By means of a leather strap it is adjusted to the shoulders. Each woman takes the shovel in her own hands, fills her can, slips her arms through the strap, shoulders the load, plods up to the scaffold where the masons are at work, and unloads her burden without assistance of any kind.

"It all seems such a cruel waste of good material—her complexion tanned and tough as whitleather, her figure robbed of every line of grace and beauty, her poor willing hands rough-grained, gross, and callous as a ploughman's, and her body bent like the pictured slaves in the galley. She wears a hempen sack tied about her waist to protect the shapeless cotton dress and a melancholy kerchief tied over her head to shield it from the broiling sun; a pair of worthless boots cover her heavy feet, and the luxury of stockings neither burdens nor bothers her. Apparently she is impervious to the weather. At eight o'clock the men rest. The women do, too, after they have brought the tankards of beer and cut the bread for the second breakfast. At noon these beasts of burden lay down their mortar cans, untie their aprons, and go home to prepare the dinner for their husbands. The meal over, the cottage is made tidy, and at two o'clock they are back at the building, where they remain until seven o'clock, toiling along the plank walk and straining under the load that seems so cruelly heavy for a woman living in this generation to be allowed to bear.

"After the day's work she has her household duties to perform. Her earnings amount to five cents an hour. If there is a daughter at home to provide for the creature comforts of the family the mother works ten hours a day. If not, the law restricts her employment to six hours. But in either instance she is in harness between 6 A. M. and 7 P. M."

CHAPTER VII.

THE JACK-AT-ALL-TRADES.

THERE are other industrial arts and activities subsidiary to those already described which were fostered in their infancy by women. Moreover, there is a higher law in culture that must not be overlooked in this connection. It is the law of co-ordination and co-operation. Among the marks by which civilization is characterized, number and variety of material used, of parts in the apparatus, and of products desired are prominent. By number is also meant the aggregate of individuals that can be brought to work out a single idea acting in harmony. By variety is to be understood the number of distinct operations that one individual performs in a given time.

It is not enough, in speaking of savage women, to say that they, as a class, do this or that. It should be also asked how many of these are performed by one woman—in short, by every woman? Recalling what was previously said about the user of an implement having to be the maker of it, one sees to what a diversity of occupations this would naturally lead.

For example, in the stone age women used, as has been shown in describing their function of food bringer, knives, hammers, mortars, cooking pots, and many other implements of stone. The lapidary art in olden time included the following operations:

1. Spalling, flaking, chipping.
2. Battering, pecking, bushhammering.

140 WOMAN'S SHARE IN PRIMITIVE CULTURE.

3. Cutting, sawing, boring.
4. Grinding, smoothing, polishing.

In the beginning every one was his own lapidary. The men performed the foregoing operations in the manufacture of whatever entered into their warrings, the women, in like manner, practiced them in their peaceful works. By and by, doubtless, there came to be cunning men and cunning women who wrought in stone alone, and then the number and variety of such workings consumed the entire life of an individual.

Fig. 42.—German Women as Housewives, Gardeners, Domesticators, Draught Animals, and Merchants. (After Chandler.)

Mr. Cushing and Dr. Palmer both say that when the women go out to quarry clay or to gather food in the cañons men accompany them, but this is for a body guard, and the custom is still kept up, though the men have been disarmed and there is no need of protection.

In his various papers on the aboriginal quarries of the United States Mr. Holmes has worked out the diversity of processes and implements concerned. When an Indian woman demanded a stone knife she might indeed knock off a sharp flake from the nearest pebble having conchoidal fracture and sufficient toughness, but no savage woman with whom ethnologists are acquainted was satisfied with such an implement. Even the Tasmanians and Fuegians and Andamanese, on the outskirts of savagery, desired something better. Knowing that stones lying on the surface and exposed to the sun are hard and brittle, and that pebbles buried in wet earth are tough and best adapted to this operation of chipping, the knife-makers sought their materials there. See now what a diversity of occupation this cutlery work involved:

1. The digging out of the pebbles or masses of rock with sticks sharpened and hardened by means of fire, frequently the breaking of masses with stone sledges and the dislodging of bowlders with rude picks of antler and with crowbars. The work of both sexes.

2. The blocking out of implements by striking one stone with another. This operation required great strength, dexterity, and patience, since not one piece in ten turned out at last to be fit for an implement. The work of men and women.

3. The carrying home of the products of this quarrying, often many miles distant. Should we find out that the digging and blocking out were done by men only, there would be no doubt concerning the back upon which the half-finished material would be loaded.

4. The turning of the blocked-out material into knives for skinning animals, scaling fish and opening them, carving meat, preparing hides, cutting leather and fur skins. This work was frequently done in exquisite fashion, and the only implement the woman used was a bit of hard bone or antler pointed at the end like a corn-husking peg.

For the second style of stone working which our savage woman was expected to do we must turn to Mr. McGuire, who has studied the uses of the stone hammer.* It is astonishing to see what a variety of work men have accomplished by simply pounding one stone with another; but here we are concerned with women. The American aboriginal millers used several kinds of mills for the reduction of food to meal or flour.

1. A hollowed log and a wooden pestle.
2. A hollowed log with a stone pestle.
3. A hollowed stone, fixed or loose, with stone or wooden pestle.
4. A flat table or *metate* of stone operated on by a muller or rubbing stone.

Now, each one of the stone elements in the four classes was always made in the way indicated—namely, by pounding off the unnecessary part of the stone. To produce a pestle the savage woman selected from the brook or the quarry a piece as nearly in the proper shape as possible. This she did to economize her labor. Then with a hard disk-shaped stone hammer she battered away the useless projections.

By the very same process she produced mortars and *metates*, only she had to be much more careful and dexterous, for some of these objects are not only shapely and symmetrical, but they are also ornamented with much taste.

In the hulling of acorns, grinding of maize and grass seeds and rice, the mortar was universally used in the temperate parts of North America. But the rubbing of food to reduce it commences at about the thirty-sixth parallel of the Interior Basin and was practiced along the Cordilleras and in the West Indies. All through Latin America the women rub one stone up and down upon

---

* Am. Anthropologist, Wash., 1902, vol. v, p. 165.

another by the same motion as the washerwoman practices on the washboard. This apparatus is now manufactured and sold as a regular article of commerce, but we are speaking of a period when the women had to batter them out for themselves. It would not do to affirm that women invented the stone hammer. The men of long ago pecked away most patiently upon their peculiar implements and weapons with this wonderful tool, and with it they worked out the rudiments of the art of sculpture. But millers and cooks and bone breakers were up and stirring quite as early in the morning of time as the fashioners of clubs and axes of stone.

James Mooney says that the Moki women have fifty ways of preparing corn for food. They make all the preparations necessary for these varied dishes, involving the arts of the stonecutter, the carrier, the mason, the miller, and the cook. The women go over to the cañons to get the stones for the mill. Having brought in a number of large sandstone slabs, they trim down the edges with hammers of hard stone. They next scoop out trenches, and in them set up the slabs, making a sort of box seven feet long and twenty inches wide, divided into four equal compartments. The box is set up near a wall, in order that the women may brace their feet when grinding. One of the women measures the right space by kneeling with her feet and back against the wall, while another marks off the line in front of the knees. After the boxes are set up the joints and corners are plastered with clay.

The stone slabs or *metates* on which the corn is to be ground are then placed one in each compartment. Each has a different granular surface, and they are placed in the compartments in order, the roughest for the coarse meal at one end, the next finest for making meal like our corn meal, and, last, a smooth stone for producing maize flour. The roller or muller that goes with each slab corresponds in grain. The metates are set in the four compartments at an angle of about forty-five degrees and plastered in firmly with clay mortar.

In grinding, the women kneel behind the box, brace their feet against the wall, throw some corn upon the sloping metate, and then, grasping the muller in both hands, bear down with it upon the corn, bending over and giving the roller a half turn at each movement. This milling is hard, slow work, but the women make it lighter by the soft, musical, grinding songs which they sing in time with the motion of their arms. They construct a furnace for baking the bread by setting up two slabs against the wall about fifteen inches apart, and placing across these as a top another slab of the same hard stone as the metates and rollers, its upper surface, upon which the bread pastes are spread, being perfectly smooth.[*]

In this connection it may be safely affirmed that steatite—called also potstone, lardstone, and soapstone—has belonged to woman from the earliest times. It has one characteristic which makes it priceless to savages—it will not crack in the fire. Used flat, it is the oldest of griddles, as it is the latest. Hollowed just a little, it is a baking pan as well as a lamp. In semiglobular form it becomes the faithful dinner pot, and in shape of a sphere it is the olla, grandmother of all teakettles.

It will be instructive to pay minute attention to this steatite art on account of the jack-at-all-trades activities which it stimulated. The mineral itself occurs in all sorts of outcroppings, but not in great abundance anywhere and infrequently free from flaws and pits. On the whole, it is a rare material, and the aborigines deserve great credit for finding and developing it.

---

[*] Mooney, The Republic, St. Louis, Mo., May 21, 1898.

After removing the surface soil from a ledge, or outcrop of the material, the quarry women proceeded with their sharp axes of quartzite to work off a block large enough to make the desired vessel, allowing a bountiful amount for waste and accidents. This block they hewed down, both within and without, into nearly the designed shape at the quarry. The marks on many hundreds of rejected pieces show that the trimming was done with an adzelike or chisel-like tool, the scars resembling those left on wood by such an implement. Thus far we have seen our workwomen handling pick, shovel, crowbar, and adzo, and next they must take up their ever-recurring burden and transport the half-finished product to their home. There they scraped down the object to its desired shape and carefully seasoned it to endure the fire.

This soapstone working is truly a stone cutting, since the marks of an edged tool are left upon it. But savage woman knows as well as any one else that one stone will grind away another, will smooth another and polish it; she also knows that nothing will give a more beautiful surface to pottery than a close-grained stone. The smoothing stone is also useful in her bark and textile art, and serves her in good stead in grinding down shells for decoration.

Before leaving the mineral kingdom as a field for woman's versatility we may pause a moment to consider the harvesting and preparation of salt. Aboriginally it was not used in preserving meat, but in seasoning food. Many animals before man had learned to look upon salt as indispensable to their happiness. As the food bringer it became woman's duty to procure salt, and there were any number of subsidiary trades involved in the getting of it.

In Mexico we are told the best salt was made by boiling the water from the saline lake in large pots. It was then preserved in white cakes or balls. The work would seem to have been done by women, since Sahagun speaks of the women and girls employed in the industry as dancing at the feast in honor of the goddess of salt in the month Tecuilpuitontli.* The fact that salt was under the protection of a goddess is also *prima facie* evidence that the industry belonged to women, as will be seen in the chapter on religion. Bancroft has gathered all the authorities upon this subject, and mentions that the Aztec kings monopolized the commodity so that the Tlascalas, who kept their independence, were forced for many years to eat their food unsalted.

In the neighbourhood of salt springs in the Ohio Valley fragments of immense earthen vessels are discovered in great numbers bearing the imprint of the well-known aboriginal twined weaving. This would further demonstrate woman's share in salt-making, and also furnish another example of composite industry. The Ohio salt boilers were weavers, potters, quarry women, and common carriers as well as salt producers.†

The connection of woman with the plant world at first was most beneficial. Unwittingly she bent her back to a burden that turned to gold and rubies. The exploitation and domestication of the fruits and food stuffs and textiles not only developed in her the most varied and refined feelings and practices of which human beings were then capable, but opened the way to the vast storage of plant materials which give to men and women in highest culture the stimulus to industrial activities and the leisure for contemplation. One can not look upon the picture of a long train of Ute women coming home with their carrying baskets full of seeds upon their backs, supported by

---

* Bancroft, Native Races, vol. ii, p. 363.
† Sellers, Pop. Sci. Month., N. Y., vol. xi, pp. 578-585.

bands across their foreheads, holding also in one hand a gathering wand and in the other a winnowing and roasting tray, without profound thought. For these women are indeed the forerunners of all farmers and barristers and thrashers and common carriers and millers and cooks. The National Museum at Washington possesses a collection of food plants used by savage women, and in the Royal Kew Gardens in London may be seen a technological museum ranged on the basis of plants. Unwittingly both these national institutions have erected a monument to the manual labor and skill of savage women.

Powers tells of Yokain women in central California cultivating little gardens of corn which belonged to themselves. They employed neither plough nor hoe, but the squaws sat down on the ground beside the hills and worked probably fifteen minutes at each one, digging the earth deep and rubbing it all up fine in the hands. By this means they tilled only an extremely small area, but they did it excellently well and got a greater yield than Americans would.*

The greatest tribute paid to savage women as tillers of the soil is by Lucien Carr. This author has noted down, after an extended reading of many years, the testimony of all the ancient discoverers and explorers of North America concerning the Indian women as farmers. It is true that they were helped by the men to clear the ground and to do some of the work. But it was the genius of the women that invoked the aid of the fire fiend to devour the forests; it was they that cleaned up the fields, planted the seeds, gave to the growing crops of maize and pumpkins all the cultivation they got, without the help of horse or dog or any other creature. The aid they received from

---

* Cont. N. A. Ethnol., Wash., 1877, vol. iii, p. 107.

the men varied, being greater among the tribes south of the Ohio and less among the Iroquois or Six Nations.*

In a general council of the magnates of the Six Nations, Brant, in a controversy with Red Jacket, taunted him with being a squaw and a coward. This was because the latter was a man of peace and had condescended to go to farming. And all along the line of history it has been the women who were willing to leave off savagery and take the higher step in the industrial pursuits.

In modern Palestine "the men do the ploughing, for you never see a woman guiding the plough; but they follow after and drop the seed—simsum, cotton, or ' white corn '—in the furrow. They also assist in reaping, and drive the mowraj round the summer threshing floor." † Civilization has changed little in the Holy Land since the days of the patriarchs. There now, as of old, the wells, the flocks, the fields, the threshing floors, are haunted by women and girls. And the country people when they pass an abandoned well or winnowing place often hear voices talking or singing as if the spirits of the dead still lingered there.

On the paddy fields of Borneo the women have their share of work. In removing the forests, the women and boys clear away the undergrowth and the men fell the trees. The land is then burned over. As soon as the ground is cool, the men dibble the soil, the women follow, drop in the paddy seed and cover up the holes by scraping the earth into them with their feet. The Dyaks have many weary duties to perform before they reap the fruit of their toil, but it too often happens that these are left to the women and children. As a rule, the women do all the weeding by themselves, and this is a laborious

---

* Lucien Carr, Ky. Geol. Survey, no date.
† Thomson, The Land and the Book, New York, 1880, vol. i, p. 50.

task. When the paddy is ripe all turn out—men, women, boys, and girls—and harvest the crop.*

The women of Teita, East Africa, are the agriculturists; they till the soil with implements of the rudest and simplest form. The land is so rich that after the undergrowth is burned off it is merely loosened with a haftless hoe and scraped up into little heaps. A small cavity is made with the finger, into which a few seeds are dropped, covered over loosely, and Nature is left to do the rest. Their planting season is anticipatory of rain, and the only further attention they give their crops after the seed is sown is an occasional weeding. In some districts they get three or four crops annually. They store up a supply in their huts, or use well-selected trees covered and almost thatched over with dried grass and banana leaves.†

East African women till the soil, care for the cattle, carry the loads, attend markets, play spy and intermediary between provinces, even in war.‡ This multiple function of farmer, herdswoman, carrier, merchant, political and military spy covers the general series of great industries in civilization. The African aboriginal tribes when discovered were further along in some lines of culture than those of temperate America. Wherever the wild beasts and more ferocious insects would allow, flocks were reared, farms were tilled with iron tools, and great markets were held.

As any student knows, there are two kinds of medical practitioners in savagery—the sorcerer and the empirical doctor. They both have a wrong theory of sickness—namely, that all disease is demoniacal possession. That can be excused, however, in view of the diversified ways

---

* Compare Ling Roth, J. Anthrop. Inst., London, 1893, vol. xxii, p. 20.

† French-Sheldon. J. Anthrop. Inst., London, 1892, vol. xxi, p. 362.

‡ Ibid., p. 350.

the doctors nowadays have of describing the *rationale* of our commonest ailments. The practice of the two schools was, however, radically different. The sorcerer invited the disease out, tried to frighten it away, coaxed it to leave, and finally proceeded to eject it by force. Among the practitioners of this school were some women, but most of them were men. The empirical school, by a kind of rude induction, ascertained the qualities of drugs and became skillful in dressing wounds, in nursing, and even in abating fevers. If the reader should be inquisitive about who these early empiricists were, let him walk about the market houses of our Southern cities. By and by he will come upon a little patch of crouching women, daughters of Æsculapius, sisters of Hygeia. They have no cup from which a serpent drinks—symbol of health—but you will find small bundles of snakeroot among the stores of barks and roots and dried herbs, whose virtues are well known to them.

The Shastas of California use the root of a parasitic fern found growing on the tops of the fir trees (*Colique noskul*) for a general medicine. In small doses it is an expectorant and diuretic; hence it is used to relieve difficulties of the lungs and kidneys; in large doses it becomes sedative, and is an emmenagogue. It relieves fevers, and is useful in uterine troubles and to produce abortion.[*] With the co-operation of the Surgeon-General of the United States Navy, there have been collected in the National Museum many hundreds of specimens of drugs used by savage tribes in their crude medical practice.

In the progress of the world from naturalism to artificialism, which is the true line of advance, domestication of animals marks a wonderful epoch. Those lands that have few tamable animals doom their inhabitants to per-

---

[*] Bancroft, Native Races, New York, 1874–'76, vol. I, p. 354.

petual savagery. Now, the first domestication is simply
adoption of helpless infancy. The young wolf, or kid,
or lamb, or calf, is brought to the home of the hunter.
It is fed and caressed by the mother and her children,
and even nourished at her breast. Innumerable references
might be given to the caging and taming of wild
creatures. The Eskimos and the Indians south of them
capture the silver fox, and the women feed them until such
time as is best for stripping off their hides. The Pueblo
people cage eagles and hawks for their feathers, and the
women feed them. Every native hut in Guiana is the
abode of many species of birds, kept for their bright plumage.
The great domestic animals left off the feral
state so long ago that no one knows their aboriginal
home. Women were always associated especially with
the milk- and fleece-yielding species of these. Before the
domestication of milk-yielding animals, and in the two
continents where they were not known in aboriginal
times, the human mother had to suckle her young two or
three years, until they were able to walk at her side and
partially take care of themselves. The effect of this
upon her nature and all social life was on one side in her
favor, but on the other dreadfully increased her burdens,
and retarded the growth of population.* The Mandans
and other Northern tribes give the care of their ponies to
the women, who allow them to graze about the wigwams
in the daytime; but at night the squaws gather the ponies
into the wigwams and feed them upon the boughs and
bark of the cottonwood. The squaws cut down the trees
and carry the branches, and the horses feed on their bark
and the tender ends. In northwestern Canada women
manage the dog teams.†

---

* See Payne, Hist. of America, New York, 1892, p. 320.

† See Coues, Lewis & Clarke, New York, 1893, vol. i, p. 233;
Warburton Pike, Barren Grounds, etc., London, 1892, p. 100.

There are certain kinds of domestication begun in savagery that are only now having their proper development. Fish ponds were very common in Hawaii, and were mostly made by women. They were formed in the small bays along the coral reefs where the outlet was very narrow. Across the entrances to the bays the natives piled pieces of coral rock so as to admit the sea water, but to prevent the fish from escaping. It was no uncommon thing to see a number of women up to their waists in mud and water, busily employed in clearing out these ponds. While they were at work their husbands and brothers were equally hard at work on sea catching the fish which were to be transferred to the pond.*

It would really seem that the first of human beings to conceive the idea of shelter for herself and helpless infant was the woman. The Eskimo snow hut is built by men. The Indian skin lodge is from first to last the work of women. The earth lodge and the pueblo are the work of both sexes; but these are not so primitive as the cave and the bark or skin shelter. In all the Malayan and Malayo-Polynesian area house building is a joint affair. The same is true of Africa, as the following example will show:

Among the Mendis, a Sierra Leone tribe, house building is a joint affair between the sexes. When the house is completed the walls and floors are smeared by the women with cow's dung, which gives a hard, smooth surface. The men do the heavy portion of the daily work and clear the bush, but the women till the ground, fetch water, go fishing, prepare and cook the food. They also spin the cotton into thread, dye it, and make mats; but the men weave, sew, and make their own clothing. The Mendis are noted for the beauty of their cloths.†

---

* Wood, Unciv. Races, Hartford, 1870, vol. ii, p. 431.
† Garrett, Sierra Leone and the Interior, Proc. Roy. Geog. Soc., London, 1892, vol. xiv, p. 433.

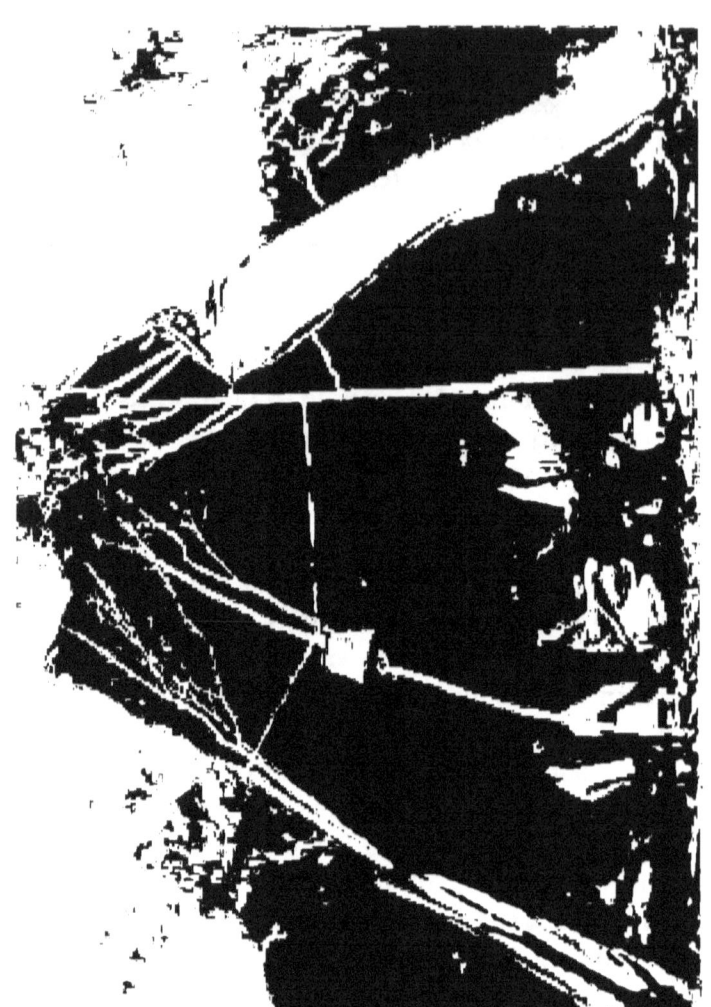

Fig. 41.—Top Equipment Studding on Hume—A Bender Profile, Montana.

In the Andaman Islands the duty of erecting the light shelters during a halt or a short visit devolved on the women. The order of arranging their huts with reference to married and unmarried women is shown in one of Mr. Man's drawings.* Not only in house building, but in other wood-working trades women assist the men.

Dr. J. F. Snyder has seen women in California assisting in felling trees. The men with the edges of their stone axes hacked around a tree, above and below, a long kerf, then pounded all around to break the annual layers. The women, with wedges of wood or antler, worked off a slab of these layers. The process was repeated until the tree came to the ground. He has also seen women with stone adzes scraping away the charred wood in hollowing a canoe.

The diversification of work or function in the life of a woman is well exemplified in the manufacture and erection of a common tepee or skin tent among the tribes of the Plains region. The tepee is a conical tent made of dressed buffalo skins. The immense amount of hard labour involved in the preparation of the hides has been sufficiently described. The separate skins are cut and fitted on the ground into a single piece resembling the cover of an umbrella. The seams are all sewed tightly from top to bottom except one, which is fastened by a lacing from the top to within four or five feet from the ground. The opening thus left is the doorway, the door itself being a buffalo robe or piece of cloth, fastened above and left to hang loose, except in bad weather, when it can be tightly stretched by thongs attached to the lower corners. The ground being selected, the tepee is spread out upon it. Three poles are lightly tied together near the smaller ends and thrust under the covering, passed through the orifice at the top, raised upright, and the lower ends

---

* Man, Andaman Islanders, London, 1883, pp. 39, 40.

spread out as far as possible. A rope or rawhide thong attached to the top of the covering is then thrown over the crossing of the poles. One woman pulls on the end of this rope, while another adjusts the tripod of poles until the covering is stretched vertically and laterally. The other poles are then carried in one by one; the small end, thrust through the top opening, is laid against the point of crossing of the first three, the large end being carried out as far as possible. When all the poles are in they are arranged equidistant, in a circle, stretching the covering as tightly as possible, a few wooden pins are driven into the ground through slits in the bottom of the covering on the outside, and the work is done. When the tepee is to be taken down all the loose poles are carried out, the rope or line holding the covering in place is loosened, the lower ends of the poles forming the tripod are brought near to each other, and the covering comes down of its own weight. Two quick-working women can put up a tepee in five minutes and take it down in three. To prevent the wind from blowing directly down the top a sort of winged cap is provided, managed from below with strings, or a deerskin fastened between two poles is set up on the windward side of the opening. It is shifted with the wind."

"The Loucheux women are literally beasts of burden to their lords and masters. All the heavy work is performed by them. When an animal is killed, they carry the meat and skin on their backs to the camp, after which they have the additional labour of dressing the skin, cutting up the meat, and drying it. They are the hewers of wood and drawers of water; all the household duties devolve upon them; they have to keep up the fires, cook, etc., besides all the other work supposed to belong to the women, such as

---

* Dodge, Our Wild Indians, Hartford, 1883, p. 288.

lacing the snowshoes for the family, making and mending the clothing of husband and children, etc. In raising the camp, or travelling from one place to another, if in winter, the woman hauls all the baggage, provisions, lodge poles, cooking utensils, with probably a couple of children on the top of all, besides an infant on the back, while the husband walks quietly on ahead with his gun, horn, shot pouch, and empty hunting bag. In the summer the man uses a small light hunting canoe, requiring very little exertion to propel it through the water, while the poor woman is forced to struggle against the current in a large ill-made canoe, laden with all the baggage, straining every nerve to reach a particular place pointed out beforehand by her master as the intended camping ground.*

Woman's connection with fire has been mentioned. No other of her activities affords such an excellent opportunity to bring out her many-sided life. With illumination she has had less to do. Dodge considers it a godsend that the Indian woman did not know how to make a light sufficient to work by at night. But the Andamanese women make torches of the resin of several plants and wrap them in the leaf of *Crinum lorifolium*, to be used in fishing, dancing, and travelling. Slow matches are procured from the heart of rotten logs of *Dipterocarpus lævis*, and tongs are fabricated by bending a strip of bamboo.†

While on the subject of house life it may be a joy to all washerwomen to know that their industry is a very primitive one. Matthews recounts the myth of an old Navajo man whose sons had been utterly unsuccessful in hunting, so he commanded them to take a sweat bath. When they had perspired sufficiently they came out of

---

* Bardisty, The Loucheux Indians, Smithson. Rep., 1866, p. 312.
† Man, Andaman Islanders, London, 1881, Trübner, p. 185; Dodge, Our Wild Indians, Hartford, 1883, p. 660.

the sudatory; this they did four times. The old man directed his daughters to dig some soaproot and to make a lather. In this he bade his sons wash their hair and the entire surface of their bodies well. It is needless to remark that the myth goes on to tell of the great success those young hunters had after that.[*]

Tools preceded machinery. The cylindrical log or rock with which a savage woman triturates foodstuffs is a tool; so is the muller, with which grain is reduced to meal on a metate. But it is next door to a machine—that is, a contrivance in which a vertical shaft is used, fixed in the upper stone and loosely piercing the nether. Hand power, beast power, wind and water power, and steam power, follow naturally. But the earliest form of this meal-producing machine is found in the hands of women whose genius, energy, or effort was arrested as soon as the powers of Nature were invoked to do their work. The first continuous motion, however, was by the spindle in the hands of women.

Dall sketches the daily round of an Eskimo housewife in early winter, and his account is abridged here, to show how many activities of our civilization are hinted at in this one poor woman's work. Rising in the early hours when a faint glimmer through the parchment cover of the smoke hole indicates the peep of dawn, her first care is to carry the necessary wooden vessels to the antechamber of the house, where the contents are preserved for tanning and other useful purposes.

This done, she removes the cover of the smoke hole and searches the hearth for embers, places some light dry sticks upon them, and, going outside, arouses the sleepers by pitching down a quantity of fuel through the aperture in the roof. Before coming in she arranges some bits of

---

[*] Matthews, Fifth Ann. Rep. Bur. Ethnol., p. 390.

wood to aid the draught through the smoke hole and
brings water for drinking or cooking. Returning, she
rolls up beds and mats. While the family are dressing
she prepares a meal of boiled deer or seal flesh or of boiled
fish with oil. The men then go to their traps or other
occupations. The remnants of the meal fall to the share
of the dogs, the dishes are cleaned, and the mistress sets
about her work, preparing deerskins for boots or clothing
or cutting and sewing the skins into garments. During
the day a morsel of deer fat or a bit of dry salmon is
eaten. In the middle of the day visiting begins and chit-
chat is mingled with instruction to the younger women.
If a stranger comes he is directed to a sitting place, one
of the women removes his wet boots and places them in
the smoke to dry, and refreshment is offered. After long
silence the visitor slowly tells the story of his journey and
the news of his village.

At nightfall the fire is made to blaze, and the whole
household go up on the roof to look for the returning
hunters. The wife receives her husband in silence, removes his weapons, puts his boots to dry, offers him a bit
of meat and fish, and when he has taken his place calls
attention to the stranger. She then trims and lights the
lamp. Conversation becomes general. All eat together,
served by the mistress of the house. At last when the
fire has burned low the good housewife tosses the large
embers from the smoke hole, carefully covers the coals,
replaces the parchment to keep in the warm air, unrolls
the beds, and when the inmates are all asleep she puts
out the light and enjoys her well-earned rest.*

In Guiana the women clean the house, fetch water
and firewood, cook the food, make the bread, nurse the

---

* Compare Dall, American Naturalist, Philadelphia, 1878, vol.
xi, pp. 8–10.

children, plant the fields, dig the produce, and when the men travel carry whatever baggage is necessary in large baskets, which fit on the back and are supported by bands across the forehead. They also make hammocks, and if there is a little time to spare they weave bead aprons, or *queyus*, their only dress, or spin cotton or weave small hammocks for their children.*

When the day has at last come to an end and the women have gathered enough wood for the fires under the hammocks during the night, they throw themselves into their swinging conches, and all talk together. Till far into the night the men tell endless stories. At last, in the middle of the narrative, the party drop off to sleep, and all is quiet for a short while. Presently some woman gets up to renew the fires or to see to some domestic work. Roused by the noise, the dogs break into a chorus. This wakes the children, and they begin to scream. The men turn in their hammocks and resume their stories for a brief time. †

It would be possible to go on multiplying the varied industries of early history, which were at first no greater than a woman's hand, fostered by the weaker sex to become afterward the sources of the world's great wealth. But something more must be said concerning this composite activity of primitive woman in which we have styled her the jack-at-all-trades.

It is not enough to say in any case, as we have seen, that she was food bringer, weaver, skin dresser, potter, or beast of burden. This view of her is absolutely misleading. It is not sufficient to say that the modern lucrative employments originated with her. We are bound to keep in mind that each woman was all of those. As in the ani-

---

* E. F. im Thurn, Indians of British Guiana, London, p. 215.
† Im Thurn, *op. cit.*, p. 216.

THE JACK-AT-ALL-TRADES. 159

mal world one part of the body performs many functions, in the social world one woman is mistress of many cares.

This diversification of duties in well-regulated homes among the civilized nations produces the matron. The

FIG. 13.—THE MATRON OF ISLETA, NEW MEXICO. (After Wittich.)

savage woman is really the ancestress and prototype of the modern housewife and not of our factory specialists. It can be seen how this versatility of talent and multiplication of industries would react on her offspring, both male and female, and bring them all at last around to her pristine industrialism.

How sharply in all the course of history does this combination of abilities in one woman stand in contrast with co-operation of many individuals at one duty or activity among men! The modern farmer with his " weight of cares" would seem to be an exception. But all his present labours were primitive woman's work from morn till eve. In co-operation women have always been weak. There are few duties that they have in common. Even as beasts of burden they seldom worked in pairs.

CHAPTER VIII.

THE ARTIST.

In the creation of the arts of pleasure what has been woman's share? That there were arts of pleasure in the remotest past, archæology abundantly testifies. The earliest people of whom there is any record at all made things shapely and covered them with decoration, which in some examples must have interfered with their use. The study of the present would guide us somewhat as to the kinds of art we should look for, but, as much of woman's ancient art is now in men's hands, their art also must be scrutinized.

As in the practical industries, so in the æsthetic, an inquiry into their origin or invention includes several questions:

1. As to the beginning and development of the art forms, at first extremely simple and little if at all removed from natural shapes. In short, if a common invention is a slight change in a natural object to improve its use, an art form is a slight change in an object to increase its beauty. The progress of beauty is an increase of complexity in those changes with higher and better defined functions.

2. As to the mental processes involved in the creation or invention of the beautiful. Here the law is the same. The first effort was extremely simple and undifferentiated; the highest effort involved the combined genius, the co-

operative effort of many minds—architects, sculptors, painters, ceramists, weavers, landscape gardeners.

3. The rewards of the artists. They are found at first in the granting by the public of some present material good or happiness or self-satisfaction. The inventor of cooking got a better husband and reared better sons. The first artists were quite similarly rewarded. The last result is the creation of a tribal or national feeling, criterion, taste, which leads the people to bestow the highest rewards upon those who give the greatest pleasure. Too much must not be expected of the savage woman in her art work. She did not sit down deliberately to compose a form, a pattern, or a song—"she piped but as the linnets sing." The determinate purpose followed up with the accumulated apparatus and experiences of the ages is always the latest manifestation of invention. The first inventor in art, like the first inventor in the industries, was the happy thinker, the acute observer, the apperceiver—the one whose senses were open to the forms and colours and movements and sounds of Nature.

No more should be expected of her than that she should be seized with pleasure in the presence of these and desire to imitate them. The first woman making a change in any natural object for the gratification which it afforded her is the starting point of three evolutions: that of the art itself, whether textile, plastic, or musical; of herself in the practice of it, growing out of a mere imitator to be a creator; of the universal or public appreciation of art, of what might be called the racial or the tribal imagination.

As we have found that in the practical affairs of life comprehensiveness is the noticeable characteristic of women, the same ought to hold true in the realm of beauty. We ought not to look for great personal specialization, but for a multitude of kinds of pleasing work done with the same pair of hands and co-operation of many in one operation. It need astonish no one to witness the plastic potter suddenly becoming a painter and then a weaver or embroiderer, nor a whole tribe of women erecting and organizing a camp. As for the drama and music, even these, as will appear later on, in the possession of women should be more homelike and less warlike.

Fig. 43.—The Origin of the Scroll. (From ancient Pueblo pottery, after Holmes.)

In considering the æsthetic element of the textile art, Holmes includes three subdivisions of phenomena, connected with (1) form, (2) colour, and (3) design.

In executing the forms, colours, and designs there are three degrees of predominance of the art idea.

1. That in which a useful object had to be made of a certain shape, but in the making the woman wrought as symmetrically and deftly as she knew how. It is as though a needlewoman of our own day had a contract to fill, but, by her own refinement, was compelled to add a touch or two not in the contract.

2. That in which a vessel or a garment or a house convenience is the object in view, and just as much decoration is added as will not interfere with use. The Apache woman covering the outside of a mush bowl with superb ornament would be an example.

3. That in which use is sacrificed to the æsthetic motif, as in all ages women have busied themselves in making textures too good and beautiful for use.*

---

* Cf. Holmes, Sixth An. Rep. Bur. Ethnol., Wash., 1888, pp. 197, 201.

The first beauty aimed at in the textile art by the savage woman is uniformity, just as the beginning of music is monotony, the prolongation and repetition of a single tone. This uniformity is concerned with the texture and the shape of the product.

As there are no piece goods woven by these primitive artisans, to be cut afterward into comely shape, the form of the product must first be in the maker's mind, at least as an intention. Piece goods begin with the cutting and making up of articles in fur and skins. The universal mat, robe, or sail, according to the material and the use of common forms everywhere prevailing, has come to have a tribal outline and proportion. These are sometimes called conventional, as though the artist were bound by conditions against which she was struggling. The fact is, that her whole effort and struggle is to be conventional. The wallet, the bowl, the tray, the pot, the jar, the bottle, the basket, after acquiring a family trait, goes on to perfection in its monotony. The fact of their being of a piece stimulates the workwoman. She must get her result now or never. In civilization there are ways of hiding a fault beneath an afterthought, but with this poor woman none.

The monotony of texture is the glory of savage women's textile work. In the great exposition at Chicago many thousands of Indian baskets were shown. Upon their surfaces hundreds of thousands of stitches or meshes had been wrought. In one example counted, eighty thousand stitches made of splints of wood, not over the sixteenth of an inch wide, were so uniform in dimensions as to excite the wonder of artists. Every sewing woman knows how much pains it requires to get at such a result with the best of needles and thread. The securing of variety, which, with unity, constitutes the charm of art, comes later. The student of primitive art will not safely follow the evolution of the former until the latter is firmly in his mind. The same is true of man's art, as any one can testify who has examined the flaking on the ancient flint blades, the pecking on the surface of granular stone implements, or the engravings on Hervey Island ceremonial adze handles.

Changes of colour on the surface are produced by varieties of the fundamental monotonies. The geometric decorations on basketry are variations simply in number and colour, the size of the mesh remaining uniform. This part of art evolution was almost exhausted by savage women. Hence one sees on basketry and on soft textiles alike patterns which the modern weaver and the jeweller are never tired of copying, which have become classic, and entered the great world-encompassing stream of art forms, pleasing to the whole species.

The Alaskan Eskimo woman selects her straws of wild rye, and adds thereto little bits of red flannel or beads. Her southern neighbour on the Pacific coast digs up the long, slender roots of the spruce tree, and splits them with astonishing uniformity. When dried, her filaments turn to a clear light-brown colour, and the surface of a watertight wallet made therefrom is a marvel of regularity. The overlaying of this surface with patterns executed in straws, coloured or uncoloured, give opportunity to secure variety in beauty.

On going southward one finds that Nature has provided dyes and natural colours in material in greater abundance, which the savage woman has been swift to recognize. In Arizona the yucca leaf presents two shades when split, a dark green on the outside and a whitish green on the inside. So the Moki woman, by wisely turning outward first one, then the other side of the fillet, creates most pleasing effects.

The California and other Indian women introduce the

stem of the maidenhair fern, the *martynia* pod, and such natural black and brown filaments into the body of their work.

The women of the eastern part of North America relied upon splints or thick shavings of tough wood, like the birch, ash, hickory, and white oak. The beauty element in these splints was their ribbonlike characteristics and the readiness with which they lent themselves to dyes, while their southern sisters had an abundant resource in the ever-present cane. In both substances, however, the rigidity and structure of the fibre held the artist within certain leading strings of manipulation.

In addition to these hard materials used in eastern North America the Indian women of the temperate belt were intimately acquainted everywhere with the willow, rhus, cedar bark, Indian hemp, bullrushes, cat-tail, vernal and other grasses, and many other kinds of filament; with their colours, and the best way of dyeing them; and, what is most noteworthy in this connection, these cunning savage women knew so well what to do with each kind, and what each kind could and could not do, that every effort to improve their methods has failed. As soon as the tropical belt is reached and the palm tree waves its graceful fronds before the quick fancy of the rudest woman of human kind, it seems to lay a spell upon her and to excite her even to the finger tips. Whether in Mexico or northern South America, or in Africa and Polynesia, the result is the same. The natural colour of the leaf and of the stem, as well as the extreme tenuity to which the filaments may be reduced, offered a variety of form and technique to the aboriginal artisans. To these delicate filaments we must add in tropical countries the *pita* fibre, cotton, *Phormium tenax*, and such other materials as could be spun into fine threads. But their use, as well as that of silk, belong a little farther along in culture than the stage here alluded to. High colours are seldom used artificially, reliance being had upon texture and surface patterns.

The textile art of Asia is more barbaric than savage, yet one can scarcely fail to note what a wonderfully refining effect the rattan and the bamboo must have had upon the primitive East Indian and Chinese and Japanese women. There is no wonder that they cling tenderly to these plants, and have never sought to improve them by artificial dyes. In very little of their work is there any effort to introduce variety of shade in the native colour. The very absoluteness of monotony gives to the surface all the embellishment it needs. The production of diaper effects is extremely easy and attractive in such ware.

Into the body of the textile the savage women of North America had learned to entwine or weave animal products —sinew thread, yarn from the dog and mountain sheep and mountain goat; and in South America there were several species of animals which yielded their fleece for the beautifying of human arts. The historic period at its very beginning on the Eastern Continent finds woman with the distaff in her hand spinning the hair of camels, goats, sheep, and other animals, and no one can tell when the Chinese did not have silk. And all these substances and productions therefrom were in their æsthetic stage when discovered. Indeed, wherever among the cults of the world the textile art is mentioned it is the Fates or the goddess who presides thereover. By this is meant that women had perfected the industry on its purely industrial side, had developed the art to a finish on the simpler æsthetic side, and had gone to live beyond the sky in the imaginations of many peoples before the days of looms wrought by men.

The Polynesian women add their coloured decoration to the tapa cloth by means of beating clubs, pencil brushes, stamps, pouring cups, ruling brushes and sticks. In Africa some of these devices are employed to lay on colour after the completion of the shape, but these fabrics are not textiles, strictly speaking. Almost universally in savagery, the filaments are coloured before the textile work begins, as before intimated, and both Nature and the dyer's art are invoked to furnish the materials.

Aside from colour, the lights and shades of the woven pattern, the innumerable varieties of interlacing within the limits of each tribal technique, and the different kinds of raw material in hand, form a group of æsthetic expressions on which the savage woman's fancy never tires of improvising.

The filaments of the textile art are either flat or roundish, rigid or flexible, coarse or fine. In the interlacing of these filaments for purely æsthetic effects the artist has her choice of making plain checker, wicker, diagonal, and diaper work. By varying the width and mixing the characteristics named above she has practically an endless variety of patterns at her disposal. In twined weaving there is the same diversity of prepared materials and the same resources. Furthermore, the two almost independent surfaces for embroidery or overlaying furnished by this style of manipulation has not been overlooked by decorators.

In the coiled work there are excellent opportunities of introducing a new element at every turn.

Now every different kind of material and style of interlacing and tribal fashion gives a new character to the textile. Upon these the fancy of savage women has run riot. The work is so easy and the leading strings are never hard to follow.

Besides the ordinary forms of textural work—basketry, matting, and cloth—there are to be found among savage women, braiding, netting, knitting, and lace-making. In every one of these beauty is secured by technique, by variety of texture, and by colour. The Indians of the Yuma stock in Arizona make their carrying baskets of coarse yucca twine, but by a kind of crocheting with figured patterns combining brown, blue, and red twine in pleasing contrast. The ordinary netting of savagery is devoid of ornament, but the women of the Sandwich Islands and of other Polynesian regions used the net as the foundation of a type of ornament soon to be described.

The arrangement of thread shown in Fig. 14, under the term "Lace," in Chambers's Encyclopedia, as produced by Lever's machine, is precisely that of a Mojave carrying basket in the United States National Museum, and the same figure has been found stamped on pottery from the mounds and graves of the Eastern United States.*

When she chose, however, and that was quite frequently, the savage woman invented processes of changing the surface of her texture, either by addition, by omission, or by elimination. The Sitka woman inserted into the outer filament of her twine in weaving, strips of grass stems, coloured and uncoloured, producing on the outside merely of the fabric rich designs of brown and yellow and black and red. This same overlaying was produced elsewhere with bark and quill and stems of various colours, of martynia and birch bark and maidenhair fern. It was, indeed, embroidery, only the work was done when the object was making, the woman being at the same instant designer, weaver, and decorator.

Furthermore, beads, and seeds, and bits of shell, and feathers, and hair of every hue were applied to the exteriors of fabrics closely or as pendants. In some cases

---

* Mason, Rep. United States National Museum, 1887, p. 204, Fig. 5; Holmes, Third An. Rep. Bur. Ethnol., p. 468, Fig. 70.

the entire surface is concealed by extraneous ornaments. "Nowhere in the world has the use of pretty feathers attained the refined magnificence seen in the Hawaiian Islands. Feather hunting was a special vocation. Sometimes nets were spread, but more frequently birdlime was smeared on the branches of trees. The arrangement of feathers on necklaces, capes, cloaks, helmets, or wicker gods was the principal occupation of noble women."*

The process of decoration by omission or by elimination is quite universal. It is simply the production of openwork suggesting lace by methods differing from tribe to tribe.†

To this omitted or reticulated fabric the workwoman superadded the combination and intertwining of the remaining warp threads in various ways. Indeed, Holmes figures one example of monochrome embroidery. "In design and method of realization it is identical with the rich coloured embroideries of the ancient Peruvians, being worked on a net foundation. The broad band of figures employs bird forms in connection with running geometric designs, and still more highly conventional bird forms are seen in the narrow band." ‡

As mentioned under the industrial side of textile work, the ornamentation of stuffs must of necessity be a matter of counting spaces. It is geometrical. So the savage basket-maker and weaver and embroiderer has brought to pass two results. She has taught the potter and the architect both geometry and a thousand plain, standard decorative features. It seems a long and tedious training, but it was a kind of kindergarten in which

---

* Brigham, Catalogue of the Bernice Pauahi Bishop Museum, Honolulu, 1899, Pt. I, pp. 9-81.

† See Mason, Basketry of the American Aborigines; and Holmes, Sixth An. Rep. Bur. Ethnol., 1888, Figs. 800-811.

‡ Holmes, op. cit.

those early imbued with a sense of beauty could be taught preparatory to free-hand work in colouring and modelling.

On the other hand, she has introduced into rectilinear network curvilinear designs. In her first artistic ventures she rounded corners to produce beauty, but in her highest flights vegetable and animal and even human figures are squared up and conventionalized to fit the texture and the spaces. These conventions analysed, figures are again seized upon by artists in other materials, plastic and hard.

It may safely be said that the whole body of decoration that has come out of the textile industry originated in woman's brain. The word "textile," in the æsthetic acceptation, includes (1) the preparation and colouring or choosing the colour of filamentary material; (2) the making of yarn, thread, string, twine, braid, and the endless catalogue of prepared material which enters into the textile art and adorns it; (3) the technique of thatching, basketry, matting, netting, lace making, weaving, sewing, and embroidery.

Another line of invention in decorative forms was followed by women working in plastic material. They had the same problems of shape and surface ornamentation to work out, but the material offered its peculiar characteristics and possibilities. It is not necessary here to repeat what was said in Chapter V on the industrial processes involved and the results achieved. But a word will not be out of place as to the primitive methods of securing pleasure through the plastic arts. In the paper by Mr. Holmes before mentioned and in Mr. Balfour's book on the evolution of decorative art the lines of the elaboration here laid down are followed, better for our purpose by the former than by the latter, because Mr. Balfour had before him in the Oxford Museum chiefly specimens wrought by men and is concerned with imitative patterns. These are later than the monotony just dwelt upon. Holmes has worked this out most elaborately, though he does not mention that in America the potter's art was exclusively woman's industry.*

With respect to the artistic element in the primitive potter's art, the most noteworthy operations are, first, the copying of natural forms such as fruits and animals and, second, the transfer of textile motives to the soft material either by taking impressions or by copying in paint.

In the matter of discipline the clay and the paint are above the textile material. The textile artist worked in grooves, the painter and the ceramist wandered at will. The former had a parallelogram of external forces to guide in forming the pattern. As children at play but poorly imitate the serious work of their elders, the earlier women colorists produced paintings which half revealed and half concealed the patterns which Nature set before them.

Ceramic inability and economy rounded a corner here, united two designs there, and in another place by a sort of artistic synecdoche made a small part of the pattern to do the work for the whole. There were also everywhere shortcomings, technical difficulties and limitations which helped to constitute the result, and for which the art student must make allowance. The mythical and religious motive is also ever present with the early potters. Looking over the tens of thousands of specimens of vessels in the United States National Museum, one is constantly reminded of the religious feeling in the artists who have thrown in a prayer in one corner, a little hymn in another, and a complimentary allusion to the friendly totem in a

---

* Holmes Fourth An. Rep. Bur. Ethnol., pp. 257–473; Balfour, Evolution of Decorative Art, Lond. 1893, Percival.

Fig. 45.—Examples of decoration on Tikopia dishes. (After Holmes.)

third. In like manner, the painters and the embroiderers of the historic past have introduced the wings of angels, the crucifix, and the star. The figure of a dipper with its decorative patterns studied out is here introduced to show how intricate the savage methods become by the processes described.

These primitive arts have come to belong to the lowest caste in the social life of the white race; yet the rich woman adorns her parlour with the ancient spinning wheel, and with the products of savage looms and potteries. Around the walls lowly implements of woman's original handicrafts have an honoured place, while the most costly museums are erected to protect and exhibit the works of her hands. More than this, modern and ancient art of the highest grade never tired of immortalizing these very artists in painting and sculpture and ceramics. Among such decorative works it must not be forgotten that figures

FIG. 45.—ANCIENT TUSAYAN DIPPER, ARIZONA. (After Holmes.)

of burden bearers and handicraft women are the pictures of real persons æsthetized.

The first achievement in music for women as well as for men was the monotone. The evolution of musical instruments includes the apparatus for the prolongation and repetition of the monotone, beginning with the savage rattle, which scarcely produces more than an instantaneous noise and ending with the toll of the bell. The evolution of vocal music, like the uniform meshes of textile work, begins also with the monotone, whose prolongation on the same key, whose repetition on the same key, whose pronunciation by many voices at once lead up to unison, and then to melody. At their work, many doing the same thing at once, in their mourning, several voices joined in wailing, we have the beginning of vocal and instrumental music. Among the modern savages men have more to do with these matters than women. For musical voices women have, in our century, been more celebrated than men, but in composition only men thus far have world-wide fame. It is only recently that women have escaped from the meshwork of the piano, and have begun to be famous with more flexible instruments.

Among the birds, it is the male that sings; the female only chatters all day long about her nest, weaving and food getting, and pursuing other domestic industries. A very careful observer informed the author that the Kaiowa Indian women have no musical instruments of their own, and that they never play on those belonging to the men. He goes further and asserts that he is not acquainted with any savage tribes in which the women have musical instruments of their own. It is quite evident, however, that he had in his mind the American savage woman and instruments producing melody; because, in describing the ghost dance, in which he participated, he mentions a large rawhide, held about waist-high by as many performers, chiefly women, as could get round it and grasp the edge of it with one hand, while they beat it with a stick held in the other. While thus drumming, they circled around, rawhide and all, keeping up one of those weird, high-pitched dance songs without meaning, so common among the prairie tribes.*

The Kiowa woman beating on the rawhide is doing the identical thing that the fine Spanish donna accomplishes with her castanets or the Italian donna with her tambourine—namely, keeping time. Every tribe of savages has its primitive and peculiar method of marking time. It may be with the naked feet, or with the hands upon the legs, or with a log of wood, or with rattles of gourds, shells, seeds, or carved from wood, or cast in bronze, or made of rawhide or parchment; the thing most convenient is utilized, and women join their efforts with men in securing unison. Let not this awkward first effort be gainsaid. Do you not see that these poor Kiowa women beating on the rawhide are themselves an aboriginal co-operating association, keeping time together, and do you not see that the men dancing there are all keeping step to the music? It is a kind of drill in which the women are the drill masters.

Melody is older than harmony, and free melody that wanders up and down the "trails" of sound is much older than the melody that climbs pentatonic or diatonic ladders. The physicists and the students of the evolution of music are now discussing the question whether there is any measurable scale for savage melodies. It is gravely hinted that instruments have compelled the human voice to go this way or that way until the fashion has become the second nature; but there were many sweet singers before Saint Cecilia.

---

* James Mooney, Am. Anthropologist, vol. v, p. 268.

It was with genuine pleasure that the author heard Mr. Cushing say that the women of Zuñi, though they never play upon any of the musical instruments of the tribe, sing songs of their own, which are invariably associated with domestic and industrial pursuits. As they nurse their children they croon a lullaby, and more novel than that are the little melodies which they chant as they plant the corn or beans or melons to encourage their growth. The theory of the Zuñi woman seems to be that there is some mysterious connection between the voices or sounds of things and their increase. When she kneels by her stone bread-making trough she sings a song which has many little imitations of the mealing stone. The theory in her mind is that the implement will do far better work under those circumstances. It is the same when she sings to her baby. Her boy she calls her little man, and speaks of all she hopes he may become, believing that these are necessary to his growth. This serious intent goes through all her music.

The following Zuñi baby songs furnished by Mr. Cushing exemplify what has just been said:

Lullaby to a Girl.

Little maid child!
Little sweet one!
Little girl!
Though a baby,
Soon a-playing
With a baby
Will be going.
Little maid child!
Little woman so delightful!

Lullaby to a Boy.

Little man child!
Little man child!
Little boy!
Though a baby,

Soon a-hunting
After rabbits
Will be going.
Little man child!
Little man, so delightful!
Oh, delightful!
So delightful!

The following instances of women associated with primitive music are contributed by Mr. Henry Balfour, of Oxford, England. In the South Pacific the "nose flute" is very generally played upon by women. A figure of a Tonga woman playing upon this instrument is shown in the account of the voyage of Cook and King. A similar figure is seen in Labillardière's Voyage de la Pérouse (Plate XXVIII) and in Melville's Four Months' Residence in the Marquesas Islands playing on the nose flute is mentioned as a favourite recreation with the females. Wilkes gives a description of the Fiji "nose flute," and states that no other instrument is played by the women as an accompaniment to the voice. Dr. Otto Finsch states that a type of the musical bow, called "pangolo" is only played upon by women of Blanche Bay, New Britain. Guppy says that the women of Treasury Island produce a soft kind of music by playing, somewhat after the manner of a jew's-harp, on a lightly made, fine-stringed bow about fifteen inches long. Livingstone speaks of women using a small musical instrument, which produced a kind of screeching sound as an accompaniment of the death wail.*

This book would be lacking in an important particular if it did not call attention to the beginnings in savagery of what may be called the fine lady—the climax of personal

---

* Travels, etc., in South Africa, New York, 1858, p. 650. Consult also Ellis, Man and Woman, London, 1894, chap. xiv, and Edith Brower, Atlantic Monthly, April, 1894.

grooming and of intellectual refinement, an ideal of supreme art in looks and behaviour.

She varies nowadays in the different European and American capitals, in Peking, Bangkok, or Pondicherry. But, wherever she be, there is no one who does not know when she appears that she is a fine lady.

It is a title to which all ambitious young women aspire, and the poorest of them dreams that, Cinderella like, she will some day come to be admired with the aid of the kind fairy. No dictionary defines her, there does not seem to be any assemblage of words that will just include all of them; but the fine lady is the beau ideal in every time and clime of what a woman ought to be. King Lemuel devotes a chapter to her charms as he saw them (Proverbs of Solomon, xxxi), and the literatures of the world abound in her portraits.

A very intelligent frontiersman once informed the writer that the ordinary voyager never sees the beauties in any land. He must be invited into the society of the place before they appear. Furthermore, it is his testimony that after living a dozen years in daily contact with a tribe one learns to appreciate the canons of beauty and understand his own surprise at first. But there is no savage people in the world that does not admire a fine air and carriage, litheness, and grace. Polynesian girls sit in a row for hours going through a Delsarte movement that is fascinating in the extreme. The habit of carrying loads upon the head, of daily exercise of every part of the body, of the study of proportion in pottery and weaving, give to most girls in savagery an unconscious *mæsia*, which heightens the beauty thereof. Indeed, among the Bechuanas, especially, it is the correct thing for an old woman to take the girls who are candidates for young ladyship to the open country, and to teach them to walk straight and to carry burdens. This reminds one of the practice in some girls' schools of compelling the misses to walk around with books on their heads. The object in both cases is the same—to secure *una bella aria*.

The industrial and humanizing element in savage culture as fostered by their women is exemplified in their tribal ceremonies. It was the author's pleasure on one occasion to witness the dance of the Kwakiml Indians, of Haeltzukan stock, which symbolizes the overcoming of the cannibal spirit. The conduct of the men was most noisy. The cannibal actor was naked as to his limbs, and wore only his ceremonial toggery. His motions were wild and ferocious in the extreme. But his performance was followed by a dance of the women. They wore long blankets of blue stranding, upon which were sewed mythic patterns cut from red flannel and decorated with rows of white buttons. They also had on aprons fringed with puffin beaks, but their small feet were bare. While the men were pounding with sticks upon a plank in front of them, the women swayed their bodies and swung half way round, to and fro, giving to their drapery most graceful motions. With their hands also they kept time, moving them to and fro by a sort of mild gymnastic.

There is a slight contrast in the matter of costume between the savage and the civilized fine lady.* But women in primitive society had their share of vanity. "Female dandies," says Im Thurn, "occur among Guiana Indians about as frequently as in more civilized communities and in as pronounced degrees. A young woman in the prime of life, conscious of a fine figure and good looks, often takes infinite pains with her person and manages to put on oils, paints, feathers, and teeth so delicately and becomingly that she gives herself exactly the neat and

---

* Thomson, British New Guinea, London, 1892, p. 68.

well-dressed appearance one is accustomed to associate with a young and well-bred lady."*

According to Ellis, the island of Tut[...]a was also fre-

Fig. 40.—[...]

quented by the females of the higher class, for the purpose of *haapori*, increasing the corpulency of the person, and removing by luxurious ease under the embowering shades

---

* Indians of British Guiana, Lond., 1883, p. 210.

of the cocoanut groves the dark tinge which the vertical sun of Tahiti might have burned upon their complexions. So great was the intercourse formerly that a hundred canoes might have been seen at one time on the beach.*

Fig. 17.—The Eye Standard of Beauty, Fiji. (After Wilkich.)

The open air was the dressing place of both sexes, and a group of females might often be seen sitting under the

---

* Ellis, Polynes. Res., Lond., 1859, Bohn, vol. i, p. 21.

shade of a clump of wide-spreading trees, or in a cool mountain stream, employing themselves for hours in arranging the curls of the hair, weaving wreaths of flowers and filling the air with their perfumes. Their mirror was one supplied by Nature, and consisted of clear water contained in a cocoanut shell.*

In the vicinity of the ancient ruins of Palenque this same devotion of women to springs of water prevails. Says Morelet: "In retired places deep excavations may be seen, where the women bathe during the heat of the day. Here they gather beneath great trees festooned with vines on mossy banks and indulge in protracted lustrations, braiding their long hair and smoking their cigarettes the while, in garb as primitive as that of the naiads. When the sun sinks beneath the waving fringe of trees they don their blue skirts, fill their pitchers, and wend homeward, chatting and laughing all the way." †

Tibetan women smear their faces with a thick black paste composed of grease and catch. They say it is to protect their skins from the drying wind. But the Lamas say it is because one of the saints commanded them to do so, to prevent their pretty faces from becoming a snare to young monks, who were commanded to keep their eyes on the ground in their walks abroad.‡

This is not the only human conduct which takes on a different color from the point of view. It is true, however, that a great many of the apparently senseless actions of peoples are thoroughly justifiable in the light of truth.

The Andamanese women mix up white clay and water and paint not only their own bodies and those of their relatives, but all their utensils. When the paint is still

---

* Ellis, Polynes. Res., Lond., 1859, Bohn, vol. i, p. 190.
† Morelet, Travels in Cent. Am., N. Y., 1871, p. 85.
‡ Rockhill, Land of the Lamas, N. Y., 1891, p. 214.

Fig. 48.—The Yuma Fish Lady, Southern California. (After Wetzel.)

wet, with the outspread finger tips the surface of the skin is decorated with patterns.*

"Nearly every morning the Patagonian men have their hair brushed out by their wives, sisters, or female friends. The women then adorn the men's faces with paint. They also paint each other's faces, and, if they possess a small piece of looking-glass, also decorate their own."† On the eve of their wedding night they cover their bodies all over with white paint, and a child on its birth is similarly whitened.‡

The introduction of women barbers into European and even into American shops recalls that in savagery women are the hair cutters and occasionally the shavers. Within a few hours after its birth the Andamanese baby has its head shaved by its mother, who uses a sharp piece of flinty rock or bottle glass, moistening the hair with milk which she presses from her breast. In fact, women are universally the barbers in the Andamans, and they not only shave one another's heads, but those of the men. The majority of women every week or ten days shave their heads almost entirely; the men have their own styles of coiffure, but only in exceptional cases, when the services of a woman are not obtainable, will men consent to operate on one another.*

A charming book could be written on the coiffures of savage peoples. This bit of vanity is not confined to either sex, but it is quite frequently women's work to "do up" the hair of the men.|

For artificial modifications of the human body, women

---

* Man, Andaman Islanders, Lond., 1883, p. 184.
† Musters, J. Anthrop. Inst., Lond., 1872, vol. i, p. 197.
‡ Op. cit., p. 197.
* Man, Andaman Islanders, Lond., 1883, Trübner, pp. 9, 114.
| Livingstone, Travels, etc., in South Africa, New York, 1858, p. 496–498.

in our day are much more responsible than men. There is not one person living in civilized society who did not when in the plastic state of infancy undergo pinchings and kneadings and sometimes surgical operations at the hands

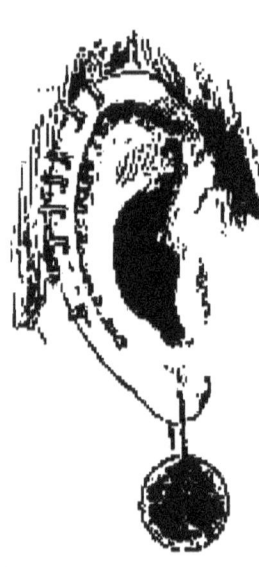

Fig. 40.—Manner of piercing the Ear—Seminole Indian Woman.

of nurses. But it is even worse in savagery. The North American Indian mother strapped her infant on a cradle board and compelled the occiput to rest on a hard substance, much to its distortion, while the Chinook baby had its forehead flattened out intentionally by means of bandages and padding.

The historians of Columbus' day tell us that the Carib women wore cotton bands on little girls' legs just above the calves, which remained there during lifetime, constricting the limb and causing the calf to swell. Among the rare treasures recovered from the caves of the Bahamas by the gatherers of bats' dung for guano is a group of figures carved from a single trunk of a tree. In these, both the arms near the shoulders and the calves are represented as constricted by bands of textile stuff. This distortion of the limbs is mentioned also as in existence among our Southern Indians.

The piercing of the lips and cheeks Dall has termed labretifery. Plugs or labrets, worn at times in the upper lip, or at the corners of the mouth, or in the median line of the lower lip, are peculiar to the women in one tribe, to the men in another, and in still other tribes both sexes decorate themselves therewith. "In most regions," says Dall, "which have been brought closely into relations with civilization the practice is extinct or obsolete." But, as one example of conservatism among women, the Tlinkit, who used to disfigure their faces with immense plugs, have abandoned them, a little silver pin representing in the lips of marriageable girls the odious *kalushka*.*

The Bongo women thrust through the upper lip a copper rivet, through the under lip a wooden labret, the latter characterizing all the married women. Copper cramps are attached to the corners of the mouths. In each nostril blades of straw are stuck.

Besides these questionable decorations of the mouth, these same women emboss tattoo marks on their arms. Incisions and punctures are made in the skin, and the healing is delayed by irritants, in order to impart to the scars, in consequence of an exuberant growth of proud flesh, the shape of embossed ridges.†

The rude and savage custom of tattooing is still in vogue among almost all classes of Hindoo females and in almost all parts of India. The face, chest, and arms are generally tattooed with varied and fantastic designs. The remnant of the savage custom of painting the person is to be seen in the red paint over the forehead among the married women of India. The up-country women, besides the tattooing and painting, bore the lower lobes of the ears and insert large wooden plugs which almost sever the lobes of the ears. The Marwaree women also ornament their upper incisors by drilling holes and plugging them with gold, and sometimes with engravings. The women of the

---

* Dall, Masks, labrets, etc., Third An. Rep. Bur. Ethnol., pp. 73-204, pl. v-xxix.

† Schweinfurth, Artes Africanæ, London, 1875, Sampson Low, pl. iii, Figs. 3, 5, 6, 19, 20; pl. xx, 1; xxi, 5. French-Sheldon, J. Anthrop. Inst., London, 1892, vol. xxi, p. 301.

Northwest Provinces, Behar, and Bengal colour their teeth black with a kind of astringent tooth powder.

Painting the foot scarlet has been prevalent among Hindoo women from a remote age. The Mohammedan and Hindoo women paint the tips of their fingers and palms with the leaves of the *Lawsonia alba*. Burmese women look down with contempt on men who fail to tattoo their persons, and would not marry a man who had not been tattooed.* To a certain extent the artistic instinct has had its own growth, because it has been trained under circumstances different from those of industrial life. But, on the whole, the daily life and activities of savage women have been the school in which they were trained.

Modern and classic art are indebted to women for the beginnings of landscape gardening, including the aviary and the zoölogical garden, for poetry and music associated with the home and its surroundings, for the cone and the dome in buildings, for the whole plastic art in ceramics and sculpture, for all geometric ornament of every sort whatsoever, for textiles, tapestries, embroideries and laces, and largely for free-hand drawing and painting.

FIG. 50.—THE MOTHER OF THE CARPENTER—LOW CASTE INDIAN WOMAN.

---

* J. Anthrop. Soc., Bombay, 1890, vol. II, p. 94.

In art, as in practical work, the necessities of the case developed in women great comprehensiveness. In the Pueblo of Oraibi, Arizona, the same woman is most skilful in three types of basketry, in loom weaving, and in pottery, with their separate forms and decorations. This characteristic struggle for beauty in every direction by every woman had a most reforming effect upon society in its infancy.

CHAPTER IX.

THE LINGUIST.

There have been many ways imagined for the beginnings of speech. The chief among them are the emotional or interjectional, the imitative or mimetic, and the responsive or intuitive, utterance of thought, will, and feeling.

When the true origin of language shall be explained, all of these theories and others will have to be taken into account, and in any event women will receive their share of credit. It will doubtless also be proved that the creation of speech was a very practical and prosy affair.

In the consideration of woman in the light of any one or of all these theories, her special part in early speech must be studied in relation to its *invention*, its *dissemination*, its *conservation*, and its *metamorphosis*. For, it must not be forgotten that language is one of the great classes of human inventions, created just as were tools, processes of activity, artistic designs, institutions, and even worships. The invention of language has followed the line of evolution pursued in other activities, beginning with almost purposeless changes, and ending with co-operative and purposeful modifications. The earliest language, at any rate, was not a set of nouns and verbs and quantifying and qualifying elements, all differentiated as in our dictionaries and grammars. It was made up of brief sentence terms, in which thoughts and emotions and wishes were couched in a single complex utterance, which was elucidated and enforced by accentuation and by gestures of the body. The sentence was the unit of speech, and the grammatic components are even now called "parts of speech." The savage tribes, the primitive men and women, invented these utterances, and, leaving out the common expressions, the very nature of the case is convincing that women developed and owned more than half of the sentence terms that were not common property.

Women, having the whole round of industrial arts on their minds all day and every day, must be held to have invented and fixed the language of the same. In our own households, two women have it in their power to converse about a dozen subjects for a long time intelligibly to each other, but entirely beyond the comprehension of men who are present. It was the same in early times.*

If women in savagery had to do with butchering and tanning, and gleaning and carrying, and milling and cooking, and the interminable list of drudgeries before mentioned then women's continual mockings or chatterings or stammerings or ejaculations thereabout, repeated and repeated to one another and to their daughters, and even to their infant sons, became a considerable addition to the general stock of speech. Furthermore, women have invented terms for men to use—at least have put expressions into the mouths of their male infants to become a part of their stock.

Dr. Brinton, in a private letter, says that in most early languages not only is there a series of expressions belonging to the women, but in various nations we find a language belonging to the women quite apart from that of the men.

Says Edward John Payne, in his History of America:

---

* On this point consult Whitney, Language and the Study of Language. New York, 1868, Scribner, p. 22.

"The steps by which language was developed are still obscure; but it may reasonably be concluded that the food quest had a considerable share in the process, and that not long after emotional exclamations and demonstrative names came primitive adjectives signifying 'good' and 'evil,' applied to animal and vegetable species with reference to the purpose of food, in the sense in which the African guide classes all plants into 'bush' and 'good for nyam' (the latter including the eatable ones, the former the residue). In the discovery of the qualities of the plants women had the largest share, the males being occupied in hunting."[*] What is said concerning the food quest would be equally true of all the substantial occupations of savage woman's life. Indeed, the Mexicans say, "A woman is the best dictionary."[†] This unpremeditated confession is based upon an early induction made by the aborigines of that country centuries ago. Savage men, in hunting and fishing, are much alone, and have to be quiet, hence their taciturnity; but women are together, and chatter all day long. Away from the centres of culture women are still the best dictionaries, talkers, and letter writers.

In the provision of names for the thousands of things that men make and that men and women have in common the latter must certainly have also chosen names of their own. For women's appliances and methods, as they appeared to the opposite sex, men also helped to enrich the languages of the earth with terminology derived from their point of view. This interchange of linguistic material still goes on in every household. One scarcely passes a day at home without hearing familiar things greeted with unfamiliar names brought in by the opposite sex.

---

[*] Hist. of America, New York, 1892, vol. i, p. 307.
[†] Dodge, Plains, etc., p. 428.

Moreover, the infinite number of gestures which are believed to be necessary for the enforcement of any thought must surely conform to woman's special employments. The pantomime of conversation is always in harmony with the subject, and so is the drama of ceremony. Men imitate the animals they hunt; women, both by voice and gesture, imitate what is theirs. I have somewhere heard of a Pueblo woman who all the time she was building up a vase imitated with her voice the ring of a sound vessel to encourage it to remain firm and not crack in the baking. This last suggestion leads on to that inquiry how far women have helped to the selection and preservation of language through onomatopœia. The female vocal apparatus is singularly adapted to the imitation of many natural sounds, and the female ear is correspondingly quick to catch the sounds within the compass of the voice. The former has harvested the sounds, the latter has garnered them. Indeed, the attempt to catch the sounds easily within woman's capabilities has necessitated the cultivation of the falsetto voice in men.

The same rule holds true with regard to the whole series of poetic figures. As every one knows, analogy lies at the basis of most savage reasoning, and is the source of many applications of words. But for one moment consider that analogy is for some fancied resemblance the applying of a term with which we are familiar to something with which it is not generally associated. The poet who compared life to a weaver's shuttle drew his inspiration from woman's work. In the use of simile and metaphor, especially all through the daily ministrations, necessarily the tropes will conform to the easiest imagery of the speaker. Whole hosts of sound combinations are constantly acquiring special meanings in the minds and in the language of women for this very reason. Many of these survive to swell the general stock of language and to add to its richness. No attempt has been made, perhaps, to separate the imagery of language naturally belonging to men from that which belongs to women. Perhaps it can not be done, and we must rest in the general statement that all the poetic imagery in language derived from the occupations of women was either devised by them or was inspired through them. In looking through any dictionary of a savage language, it will be found that while things change, names endure. The point in this assertion is that many arts originated by women in savagery passed afterward into the hands of men and became theirs; but the name survived. The modern Navajo *hogan*, or house, is supposed to be the descendant of a brush hut covered with earth. It is frequently built of stones and mud. The Zuñi name for the *hogan* is *ham'-pon-ne*, a "brush or leaf shelter." And long, long ago the Zuñi probably so built their houses. At any rate the old name endures.

These facts come out in a remarkable manner in the rise and application of what in the classical languages is termed grammatic gender. This differentiation in the forms of speech does not exist in the lower languages, the separation of words into classes being upon a quite different basis—namely, the possession of life or some imaginary characteristic. As will appear more clearly in the chapter on religion, personification is the most common act of the primitive mind. Men and women personify alike the thoughts and the things which they use in common. Men personify the results of women's labour. Women personify the observations and the results of their own and of men's labour. In each case the appropriate sex word, whatever it may be, comes to be joined with the root word. Real gender and some way of indicating it in speech have always been known to men and women, and it is not to be supposed that there was ever a language in which its distinctions could not be clearly stated. To transfer this method, whatever it may be, this mark of personality to impersonal things and this mark of gender to things associated with males and females is the most natural instinct in the world.

No one knows how far back the custom goes of giving gender to things by reason of association with them. The modern sailor calls his ship "she" because he is attached to her, and so also did the Roman sailor and the Greek sailor before him. They are in a sense married to the ship. Among the ignorant men in civilization almost every object with which they have to deal gets the sobriquet of "she." This custom does not prevail so far as is known among women. But the fashion of grouping things in pairs as belonging to opposite sexes is common.

In a special sense, and in innumerable ways, not only objects, but men and women are united socially, intellectually, religiously. In his Essays of an Americanist, Dr. Brinton devotes one chapter to the conception of love in some American languages,* especially the Algonquin, Nahuatl, Maya, Quichua, and Tupi-Guarani stocks, with the following results: In three of the stocks the terms of love are simply cries of emotion. In four of them the expressions are built on a "root like *amare*, which brings us to the Greek ἄμα, ὁμός, both of which spring from the Sanscrit *sam*; from which the Germans in turn get their words *sammt* and *zusammen*, while we obtain *similar* and *same*." Three of the stocks yield terms asserting union, conjunction, attachment, and four of them have words asserting wish, desire, longing. The Cree, an Algonquin language spoken in central Canada, contains expressions for all four ideas, and hence we infer from the studies of the

---

* Brinton, Essays of an Americanist, Phila., 1890, pp. 411–431, referring to Carl Abel, Linguistic Essays, Lond., 1882.

distinguished Americanist—the superficial observations of travellers to the contrary—that among American aborigines of both hemispheres the distinctions of which I have been speaking existed already. It is to be regretted that our studies must end with this general assertion. The share of women and of men in developing the sentiment, and then the language of the sentiment, and then the transfer of the language of this sentiment to associated things, and finally, through poetry, to ideals, must remain to be studied later.

Dr. Brinton says: "A most instructive fact is that these notions are those which underlie the majority of words for love in the great Aryan family of languages. They thus reveal the parallel paths which the human mind everywhere pursued in giving articulate expression to the passions and emotions of the soul. In this sense there is a oneness in all languages which speaks conclusively for the oneness in the sentient and intellectual attributes of the species." That the lowest peoples have not attained the highest comprehension of this term, but have been engaging themselves in giving definition to its lower and material inclusions, is exactly in line with all the studies we have been making thus far.

This brings us to the invention of written or recorded speech. The first written speech was in the form of pictures. The artist was unskilled, the pencils were not of the best, and repetition of the same design was out of the question. Mr. Henry Balfour makes this very apparent in his work on the evolution of art. He made a sketch of a snail crawling over a stick and gave it to a friend to copy. The copy he gave to a third, and so on to twelve persons in turn. The result is the drawing of a bird perched on a limb. Pictography has in the long run undergone a similar evolution. Pictures, bad enough, were succeeded by abbreviated pictures, and these by further curtailments, with by and by not a suggestion of the original. Finally came hieroglyphs, then logographs, then syllabaries, then alphabets. But what has all this to do with women?

We have studied minutely enough the associations of women with textile and with plastic art to discover how on baskets and blankets and robes and pottery she spoke a language eloquent to the eye. Men modified their pictographs because they could not draw. Women first modified theirs because they were in leading strings. But when they came to the ceramic art they were in the best field for pictography. The honours were divided between the pointed stick and the rude paint brush.

The robes of buffalo hide on which a great deal of picture writing was done were all wrought by women, and Dr. W. J. Hoffman, one of the acutest observers, who is familiar with the picture writing of the American aborigines, says that the first pictograph he ever saw made was executed by an Arikara woman. Birch-bark love letters indited by Indian maidens are in existence.

Tattooing is a species of sign writing or pictography. There are many tribes in which women alone tattoo, and in those where it is common to both sexes the women do their own share of the work. In many cult societies they record the songs, and the assertion has been made, but it can not be proved here, that among the Plains Indians the women have a picture language unknown to the men.

Both gestures and pictures obey the usual law. There are very many that are common to the sexes, and some that are peculiar to each.

An excellent example of the species of sign language or telegraphing growing out of the work of women exclusively is given by Brigham, in speaking of the tapa-cloth making in Hawaii, who says: "I have usually seen the old women establish their *kua kuku* (beating logs) under some tree near a brook or kalo patch. It is interesting to note that the women engaged in the beating had a system of signalling by blows and intervals from valley to valley."*

This is a very primitive kind of telegraphy or signalling, which finds its parallel in our modern marine and military language of signs. The drum languages of Africa, understood by both men and women, will recur at once to the reader.

In the dissemination of speech in primitive times it is almost safe to say that woman had the larger share—at least before the commencement of that world-encompassing commerce which mingled the languages as it did the productions of the nations. In Australia, in Africa, in America, tribes belonging to different linguistic stocks over and over again pressed on each other's boundaries and went to war.

But in these conflicts women were not killed as a rule. They were seized as spoils, and either enslaved or adopted into the conquering tribes. Indeed, with many tribes and nations systematic kidnapping of women was carried on. They took with them to their new homes mouths full of words and hands nimble in arts that were perhaps unknown to their captors.

If the migrants were in considerable numbers, as happened many times, they kept up conversation in their own tongue and learned the new one. Whatever novelty they brought with them for which there was no word in the new home they supplied with the old name, and that became a loan word in the new tongue. Just as the German women who came to America have given us both the name and the thing *pretsel*, so this endless train of captive

---

* Brigham, Cat. Bishop Mus., Honolulu, 1892, p. 29.

women who for many thousands of years wandered over the earth in dreary exile unconsciously enriched each tongue from the vocabularies of the others.

The phenomenon to be witnessed in the North Central States of the Union of foreign mothers keeping alive the native speech among children to such an extent as to require the intervention of the laws to have English taught in the schools is common enough. But there are localities where the matter enters into politics and the law has been defeated.

A historic example of the same character among aborigines is furnished by the Arawaks, of whom Brinton says: "They were the first of the natives of the New World to receive the visitors from European climes, and the words picked up by Columbus and his successors on the Bahamas, Cuba, and Hayti are readily explained by the modern dialects of this stock."[*]

Now these Arawaks had just before the discovery of America been driven from many of the southern islands of the West Indian archipelago by the Caribs. Yet on these very islands two languages were spoken—the Arawak by the women, and the Carib by the men.

Mrs. French Sheldon assures us that the women in those parts of eastern Africa which she visited played the part of intermediary between tribes in the times of peace and acted as spies in war. For this work they are peculiarly fitted both by their common duties and by their knowledge of the languages.[†]

Between the Klamath and the Mutsun, of northern California, languages belonging to different stocks, the

---

[*] Brinton, The American Race, New York, 1891, Hodges, p. 242; Trans. Am. Phil. Soc., 1871. Lucien Adam, Du Parler des Hommes et du parler des Femmes dans la langue Caraïbe, Extr. d. Mém. de l'Acad. Stanislas, 1878, Paris, 1879.

[†] J. Anthrop. Inst., London, 1892, vol. xxi, p. 350.

only corresponding words are *tchāyu*, shallow basket in the former, and *tchálu* and *tchakeln*, two kinds of root baskets in the latter. Compare also Selish *ténas*, young; Klamath, *tú-initwi-ash*, young woman; *ténase*, infant in Aht of Vancouver Island; Klamath, *kuhi*, female animal; Maidu, *kille*, *kúle*, woman, wife, female animal.*

This is an interesting fact in connection with another regarding language. The American Indians practiced tribal or national endogamy—that is, marriage within the tribe or nation. The introduction of strange women was practiced, but it was not the rule. Hence these American linguistic stocks are distinct and easily classified. The student has little trouble in keeping them apart. As Brinton has shown, however, the tribes or nations of middle America were more mixed and foreign women were more frequently brought in. The consequence is the multiplication of loan words. Now in Africa the language problem is in a very different condition. Over immense regions there are groups of languages that are akin. Omitting the Earafric element in the North, the Semito-Hamitic element in the Northeast, there are at least three types which must be grouped together—the Soudanese, the Bantu, and the Hottentot. In these three areas borrowing and lending both wives and words, through war and slavery, have gone on for ages. This, however, has not been worked out carefully either by the students of marriage or by the philologists. The existence of widespread language types is a proof of constant communication of some kind, especially where this diffusion is in spite of blood, latitude, climate, natural scenery, and resources. In the absence of writing and through change of living, two members of the same tribe soon

---

* Gatschet. Cont. to N. A. Ethnol., vol. ii, p. ii *et seq.*

forget the mother tongue, except the numerals and the commonest words for things familiar.

Tylor says that "civilization is a plant much oftener propagated than developed," and Arthur Mitchell holds that "no man in isolation can become civilized," which opinions Mr. Gomme strenuously maintains in his work Ethnology and Folklore.*

These statements should be held to mean that every civilization is stimulated and enriched by new arts and new thoughts and new words from without. And this scattering has been largely woman's work. A curious illustration of the share of woman in the scattering of language is furnished in Australia. The whole nation is the *supremum genus*. "A native who travelled far and wide through Australia stated that he was furnished with temporary wives by the various tribes with whom he sojourned in his travels; that his right to these women was recognized of course, and that he could always ascertain whether they belonged to the division into which he could legally marry, though the places were one thousand miles apart and the languages quite different. Hence it often happens that husband and wife speak different languages, and continue to do so after marriage. Indeed, in some tribes of western Victoria a man is actually forbidden to marry a wife who speaks the same dialect as himself; and during the preliminary visit which one pays to the tribe of the other neither is permitted to speak the language of the tribe whom he or she is visiting." †

In China, on the contrary, where women do not migrate notably, the dialects are extremely unlike—so much so that a man from one province can not read aloud to

---

* Tylor and Mitchell, quoted in G. L. Gomme, Ethnology and Folklore, New York, 1892, D. Appleton & Co., p. 9.
† J. G. Frazer, Totemism, Edinburgh, 1887, p. 67.

one from another province a document which either one could read to himself. In this same line of inquiry the capabilities of women in all ages as linguists and players upon language as an instrument in literature may be examined. Between savagery and our modern civilization there was an age of sentimentality in which women's tongues became atrophied. But it was not so from the beginning. The Hindu woman, as set forth in the following extract, represents the feeble type. But the share of woman in the creation of language and its dissemination shows how capable she should be in its management.

In 1679 was born, near Pandharpur, Shridhur, the famous poet who gave to the people the stories of the Ramayana and the Mahabharata in the popular Marathi. He tells us that he wrote his poems for the weaker sex. Said he: "Women do not understand Sanskrit, and in this respect their helplessness may be likened to that of a weak person distressed with thirst standing at the mouth of a deep well. Now, if that person has no rope and pot, how will he draw water to quench his thirst? Whereas, if he comes to a tank he can quench his thirst at once. In the same way to quench the thirst of the weaker sex and lead them into the paths of salvation the Almighty has ordained that works shall be composed in the Prakrit tongue. It is true that the original story of Rama being in Sanskrit, it is better to peruse it in Sanskrit. But the weaker sex can not master that language any more than an elephant can be restrained by a rope made out of the fibres of a lotus. If the weaker sex can not understand, how will they be saved?" *

The fact is that women are naturally more voluble

---

* J. Anthrop. Soc., Bombay, 1890, vol. II, p. 511. A modern book equally silly in tone is William Alexander's History of Women, published a hundred years ago in London.

than men, have more things to talk about, are captured and carried about more, and spread the seeds of new words and their underlying thoughts. In an equally remarkable degree women have been the conservators of speech. The conservation of speech is quite as necessary as its invention. Women very early invented industries which were to last until the end of time. That they worked at them day in and day out without talking about them is not to be supposed. They did prattle about them, and gave names to them and to all the raw materials and tools and apparatus and methods and rules and productions and their thousand and one uses. As all these were to endure, the words and sentences which were attached to them became an integral part and symbols of them, and had the best chance of preservation. Over and over again women have been characterized as the conservative sex. In the light of these studies they could scarcely be otherwise. The Hindu god Vishnu is called the preserver of forms, not because he has been requested to hold all things together, but he got his name by reason of all his good deeds in this direction. The name came after the fact. It is no violation of language to call her the conservator of language whose words endure. Without noticing the reasons here assigned, Buckle dwells on the same thought and quotes from a multitude of authorities.[*]

A casual glance at any list of old-time verbs in the English and other cultural languages—*sow, sew, sweep, spin, weave, grind, wind, wash, bake*, and so on to the end of the list—confirms the suspicion that a goodly stock of enduring words have come to us in the occupations of women. Indeed, that most brilliant of linguistic achievements, the identification of Indian, Iranic, and European languages, rests upon the common heritage of

---

[*] Buckle, Works, and Fraser's Magazine, London, April, 1859.

words, most of which belong to women. "It is only the most rudimentary terms connected with agriculture that agree in Greek and Latin. The names for the various species of grain, for the various parts of the plough, for the winnowing fan, for the handmill, and for bread, are all different. So also are the words denoting the most elementary legal and political conditions, as well as the words relating to metals, seamanship, fishing, and war, the names of weapons, ... none of them can be traced in Greek."*

It is a threadbare fact that among dying tribes the ambitious linguist generally finds at the last moment one old woman who still holds on to a part of her vocabulary. Of Minnie Froben, a Klamath woman, Mr. Gatschet says: "She and Subchief Hill were the most important contributors to my mythic and other ethnologic anthology, and the pieces dictated by her excel all others in completeness and perspicuity. Moreover, I obtained from her a multitude of popular songs, the names and uses of esculent roots and plants, the Klamath degrees of relationship, etc." † Lalla Rookh, last of the Tasmanians, and others will occur to those familiar with collecting vocabularies.

In the conservation of the history of language women have played a prominent part through what is commonly termed folk speech. The folklore that abides in the minds and habits of cultivated persons came there in childhood, largely introduced into nursery instruction by mothers and servants. Nursery rhymes, Märchen, riddles, and jingles, infolding bits of ancient philology, are passed from nurse to child, and have been for centuries. While many thousands of books have perished, these traditional

---

* Isaac Taylor, The Origin of the Aryans, London, 1892, Scott, p. 104.

† Gatschet, Cont. to N. A. Ethnol., vol. ii, pt. i, p. 7.

examples have endured with a tenacity of life that is truly astonishing.

Lastly, besides producing profound modifications of language through its dissemination, women have themselves taken part in those changes of form and meaning in words and the construction of sentences that constitute its life history. Many schools in our country employ both men and women to teach French and German, because the two sexes do not, in fact, speak these languages alike.

To begin with, the vocal apparatus is different, and has not undergone a great deal of modification since the days of savagery. Mr. Mooney's Kiowa women beating upon a rawhide for a drum were singing treble, uttering their own fancies and dreams and experiences and hopes. There is no tribe where music awakens the same sounds or words among the sexes. As a matter of fact, savages are not so stationary as the civilized nations. The women of an Athapascan tribe in central Alaska, in that cold and barren land, exclaimed and mocked with their voices the things of Nature around them, and uttered the thoughts that arose in them by reason of their environment. When they moved over the coast ranges and southward to California and Oregon, they gave to old roots new meanings and found a new heaven, a new earth, a new climate and a new soil, new minerals, plants, and animals. These excited, proposed, and awakened a new batch of words and sentences and gestures. When the tribes of the same stock wandered into Arizona, another entirely new series of forces created further changes in vocabulary. Lastly, one half of the Southwestern tribes became pastoral. Hence the Tinné woman, working in birch bark and quills; the Hupa woman, gorgeously dressed in piñon-seed skirt and hat of hazel twigs and pine root and fern stalk; the Apache woman, loaded with gaudy jewellery in a desolate land; and the Navajo woman in highly-coloured blankets of her own dyeing and spinning and weaving, though of the same blood—have been tutored of different climates and environments. There is enough of the primitive Athapascan left in them all to confirm their unity, but the charming part of the study of them all is the curious metamorphosis of old words, their adaptation to new uses, and the variety of new forms of speech which each set of natural conditions has effected.

Furnished with a vocal apparatus differing from that of men, engaged in industries growing more and more complex and tabooed to men, talking to one another more than to men from day to day, women have modified language and fixed its colloquial form at home as well as by dispersion. Theirs is the speech of common parlance largely—that which all children learned from them to prattle, the vulgar dialect, the ungrammatical and greatly abbreviated talk of the day. But all observers tell us that in their councils the men spoke a different tongue—more sonorous and oratorical, and frequently incomprehensible to women.

CHAPTER X.

THE FOUNDER OF SOCIETY.

If there is in savagery any operation in which the women have always and everywhere "trodden the winepress alone," it is in the supreme moment of motherhood. The following quotation, if the tribal name were erased, might have been written among any aborigines in the world: "Upon the approach of childbirth the Quissama woman [Angola] departs from home, as she has the idea that neither man nor woman should see her, into the forest, where she remains until she has succeeded in delivering herself of the child. Shortly after the birth she returns to her hut, and no questions are asked."*

Among the Indians of Guiana before the birth of a child the father abstains from certain kinds of animal food. The mother works up to a few hours before the infant is born. At last she retires alone, or accompanied only by some other women, to the forest, where she ties up her hammock, and then the babe is born. Then in a few hours the woman gets up and resumes her ordinary work. No sooner is the event announced than the father takes to his hammock, and, abstaining from every kind of work, from meat and all other food except weak gruel of

---

* J. Anthrop. Inst., London, 1872, vol. i, p. 159. In the Index Catalogue of the Surgeon General's Library, Washington, under the appropriate catch words, many hundreds of references to this fact will be found.

cassava meal, from smoking, from washing himself, and, above all, from touching weapons of any sort, is nursed and cared for by all the women of the place. The child is not weaned till a late age, sometimes not till the third or fourth year. When there are too many children claiming food from one mother, the grandmother occasionally relieves her of the elder. The mother, even when working, carries the child against her hip or slung in a small hammock from her neck or shoulder. As soon as children can run about they begin to mimic their parents. Even the youngest girls can peel a few cassava roots, watch a pot, or collect a few sticks of wood.*

This practice of putting the father to bed is called *couvade*, and is of extreme antiquity, as the following quotation from Apollonius shows:

> In the Tibarenian land,
> When some good woman bears her lord a babe,
> 'Tis he is swathed and groaning put to bed;
> Whilst she arises, tends his baths, and serves
> Nice possets for her husband in the straw.†

The fate of the tiny creature thus ushered into society depends with savages upon a number of circumstances. The first question is, whether it shall live or die, and this question, wonderful to relate, is not infrequently raised by the mother herself. Among the Eskimo, in times of scarcity, if a child be born for whom food can not be provided, it is exposed to die of cold, having its mouth stuffed with a bunch of grass to prevent it from crying. This is done as a matter of duty. The child must not cry, or its voice will be heard about the house. One of these

---

* Im Thurn, Ind. of British Guiana, London, 1883, p. 219.

† Apoll. Rhod., ii. 1012, quoted by H. Ling Roth, in J. Anthrop. Inst., London, 1893, vol. xxii, p. 214. The whole paper on couvade by this author should be consulted (Ibid., pp. 204–244).

FIG. 51. THE MAIDEN IN NATAKSHI.

little ones picked up and adopted owes lifelong service to the foster parent.*

The very same thing would be done by any other primitive people, and for similar reasons, without exciting horror. The Australian mother or father would fill the baby's mouth with dry sand; the poor woman in a great city would place her hand over its mouth, wrap it in a coarse cloth, and lay it in some dark alley, the motive in many cases being the same. Infanticide, however, is social suicide in any way, shape, or form, and female infanticide is the worst form of the infatuation. Price says: "There are few women in comparison to the number of men among the Quissema, Angola, which I think would be accounted for if we could determine that at some time past they destroyed their female offspring."† Of the Angola people Livingstone also writes: "The height of good fortune is to bear sons. The women will leave their husbands altogether if they bear daughters only, and childless women often commit suicide."‡ That men should dote on male children is natural enough, and that they on occasion weed out the females has over and over again been shown; but the curious attitude of the Angolese women toward girl babies is worthy a moment's reflection, in the light of what civilized women say and do on the same subject.

The little girl in savagery, if her life was to be spared, grew up at the side of her mother and her mother's sisters. The time she passed between her third and her thirteenth year was the period of her education. She was then expected to be ready to fill a woman's place. Ten years of pupilage had their effect upon her physical edu-

---

* Dall, Am. Naturalist, Philadelphia, 1878, vol. xii, p. 6.
† Price, J. Anthrop. Inst., London, 1872, p. 189.
‡ Travels, etc., in S. Africa, New York, 1858, p. 446.

cation, her mental training, her morals. In the different races there were characteristic codes of child training. Climate also, and even religion, entered into this savage pedagogics.

In all of them, however, as the little girl grew to be the maiden, there was no home circle to guard her morals. Her ears were saluted with talk that hardened and vulgarized her mind. Yet her education was of the most practical character. You have only to look in the great museums to find among savage woman's handiwork innumerable examples of tiny pieces of basketry, pottery, bread, or weaving, labelled "children's work." In the industrial schools of the times the little hands learned dexterity. In the Mexican codices, mother and child are represented as teacher and scholar through years of tutelage, with the rewards and punishments clearly set forth.

In ancient Mexico, annexed to the temples, were large buildings used as seminaries for girls, a sort of aboriginal Wellesley or Vassar. They were presided over by matrons or vestal priestesses, brought up in the temple. Day and night the building was guarded by old men. The maidens could not leave their apartments without a guard, and if any one broke this rule her feet were pricked with thorns till the blood flowed. When they went out, it was together, and accompanied by the matrons. The maidens had to sweep the precincts of the temple occupied by them, and attended to the sacred fire; they learned how to make feather work and to spin and weave mantles; they were obliged to bathe frequently, and to be skillful and diligent in all household affairs; they were taught to speak with reverence, to humble themselves in the presence of their elders, and to observe a modest and bashful demeanour at all times. They rose at daybreak, and whenever they showed themselves lazy or rude, punishment was inflicted. At night the pupils slept in large rooms in sight of the matrons. The daughters of nobles, who entered the seminaries at an early age, remained there until taken away by their parents to be married.*

In the old tribal life of the Omahas the girl was kept in a state of subjection to her mother, whom she was obliged to help when the latter was at work. When she was four or five years old she was taught to go for wood, etc. When she was about eight years of age she learned how to make up a pack, and began to carry a small one on her back. If she was disobedient she received a blow on the head or back from the hand of her mother. As she grew older, she learned how to cut wood, to cultivate corn, and other branches of an Indian woman's work.†

The Quissama women [Angola] have an excellent way of bringing up their pickaninnies. In order to keep them out of harm's way, all the children belonging to the many scattered huts of a district are brought together every morning, and are kept under the strict supervision of an old woman during the day; at night they return to their parents. This arrangement enables the parents to attend to their agricultural pursuits, of which both sexes are very fond. The women, while doing field work, always have the young infants strapped upon their backs.‡

As will be seen a little farther on, girl children are named in some of the lowest social units more surely than boys. They bear forever the clan name. But the custom

---

* Bancroft, Native Races, New York, 1875, vol. II, p. 246.
† Dorsey, Third An. Rep. Bur. Ethnol., p. 263.
‡ Price, J., Anthrop. Inst., London, 1872, vol. I, p. 188. The same author describes a girl with a calabash of mandoc, palm oil, and mealies feeding a row of these babies hung up in their frames upon beams, just as they had been unharnessed from the mothers' backs (op. cit., p. 191).

is well-nigh universal of adding to this name others as they grow older and to accompany the giving of the name with a religious ceremony. Indeed, the parents frequently receive a title from the child named, so that they are known as the father or mother of such a one. The following custom, taken from a very lowly people, would find its counterpart anywhere:

When the Andamanese girls arrive at the period which divides childhood from maidenhood they receive "flower" names. There are eighteen prescribed trees which blossom in succession, and the "flower" name bestowed in each case is taken from the one in season when the girl attains maturity. This, added to her prenatal name, constitutes the personal address of the girl until she marries and is a mother, when she receives the more dignified title of *Chāna* (madam or mother).*

The training completed, the girl graduate had to pass through a ceremony of initiation, a kind of "bringing-out" ordeal. This was oftentimes painful, but never so terrific in its tortures as those which young men had to endure on reaching manhood. In some tribes a girl had to begin in her eleventh year to fast and to abstain from doing this or that. The things she ought not to do were quite as many as are the interdictions on the modern miss. She had to walk ever-increasing distances with a jar on her head and to carry burdens made heavier every day. In fact, she was drilled in endurance and skill and every wifely exercise.

A life of single blessedness is possible in savagery, but far less happy than in civilisation. It is doubtful whether a single human being could prosper for any length of time alone in any part of the earth. And this state would be worse for a woman than for a man. A definition of civili-

---

* Cf. Man, Andaman Islanders, London, 1883, Trübner, p. 60.

zation might be framed as "the ever-increasing possibility of the number of unmarried females that might exist in a community." Dall narrates the story of two Eskimo women who, eschewing the tribal customs, set up establishments of their own, and Hearne tells of a regular woman Crusoe in the Hudson Bay region of Canada.

A young Eskimo woman, fine looking and of remarkably good physique and mental capacity, held herself aloof from the young men. She said she was as strong as any of them, as they could testify. She could shoot and hunt deer as well as the men, and set snares and nets. She had her own gun, bought from the proceeds of her trapping. She did not desire to do the work of a wife, preferring that which custom allots to the men. When winter came, having made a convert in a smaller, less athletic damsel, the two erected their own house, and here lived and traded in defiance of public sentiment. When on one occasion they were off on a deer hunt " outraged public opinion combined in a mob which reduced their winter quarters to a shapeless ruin. The next year they gave up the unequal contest and returned to the ways of the world."*

Though cut-and-dried marriages are the rule in savagery, as some would have them with us, these do not lack a cloud of witnesses to the existence of romantic love among lowly peoples.

Ellis relates a charming account of this phenomenon at Tahiti. A chief of Eimeo, about twenty years old and of great personal beauty, became attached to the niece of the principal *owhira* in the island, and tendered proposals of marriage. She declined every proposal, though no means to gain her consent were left untried. He was seized with the deepest melancholy, and leaving the other

---

* From Dall, Am. Nat., Philadelphia, 1878, vol. xii, pp. 4–6.

members of the family to follow their regular pursuits, from morning to night he attended his mistress, performing humiliating offices. At length she relented, accepted his offers, and they were publicly married.*

The day of days to all young women who enter the current of human activity is that of their wedding. Mr. Man thus describes the ceremony among his Andamanese: "On the evening of the eventful day the bridal party assemble at the chief's hut, or in one of those occupied by unmarried women. The bride sits apart, attended by one or two matrons, and the bridegroom takes his place among the bachelors until the chief or elder approaches him, whereupon he at once assumes a modest demeanour and simulates reluctance to move; however, after a few encouraging and reassuring remarks, he will allow himself to be led slowly, sometimes almost dragged, toward his fiancée, who, if she be young, generally indulges in a great display of modesty, weeping and hiding her face, while her female attendants prepare her by straightening her limbs. The bridegroom is then made to sit on her lap, and torches are lighted and brought close to the pair that all present may bear witness to the ceremony having been carried out in orthodox manner, after which the chief pronounces them duly married, and they are at liberty to retire to the hut that has been previously prepared for their occupation. On the morning after the marriage the parties are painted by their mutual friends. It often happens that a young couple will pass several days after their nuptials without exchanging a single word or even looking at each other." †

The marriage relation in its broadest sense must be

---

* Ellis, Polynes. Researches, London, 1850, vol. I, pp. 267-269. See also Musters, J. Anthrop. Inst., London, 1872, vol. I, p. 201.

† Man, Andaman Islanders, London, 1883, Trübner, p. 60.

studied in Morgan, Lubbock, Tylor, McLennan, Letourneau, Starcke, and Wake. Their comprehensive works abound in references to original observers, and form an encyclopædia on this topic.

Here, briefly, it is designed to observe how the civilized woman stands related to primitive woman in this regard, and how little by little the condition of the latter came to be that of the former. It is said that woman was first the wife of any, then the wife of many, and then one of many wives. In this last condition her nuptial period has been growing more and more stable.

The evolution of matrimony has been woman's work in more ways than one. Of any bird or beast there is no difficulty of telling who is the mother. The longer the mother's care of the eggs or of the young was demanded, the longer was it possible to vouch for the identical mother day after day. Matrimony in all ages, then, is an effort to secure to the child the authenticity of the father. So the poor female, always the mother well known, has had curious ups and downs as regards her spouse. The evolution of the husband, then, is the history of matrimony. The motives of this evolution will appear as the various standings of woman in this regard are unfolded. Paternal feeling is just as strong as maternal affection, but its existence and strength depend upon the identification of paternity either in a group or an individual.

In every social state a good wife, as wifehood goes, has ever been considered among the most precious possessions. Whether the bliss of undivided companionship be the point of view or the gain of profitable service to him alone, the man has always looked upon the best woman as the pearl of great price. Hence the family or the clan that owned the young woman, as well as the man who desired the young woman, could not fail to see that he who loses the service and he who gains the exclusive right are dealing with commodities of acknowledged values. In the higher forms of culture presents are given to the bride, but down the hill a little way they demanded them.*

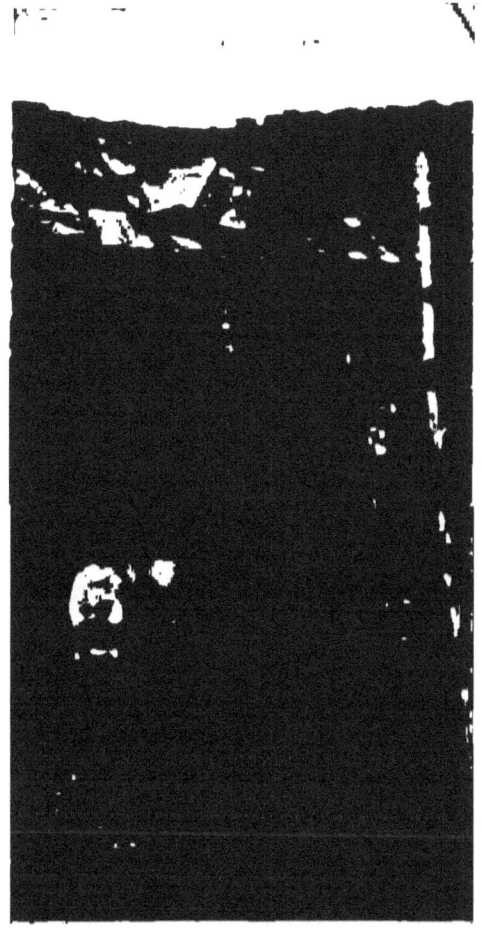

FIG. 52. THE FOUNDER OF SOCIETY, THE PRIMITIVE SOCIAL UNIT.

It will appear farther on why a present was demanded by the bride's family. Even in our own day the union of

* See Bancroft, Native Races, New York, 1874-'76, sub voce Woman, vol. v, p. 782, for numerous kinds of wife purchase or claiming among North American tribes.

young people in wedlock is not without its commercial elements, especially where property is involved. But in primitive aggregations the motive was more apparent and the means more direct.*

Among the ancient Germans the wife did not bring a dowry to her husband, but received one from him. "The parents and relations assemble and pass their approbation on the presents—not adapted to please a feminine taste or to decorate the bride, but oxen, a caparisoned steed, a shield, a spear, and a sword. By virtue of these the wife is espoused; and she in turn makes a present of some arms to her husband. That the woman may not think herself excused from exertions of fortitude or exempt from the casualties of war, she is admonished by the very ceremonial of her marriage that she comes to her husband as a partner in toils and dangers; to suffer and to dare equally with him, in peace and in war. All this is indicated by the yoked oxen, the caparisoned steed, and the offered arms. Thus she is to live; thus to die." †

From the point of view of this book the study of marriage involves the following questions, based on the constitution of the tribes in which it exists: 1. Who may marry a woman? 2. How many women may he marry, or how many men may she marry? 3. For how long a time may the woman marry the man—that is, after how long a time, and under what circumstances may he put her away or may she dissolve the union? Now, the answer of these questions, as hinted, depends largely upon the way in which the community is held together, upon its constitution and government. The patriarchal family is insepa-

---

* See Livingstone, Travels, etc., in South Africa, New York, 1858, pp. 543, 687, 663. On the subject of wife purchase consult also Wake, Marriage and Kinship, London, 1889, Redway.

† Tacitus, Germania, chap. xviii, Harper's Class. Ser., vol ii, p. 809; other notes referring to German women.

rably connected with the patriarchal government, the clan marriage can not be severed from the clan government, and so on. We shall now examine some of these forms of wife holding under the titles that have been adopted by distinguished writers. As studied by the eminent authorities above mentioned, society presents itself to us in different phases with reference to wife holding or husband holding. The following are the principal conditions, imaginary or real, that have been considered necessary to a complete study of the subject: 1. A primitive condition, of which nothing is known, in which unions were not for life, wherein any man might marry any woman, or as many women as he pleased and *vice versa*, as long as it suited them, or until the child was weaned. In such a state our young woman was the wife of any. 2. A condition in which female infanticide was practiced, causing men to become much more numerous than women. This led to several kinds of *polyandry*, in which all the men of a community held all the women in common, or in which several men attached themselves specifically to each woman. Here she became the wife of many. 3. A condition in which, to increase the number of women, those of other tribes or communities were carried off by force. Here *polygamy* has an opportunity of arising legitimately, but as yet there would be no law as to whom a woman should marry. In such a state she is one of many wives. 4. A state of things in which the daughters of the same mother, at least, are not lost in the general *mêlée*. It will be learned that such a time was the dawn of social history. There is no lower condition known. This was the foundation of the gentile system, in which the young woman is fenced by tribal restrictions. 5. A state of society in which men began to lead industrial lives, to assume the *rôle* that had been woman's alone, to have property, and to think it worth

FIG. 51.—CHE-MAH-RAH-VIN FAMILY, HATCHITAS MOUNTAIN, CALIFORNIA.

their while to own their daughters. Here began father right, leading finally to the monogamian family.

The old voyagers assert that many aboriginal peoples practiced communal marriage—that is, any man and any woman might be man and wife for just as long as they pleased, and there was no social let or hindrance. The old idea that everything came from nothing seems to demand some such state of marriage at first in our species. Closer study by patient scholars reveals the fact that no such practice exists anywhere. Even pigeons mate for as many as fourteen years, and hawks are monogamous for life. The animal world had got further along when the human race appeared. Of the Andamanese, frequently referred to in this book as among the lowliest of the lowly, "so far from the contract of marriage being regarded as a temporary arrangement, to be set aside at the will of either party, no incompatibility of temper or other cause is allowed to dissolve the union, and, while bigamy, polygamy, polyandry, and divorce are unknown, conjugal fidelity till death is not the exception but the rule, and matrimonial differences are soon settled, without the intervention of friends." *

So far from promiscuity in married life are all the savage tribes known on earth at present that the lower down we go the more stringent are the rules about who shall take each young woman to himself. The modern physiologists are unanimous in declaring against the marriage of cousins and those near of kin, and civilized nations have enacted laws to prevent its occurrence, but customs far more exacting and penalties far severer universally guard the young female in savagery.

True, there may be no law against the children of brothers marrying; but in such tribes sisters' children

---

* Man, The Andaman Islanders, London, 1883, Trübner, p. 67.

only are deemed brothers and sisters, and these never marry.

Who invented this benign arrangement is not known. Even before marriage young savages are taught to heed this rule, and relatives so near of kin as true cousins according to the prevailing idea avoid one another as they grow up.

Now, a moment's reflection shows that this subject of who may marry depends largely on the limits of identification of relationship. The American Indians had one method, the Polynesians another, and the Australians a third, but they were all struggling with the same difficulties.

Among the American Indians and in certain parts of Asia the gentile system of marriage prevailed, called by Morgan the *gussowanian* or "bow-and-arrow" system. In each tribe of Indians were several *gentes* or clans named after some class of natural objects called their "totems." Each clan was composed of a supposed female ancestor and all her descendants through daughters. Descent was in the female line, and the name of the totem adhered to females forever. Under this system in its simplest form a man went to marry a girl. The children bore her name. A man could not marry a woman of his own clan. He must marry into another totem.

"The social corner stone of the Pueblo," says Lummis, "is not the family, but the clan, and this was almost universally the rule in America. Husband and wife must belong to different *gentes* and the children follow the clan of the mother. The spheres of the sexes are clearly defined. The woman is complete owner of the house and all it contains save his personal trinkets; and she has no other work to do than housework, at which she is no sloven. Should her husband ill treat her she could permanently evict him from home, and would be upheld in so doing.

Fig. 14.—The Australian Family.

The man tills the fields, and they are his; but after the crops are housed she has an equal voice in their disposition."*

Some notion of the effect of this clan system or its equivalent in defending women among lower peoples may be had by the custom of slavery before the civil war. Frequently a slave man desired to marry a slave woman on the adjoining plantation. This could be done with the consent of both masters. In every case the children belonged to the owner of the mother. The father could not punish his own child, because he would be striking the property of another man, who in this case stood for the *gens*; neither could he in any way abuse his wife for the same reason. Even the mother and her kin would be restrained in their violence through fear of a higher power.

Perhaps the lowest people on the face of the earth are the Australians. They have a marriage system which decides just where every woman must look for a mate. In Wake's Marriage and Kinship, as well as in Morgan's Ancient Society, the scheme has been worked out for the Kamilaroi people of Darling River district. There are eight classes of persons—four male and four female—recognized, just as though there were only eight family names in the United States. The Australian class titles are as follows: Males, Muri, Kubi, Ipai, Kumbu; Females, *Butha, Ipatha, Kubitha, Matha*. In the following description, in order to give them prominence, female names will all be in italics. The tables will show whom each one must marry, what will be the names of the children, and how the generations return into themselves.

---

* Lummis, Scribner's Magazine, Sept., 1892; also Dorsey, Third Ann. Rep. Bur. Ethnol., Wash., 1884, p. 260.

Name of male.	Must marry female.	Their children.	Their nephews.	His father's sister's and his mother's brother's son or daughter. Cousins.	Brothers and sisters of man.
1. Muri.	1. Butha.	1. Ipai. 1. Ipatha. 2. Kumbo. 2. Butha. 3. Muri. 3. Matha. 4. Kubi. 4. Kubitha.	1. Kubi. 1. Kubitha. 2. Muri. 2. Matha. Kumbo. Butha. Ipai Ipatha.	Kumbo. Butha. Ipai. Ipatha. Kubi. Kubitha. Muri. Matha.	Muri. Matha. Kubi. Kubitha. Ipai. Ipatha. Kumbo. Butha.
2. Kubi.	2. Ipatha.				
3. Ipai.	3. Kubitha.				
4. Kumbu.	4. Matha.				

Note also that all Muris are hypothetically brothers and all Mathas are sisters, and Muris and Mathas are brothers and sisters, though most of them never saw one another. Furthermore, when it is said that a man is compelled to marry his cousin—that is, his father's sister's daughter or his mother's brother's daughter—he would probably not actually do that thing, but simply take a woman belonging to that class. If there were only eight names in the United States, four for males and four for females, and they were compelled to obey the Australian system, the family tree would look like the following: The eight names are Green, *Greenway*; White, *Whiting*; Smith, *Smythe*; Brown, *Browning*. The tables show how they must marry and what would be the result, and, in order to trace the part that we are interested in, the feminine names are in Italics.*

---

* This can be traced out at length in Morgan's Ancient Society, New York, 1877, pp. 51–61, and in Wake's Marriage and Kinship, London, 1890, p. 95 *et seq.*, p. 324.

Men.	Must marry.	Sons.	Daughters.	Cousins. His father's sister's or his mother's brother's children.
Brown.	*Whiting.*	Green.	*Greenway.*	White and *Whiting.*
Smith.	*Greenway.*	White.	*Whiting.*	Green and *Greenway.*
Green.	*Smythe.*	Brown.	*Browning.*	Smith and *Smythe.*
White.	*Browning.*	Smith.	*Smythe.*	Brown and *Browning.*

The Punaluan Family.—In this system of intermarriage several sisters, own and collateral, have one another's husbands in a group, the joint husbands not necessarily being kinsmen to one another; or several brothers, own and collateral, have one another's wives in a group, these wives not necessarily being of kin to one another, although often the case in both instances. In each case the group of men were conjointly married to the group of women.* This form of marriage was common in Hawaii, and perhaps throughout Polynesia.

Polyandry—In the *punaluan* system there may be a plurality either of wives or of husbands. If under such a system the husbands in each case were reduced to one, that would give us an example of polygyny; but if the number of wives be reduced to one, we should have an example of polyandry. And the different phases of *punaluan* marriage reduced would give us the two forms of polyandry—namely, that in which the husbands were brothers or members of the same totem or blood kinship, and that in which they did not claim such relationship. The former type is called Tibetan polyandry, the latter the Nair polyandry, and between the two are many intermediate varieties. Chinese authors ascribe the custom of polyandry to the superiority of the women; Rockhill believes it is due to the small extent of

---

* *Cf.* Morgan, Ancient Society, New York, 1877, Index, *Punaluan.*

family possessions in lands no longer capable of subdivision; McLennan regards polyandry to be one of the fundamental and widely prevailing systems of primitive wedlock. Among the Nairs of the Neilgherry Hills, India, a simpler form prevails, wherein several unrelated men have one wife in common. In the Tibetan region polygamy prevails among the pastoral people and the rich, so that there is a general provision for a home to each one.

Under the Tibetan system, "whatever be the marriage custom," says Rockhill, "the wife is procured by purchase, and as soon as the woman has entered the home of her husband she assumes control of nearly all of his affairs; no buying or selling is done except by her or with her consent or approval. She is the recognized head of the house. This pre-eminent position of women in Tibetan society has been from of old one of the peculiarities of the race, of which parts have frequently been governed by women. One state of eastern Tibet is always ruled by a queen, and to-day the principality of Pomo has a female sovereign."*

Polygyny, from Greek roots, meaning several women, is the type of marriage in which a group of females are married to one man. If these women should be akin, the union would be a variant of polyandry. If they are not necessarily akin it would be polygamy, and the family would be patriarchal.

"The simplest form of polygyny is that in which several sisters become wives of the same man. It appears to have been known to the natives of America, it is practiced among the Australian aborigines, and also by the Ostiaks of Siberia and some of the Malayan tribes. It was not unknown to the early Semites, as appears by

---

* Rockhill, Land of the Lamas, New York, 1891, Century Co., p. 218; also appendix, p. 339, on the Kingdom of Women.

the marriage of Jacob with Rachel and Leah." Darwin affirms that most savages are polygamists, and that polygamy is almost universally followed by the leading men in every tribe.*

What is usually called bigamy or polygamy is in reality polygyny, because, as was shown under monotomy,

Fig. 56. Mexican Indian Family.

the having of several legitimatized husbands by the same wife is one of the rarest things in the world.

But the possessing of several wives occurs in different forms, and may grow out of very different social systems. "In the Australian tribes the monopoly of the women by the old men is very common.

---

* Descent of Man, quoted by Winks, op. cit., p. 484.

"The Fijians belong to the race of Oceanic negroes. Polygyny is said to be universally practiced by them, and a man's social position depends on the number of his wives, all of whom, however, except the first, would be treated as slaves."[*] In America, as appears from the description of clan or punaluan marriage, when a man went to live with the clan of his wife the possibilities of practicing polygyny were limited almost solely to the first kind—namely, that in which the wives were of the same totem. But everywhere on the continent the system of mother right was interrupted by father right, and the man took the wives to live in his lodge.

The practice of polygyny appears to be known to all the tribes of the Pacific coast, where the husband does not live among his wife's relations.

"Among the Mexican nations either polygyny or concubinage was allowed. In addition to the principal wife, a man might have less legitimate wives, with whom the 'tying of garments' constituted the whole of the marriage ceremony. According to Garcillasso de la Vega, the Inca of Peru had three kinds of children, placing women in three marital attitudes: 1, Those of his wife, who, as legitimate, were destined for succession to the chieftaincy; 2, those of his relations, who were legitimate by blood; 3, bastards born of strangers in blood."[†]

In the Asiatic continent polygyny is not prevalent among the Mongolian and other peoples of Central Asia and Siberia. The Ostiaks occasionally practice polygyny, but not frequently, as wives are too expensive. A man may marry several sisters, and a younger brother is bound to marry the widow of an elder brother.[‡]

---

[*] Wake, Marriage and Kinship, London, 1889, p. 182.
[†] Hist. des Yncas, Fr. trans., 1700, vol. 1, p. 854, quoted by Wake, p. 183 et seq.
[‡] Castren, quoted by Wake, op. cit., p. 186.

The Mongols proper have one legitimate wife. There may be also secondary wives, but their children have to be legitimatized by law.

Among the Chinese polygyny may be permitted under certain conditions. The wife chosen for a man by his father and mother is the principal wife. He may have other wives, who, although legitimate, are subject to the first wife, and their children have the right of succession. Doolittle supposes that the second or inferior wife is generally married with the consent of the principal wife when the latter is childless, the desire to have male children "to perpetuate one's name and to burn incense before one's tablet after death" having great influence over the Chinese mind. The children of the inferior wives would appear to belong in law to the first wife.*

This same general system of having one principal wife, with any number of secondary wives, is prevalent all over Japan, Corea, Farther India, and, indeed, among all Buddhist peoples of the Indo-Chinese peninsula. Wake quotes Sir John Bowring, as saying that there are said to be in Siam four classes of wives: the first is the wife of royal gift; the second, the legal wife; the third, the wife of affection; the fourth, the slave wife—that is, the handmaid who has borne children to her master, and in consequence is manumitted.

The Jenadies of southern India are polygynists, owing to the women being more numerous than the men. The Dravidian Malers of Rajmahal favour polygyny, and if a man leaves several widows they are distributed among his brothers and cousins. The Santhals favour monogyny, and where it is otherwise the first wife is honoured as the head of the house. The Juangs of Singbum permit polygyny

---

* Doolittle, Social Life of the Chinese, 1866; Edkins, Religious Condition of the Chinese, p. 163; Douglas, China, 1882, p. 78.

only where the first wife has no children. Many Assam tribes practice both polyandry and polygyny. Among the hill Muris, the chiefs practice the latter, and when a man dies his wives descend to his heir, who becomes the husband of all except his own mother.

In Madagascar polygyny prevails, with Malayan and far Asian characteristics, as one would expect.

Polygyny seems to have been universal in Africa among the negroes. In Uganda the Wahuma men often obtain wives by exchanging daughters. The royal harem is supplied by women received in tribute from neighboring chiefs, and governors are presented by the King with women who are captured abroad or seized from offenders at home.*

A similar practice was in use among the Ashantees, of whom the higher classes had many wives, and the King thirty-three hundred and thirty-three, which number was carefully kept up in order that he might be able to present women to distinguished subjects. Among the Kaffirs and Bechuanas, women are valued in cattle and girls pride themselves on the high price they fetch. The first wife has pre-eminence, all the cows which a man possesses at the time of his marriage are the property of his wife, and after the birth of her first son they are called his cattle. If the first or any subsequent wife furnishes the cattle to purchase and endow a new wife, she is entitled to her service and calls her "my wife." †

In ancient Egypt the priests married only one wife; but other citizens could have as many wives as they pleased, and all the children were legitimate, even those of slave mothers. ‡

---

* Speke, quoted by Wake, op. cit., p. 191.
† Shooter, Kafirs of Natal, 1857, quoted by Wake, op. cit., p. 191.
‡ M. Ménard, La vie privée des Anciens, vol. 3, p. 3, quoting Diodorus. Other references in Wake, op. cit., p. 162.

In modern Egypt a man may, according to the Koran, have four wives, but if he has only one wife he can divorce her and take another whenever he chooses. He has only to say to her "Thou art divorced," and she must return to her friends.[*]

Among the ancient Jews, although polygyny was practiced, monogyny was the rule.[†]

The Moors of Northern Africa and the Berbers are usually monogynous.

In Persia, says M. Ménard, "the royal harem, raised to the dignity of a state institution, had an immense development and magnificence without equal."[‡]

The practice of polygyny was not allowed by the ancient Iranians, and the same must be said of the Aryans of India and of the early Greeks and Romans. The first polygynist named in Roman history was Mark Antony. In 726 a decretal of Pope Gregory II allowed a man to marry a second wife. The primitive Slavs were polygynists. The chiefs of families even now marry their sons of eight and ten years of age to women over twenty and hold these as their own wives until the boys become of age.[#]

Wake sums up the phases of polygyny as follows:[|]

1. Those in which all a man's wives have equal rights.
2. Those where there is a superior wife or wives and inferior ones, the latter being sometimes legal wives, and at others slave wives or concubines.[▲]

Syndyasmian Family.—This type of family life was

---

[*] Lane, quoted by Wake, op. cit., p. 192.
[†] Weill, La Femme Juive, quoted by Wake, op. cit., p. 193.
[‡] La vie privée, etc., quoted by Wake, op. cit., p. 194.
[#] Wake, op. cit., p. 196.
[|] Op. cit., p. 197.
[▲] The operation of polyandry on the condition and happiness of women is set forth in Wake, op. cit., chap. vi, pp. 179–225.

based on marriage between single pairs, but the union continued during the pleasure of the parties. As every form of primitive culture survives into our day, the parallel of this will be found in civilized countries in the case of those women who, through divorce laws or in spite of legislation against bigamy, become the wife of a second husband while the first is living. If she remained with both at the same time we should have an example of polyandry. This form of marriage existed in some communal households of American aborigines, and, in spite of laws against bigamy, may yet be seen in full bloom among the negroes of the Southern States.*

Monandry.—This is a form of primitive marriage in which one man and one woman are joined together in the family. The more exalted form of monandry is monogamy, as practiced among the most civilized. It will be readily seen that where other forms of marriage prevail, since there are very nearly the same number of men and women in each tribe, if some men have a plurality of wives exclusively to themselves others must go without. The same is true in polyandrous countries. Under *punalua* the cases would be balanced; but, after all, the foreshadowing of our present system existed in lowest savagery. There were monogamous marriages under all the systems, but they could be broken up at any time, either by divorce or by returning to the other forms in vogue. A little higher up in civilization we come upon the monandry of the Chinese, the Japanese, and of the ancient Greeks and Romans. The minute development of these would require too much of our space. In China the women are still subjects of purchase, and under the teachings of Confucius man is the representative of heaven,

---

* Consult Morgan, Ancient Society, New York, 1877, Holt, part iii, chap. iv.

and woman must obey his instructions. "When young she is to obey her father and elder brother; when married she must obey her husband; when her husband is dead she must obey her son."*

Divorce.—In the United States during 1867–'86 there were 328,716 divorces granted—216,738 to wives. The dissolution of the marriage tie is practiced by every people, in every age, and among all grades of culture. But in savagery, where every man and woman and child is billeted somewhere, there is no such thing as thrusting man or woman out into nowhere. Every social movement has a starting point and a destination. If A sells his daughter, or if a clan or council assign a young woman to a man, property is exchanged and value given. Should the man wish to repudiate his wife, she can not be sent out into the jungle or forest; she must be returned to somebody. So that while in savagery divorces are easier and more common, they are also more according to rule. Confucius allowed seven grounds of divorce—to wit, disobedience to a husband's parents, not giving birth to a son, dissolute conduct, jealousy of her husband, talkativeness, kleptomania, chronic disease or leprosy. For these reasons the man may put away his wife, but for no reason, in China, may she put him away. Even in China, however, the savage's rule obtains. The husband may not thrust the wife forth if she have no refuge.†

"The first recorded case of divorce at Rome was that of Carvilius Ruga, who put away his wife because she had not borne him children."‡

When we cast our eyes backward over the tyranny, we

---

* Wake, op. cit., p. 232.
† Legge, Life and Teachings of Confucius, 3d ed., p. 106, quoted by Wake.
‡ Consult Wake, op. cit., for references to Ménard, De Coulanges, Herodotus, Code of Menu, etc., p. 449, et seq.

might call it, with which woman has been held to the marriage relation, which she has scarcely ever been able to escape, and from which it has been most difficult for her to break away, we are momentarily filled with pity. But in this very discipline are to be found the groundwork and the reason for that high moral purpose and purity which mark her in the family life of cultured society. Most surely, society of our day is not looking to divorced women for its reclamation. Stable society in the past has been solidly constructed around the woman, who has been taught that to escape the responsibilities of her position was next to impossible.

How do savages provide for widows? Remember that the widow usually is one who has not changed her clan in marriage or her name. She has therefore two means of support secure even though she may not seek self-support. Her husband's brothers are all eligible husbands for her, because they belong to the same clan with him and not to her clan. And among many very uncultured tribes it is the law for a bachelor or widower to propose to the childless widow of his elder brother or cousin. Should no such person exist, she may marry whom she will out of her clan or in a clan prescribed for her clan. Finally she may go back among her own clan, and that would support her as one of its members, or, at the very worst, perform for her the clan funeral rites.

This review of the struggles of humanity about the possession of women in marriage leads naturally to a second question: What were her duties, her rights, and her pleasures in this state? Or, to put the question more in accordance with our present study, What opportunities did it afford her for advancing culture? It is not here assumed that the marriage state is yet perfected when

Woman sets herself to man
Like perfect music unto perfect words;

but enough progress has been made to render it profitable to inquire by what steps we have climbed so far.

In the natural world the male takes very little care of the female. She defends herself and provides for her offspring. Indeed, in the lower forms of life he plays an inconspicuous part. Mr. Darwin wrote to Sir Charles Lyell in 1849: "The other day I got a curious case of a unisexual cirripede, in which the female had two pockets in the valves of her shell, in each of which she kept a little husband." *

In the higher mammalian forms "the greater size and strength of the males, together with their powerful weapons, have not been acquired for the purpose of protecting the dependent females; they have been acquired entirely for the purpose of combating rivals and winning females. In very few such animals do the males ever attempt to protect the females, even where the latter have their young to take care of.†

The most primitive tribes known to us were living under a social system in which woman held a place most interesting for this study. She was not in the condition of the spider exactly, wherein "the miniature male is seized and devoured during his courtship by the gigantic object of his affections"; nor in that of the hen, who never thinks of calling upon her pompous husband either to scratch or fight for her young; nor in that of the female bird, who builds her own nest and cares for her own young. The division of labour among the sexes foreshadowed by some of the higher animals was perfected early in the human period. And in this primitive society the offices for woman to hold and the duties for her to perform were laid down by the structure of the clan or family and

---

* Quoted by Ward in the Forum, 1888, vol. vi, p. 274.
† L. F. Ward; Forum, 1888, vol. vi, p. 269.

by her function of childbearing. Could anything be more perfectly devised than the modern family, especially in rural life? The father goes out to his daily labour accompanied by his sons, the youngest of whom has some little task assigned; the mother remains at home, queen of the household, with her daughters around her, each bearing a burden suited to the back. In the earliest social condition known to us this form of monogamic society did not exist and there were no cleared fields to plough, no great mines or factories or warehouses. The man had to go out and war with Nature at every point with weapons. He had no ploughshare, but had to wield his rude sword; instead of pruning hooks were spears.

He was often gone several days, and many times he did not return at all. The women in such a group were like the balance wheel on a machine, gathering up the spasmodic labours of the men and distributing them evenly and smoothly over each day, month, or year. They did not have to be self-supporting, like the hen, and yet their vegetal food quest was an excellent discipline in developing that steady-going industry which lies at the foundation of the great business of the world. The drying of meat and the curing of fish were activity along the same line.

Hearne relates an excellent account of a Canadian Indian woman thrown on her own resources. "On the eleventh of January, as some of my companions were hunting, they saw the track of a strange snowshoe which they followed, and at a considerable distance came to a little hut, where they discovered a young woman sitting alone. On examination, she proved to be one of the western Dog Rib Indians who had been taken prisoner by the Athapuscow Indians in the summer of one thousand seven hundred and seventy; and in the following summer she had eloped with an intent to return to her own country, but the turnings and windings of the rivers and lakes were so numerous that she forgot the track. So she built the hut in which we found her, and here she had resided from the first setting in of the fall. From her account it appeared that she had been near seven months without seeing a human face. During all this time she had supported herself very well by snaring partridges, rabbits, and squirrels. That she did not seem to have been in want is evident, as she had a small stock of provisions by her when she was discovered and was in good health and condition, and I think one of the finest women of a real Indian that I have seen in any part of North America. The methods practiced by this poor creature to procure a livelihood were truly admirable. When the few deer sinews that she had taken with her were all expended in making snares and sewing her clothing, she used the sinews of the rabbits' legs and feet. These she twisted together for the purpose with great dexterity and success. The rabbits, etc., which she caught in those snares not only furnished her with comfortable subsistence, but of the skins she made a suit of neat and warm clothing for the winter. All her clothing, besides being calculated for real service, showed great taste and exhibited no little variety of ornament. The materials, though rude, were very curiously wrought and so judiciously placed as to make the whole of her garb have a very pleasing though rather ornamentic appearance. Her leisure hours from hunting had been employed in twisting the inner rind or bark of willows into small lines like net twine, of which she had some hundred fathoms by her; with this she intended to make fishing nets as soon as the spring advanced. Five or six inches of an iron hoop made into a knife and the shank of an arrowhead of iron which served her as an awl were all the metals this poor woman had with her, and with these she had made herself complete snowshoes and several other useful articles. Her method of making fire was equally curious, having no other material for that purpose than two hard sulphurous stones. These by hard friction and long knocking produced a few sparks which at length communicated to some touchwood. But as this method was attended with great trouble, and not always with success, she did not suffer her fire to go out all the winter. Hence we concluded that she had no idea of producing fire by friction in the manner practiced by the Eskimos and many other uncivilized nations."*

The remarkable cleverness of this woman is not mentioned to show how the average female supported herself in primitive life, but to demonstrate what kind of women it produced. It also serves as an offset to the notion that all savage women are so brutalized as not to have a thought of their own.

Social progress with primitive women was stimulated and encouraged by their relation to home life, to dress, and to manners. We have already alluded to the women as the authors of the home or shelter. It is the female bird that makes the nest, the female mammal that digs the burrow for her young, and the female bee that makes the honeycomb as a home for hers.

The human female more than all the rest created her home. But not only is this true, but she differentiated the home, and all the parts of the most elaborate establishment were instituted by her or on her account. The first homes were cheerless caves. Fire could not be made in them because of the smoke, so the woman sought out a cave with an opening in the rear or a rock shelter with a high curved roof.

When she became a dweller in a tent she searched for

---

* Hearne, Journey, etc., Lond., 1795, Strahan, p. 202. Recall the incident of the Ayacanora in Kingsley's Westward Ho, her claims to be as good as a man, her hatred of marriage, and her Amazonian exploits.

the oldest wood, learned the mysteries of the fuel problem, and even invented the coral to induce the wind to draw a little of the smoke therefrom, and to increase her comfort.

In houses built of mud, adobe, loose stone, or brick she invented the industrial portion, while the men invented the defensive portion. Indeed, it may as well be said here as elsewhere, that while a man's house is his castle, and always has been, a woman's house is her home and the scene of most of her labours. The principles of militancy and industrialism manifest themselves here as elsewhere.

To the women of the household we are indebted for the oven, the chimney, and the chimney corner, the kitchen, the dining-room, the family room, the separate bedchamber. It has been a wonderful evolution, resulting in comfort, taste, and morality.

A remarkable result of abstinence and morality is the fact that neither in America nor in Africa nor in the Indo-Pacific were women guilty of indulgence in the native forms of intoxication. In the New Hebrides and elsewhere Turner found that the women and girls were total abstainers from drinking kava.* "Drunkenness," says Dodge, "is not a female vice. In all my experience I have never seen a drunken Indian woman."†

Similar testimony could be gathered concerning beer drinking in Africa.

The seclusion of women and their always eating apart by a roundabout way tended to their refinement and advancement and protection. It called for more services, and time in service. It consumed the hours in organized and regulated labour. It was discipline. In this coterie were included frequently the children and the

---

* Turner, Samoa, London, 1884.
† Dodge, Plains of the Great West, New York, 1877, p. 336.

old men. It is said that in times of scarcity the women were pinched with hunger first, but no one ever heard of a cook starving to death. This seclusion is also an evidence of the great independence and self-help developed in the prison women.*

In the old Vedic civilisation women enjoyed a high position, and some of the most beautiful hymns of the Rig Veda were composed by ladies and queens. Marriage was held sacred. Husband and wife were both "rulers of the house" (*dampati*), and drew near to the gods together in prayer. The burning of widows on the husband's funeral pile was unknown, and the verses in the Veda which the Brahmans afterward distorted into a sanction for the practice have the opposite meaning. "Rise, woman," says the sacred text to the mourner, "come to the world of life. Come to us. Thou hast fulfilled thy duties as a wife to thy husband." †

In the evolution of clothing as a covering of the body women in primitive life were in advance of men. The Andamanese men go practically nude as regards clothing, but it is otherwise with the women, who never appear without an *obunga* or small apron of leaves, which is kept in place by the *bōd* or cincture. While men are usually content with one girdle, women almost invariably wear four or five. Experience tends to prove that the females of the tribes of South Andaman are strikingly modest. So particular are they in this respect that they will not remove or replace their apron in the presence of any person, even though of their own sex.‡

The first *modistes* were undoubtedly women, and in the application of the peculiar lace work of colour called

---

* Cf. Brigham, Cat. Bishop Mus. Honolulu, 1892, vol. ii, p. 11.
† Hunter, Gaz. of India, London, 1886, Trübner, vol. x, p. 73.
‡ Man, Andaman Islanders, London, 1883, Trübner, p. 110.

tattooing they were among the first artists. They knew how to insert pigment under the cuticle by gashing with a bit of flinty stone or obsidian, by drawing threads under the skin, and by pricking or puncturing. In Polynesia professional tattooers were employed, but even there the poor sufferer lay with his head in his sister's lap, while she and her youthful female companions sang to him to lull his pain. This was, indeed, a curious sort of comfort by primitive sisters of charity not to be overlooked.*

Major Austen, Surveyor of India, says of the Khasi Hill tribes on the northern border of the Bengal Presidency: "They have the feeling of modesty strongly developed, and are quite as particular about the exposure of their persons as the people of India proper. I can speak for the Garo women being particularly quiet and modest in their demeanour." †

In every American tribe, from the most northern to the most southern, the skirt of the women is longer than that of the men. In Eskimoland the *parka* of deerskin and seal skin reaches to the knees. Throughout central North America the buckskin dress of the women reached quite to the ankles. The west coast women, from Oregon to the Gulf of California, wore a petticoat of shredded bark, of plaited grass, or of strings, upon which were strung hundreds of seeds.

Even in the most tropical areas the rule was universal, as any one can see from the codices or in pictures of the natives.

The same rule holds good throughout Africa and in the Polynesian area. Even in abject Australia the efforts that are made toward modesty belong to the women. ‡

---

* Compare Landa, Relacion, in Bancroft, Native Races, vol. II, p. 685.

† J. Anthrop. Inst., London, 1872, vol. 1, p. 128.

‡ Compare David Kerr Cross, Proc. Roy. Geog. Soc., Feb., 1891.

The longer one studies the subject the more he will be convinced that savage tribes can now be elevated chiefly through their women. When higher civilization comes upon the lower it brings to the men the gun for the bow and arrow, or the slowly and painfully made device for the capture and killing of animals; it also commands him to stop hunting and warring, and to take up woman's work. He would rather die than do this, so he becomes an idler. But it brings to the woman only better tools and processes for doing her old work, and she is lifted up. A great impediment to the present disarmament of Europe is the fact that the men would have to do woman's work when they laid down the musket.

Even among the lowest peoples women have been possessed of personal courage and noble sentiments regarding their tribes.

In Samoa the wives of the chiefs and principal men generally followed their husbands wherever they might be encamped, to be ready to nurse them if sick or wounded. A heroine would even follow close upon the heels of her husband in actual conflict, carrying his club and some parts of his armour.*

The New Caledonian women went to battle. They kept in the rear and attended to the commissariat. Whenever they saw one of the enemy fall it was their business to rush forward, pull the body to the rear and dress it for the oven.†

So centuries ago Tacitus wrote: "It is a principal incentive to their courage that these squadrons and battalions are not formed by men fortuitously collected, but by the assemblage of families and clans. Their pledges are also near at hand; they have in hearing the yells of their women and the cries of their children. These, too,

---

* Turner, Samoa, London, 1884, p. 190.   † Ibid., p. 344.

are the most revered witnesses of each man's conduct, these his most liberal applauders. To their mothers and their wives they bring their wounds for relief; nor do these dread to count or to search out the gashes. The women also administer food and encouragement to those who are fighting.

"Tradition relates that armies beginning to give way have been rallied by the females, through the earnestness of their supplications, the interposition of their bodies, and the pictures they have drawn of impending slavery, a calamity which these people bear with more impatience for their women than for themselves; so that those states who have been obliged to give among their hostages the daughters of noble families are the most effectually bound to fidelity. They even suppose somewhat of sanctity and prescience to be inherent in the female sex, and therefore neither despise their counsels nor disregard their responses. We have beheld in the reign of Vespasian, Veleda, long reverenced by many as a deity. Aurinia, moreover, and several others were formerly held in equal veneration, but not with a servile flattery, nor as though they made them goddesses." *

Intimations of this personal bravery are given in the conduct of most female birds and mammals about their young. As to their fighting for their male companions the testimony is not so convincing. †

The two most brilliant periods in the career of the

---

* Tacitus, Germania, vii and viii, Trans. Harper's Classical Series. New York, 1882, ii, p. 290, with references to Cæsar, Suetonius, Statius, Strabo; consult also Germania, xvii-xx, xlv. "When Marcus Aurelius overthrew the Marcomanni, Quadi, and other German allies, the bodies of women in armour were found among the slain." —Fourniere, p. 206.

† Plutarch, Concerning the Virtues of Women, Morals, Boston, 1870, i, pp. 340-384.

most comprehensive nationality this world has ever seen were the Elizabethan and the Victorian. England acquired her globe-encircling empire under the reign of women. Brilliant examples of women skilled and potent in statecraft are not wanting among all civilized nations. The testimony of the best observers is to the effect that in primitive society there were queens in fact if not in name. Nothing is more natural than that the author of parental government, the founder of tribal kinship, the organizer of industrialism, should have much to say about that form of housekeeping called public economy.

Among the Wyandottes, an Iroquoian tribe, each gens or clan of the tribe occupied a tract for the purpose of cultivation, set apart by the council of the tribe. The women councillors partitioned the gentile land among the householders, and the household tracts were distinctly marked by them. Cultivation was communal—that is, all the able-bodied women of the gens took part in the cultivation of each household tract in the following manner:

The head of the household sends her brother or son into the forest or to the stream to bring in game or fish for a feast; then the able-bodied women of the gens are invited to assist in the cultivation of the land, and when the work is done a feast is given.

The wigwam or lodge and all articles of the household belong to the woman—the head of the household—and at her death are inherited by her eldest daughter, or nearest of female kin. The matter is settled by the council women.*

---

* Cf. Powell, In Abstract, etc., Anthrop. Soc., Washington, 1891, p. 54.

CHAPTER XI.

THE PATRON OF RELIGION.

In a general sense, religion is the sum of what is thought or believed about a spirit world and what is done in consequence of such thinking. What is thought about such a world constitutes *creed*, what is done or what a people does under its inspiration constitutes the *cult*. The *creed* and the *cult* together form the *religion* of any individual or people.

No one can fail to see, therefore, that the religion of women has been different from that of men and at the same time similar. By all those thoughts and acts which the sexes have in common, especially in the book religions, their creed and cult are one. By all those thoughts and acts which are theirs by reason of the differences of life growing out of sex, their religion will not be the same.

It will be especially interesting, therefore, to take notice of the savage woman gazing at the spirit world. To her, as to her mate, it is never far away. Her heaven is around her, perhaps beyond some mountain or stream of water, but never out of sight or hearing. And in that spirit world or heaven there are female inhabitants. Men and women in our world have had thoughts about them and have shaped a great deal of conduct in accordance with those thoughts.

The two parts of this study, indeed, are the religion of

women in this life and the description of the female inhabitants of the spirit world. The two are correlated in many ways, and influence each other to a large degree in savagery.

From the point of view of science, it is only the phenomenal aspect of religion—that is, its visible creed and cult—with which the student has to do at first. Of its unseen elements and the great forces at work to produce religion nothing can be discovered. Whether men or women are more divinely inspired and directed there are no technical means of knowing; but women have always seemed to be more under the domination of fixed and declared beliefs and have practiced with more fidelity the prevailing cult. In Christian countries it is the women who throng the churches, and the survival of the more primitive forms of belief and custom, called folklore, is chiefly among the unlettered women of a community. In the ultimate science of religion the fundamental principles will have to be considered. "Unter der Hülle aller Religionen liegt die Religion selbst," said Schiller; but in this chapter it is better to remain within the area of common observation, and consider only phenomena carefully with a view to a better opinion concerning the underlying law.*

The type of religion in the sense just indicated, wherein savage women and men find themselves, has been called by Tylor "animism," because every object is believed to be ensouled, consciously alive and full of purpose and feeling.

How unspeakably near must such a world of spirits be

---

* Consult Brinton, The Religious Sentiment, New York, 1876, Holt, p. iii; Andrew Lang, Myth, Ritual and Religion, London, 1887, Longmans, etc., 2 vols.; and J. G. Frazer, The Golden Bough, London, 1890, Macmillan, 2 vols.

to women like unto these! They walk hourly among the gods. Heaven does not so much come down their souls to greet, as they exist on a narrow island between the two oceans, indistinguishable to their untutored minds.

As time went on and the game of science began to be played, the more common objects, coming to be familiar acquaintances, dropped out of the rôle of gods and goddesses, and were won over to the side of the known.

In the arts considered in the foregoing chapters the materials, the tools, the forces, the processes, and the products of each industry were carefully scrutinized in order to understand woman's connection therewith. But not more than half the truth has been told. With every operation of the primitive workwoman there was a quasi-religious ceremony. The commonest performance, not more dignified, perhaps, than washing dishes, was under the eye of any number of gods and witnessing spirits. There was a choice of seasons, a time of day, an attention to propitious and unpropitious omens, a desire to please, a dread to offend the gods, a formula, a ritual, a song. The uninitiated observer overlooks all these, and yet they

Fig. 56.—Zuñi Priestess Plaiting the Ears of the Young Corn which are Plaited.

constituted the aroma, the bouquet of the savage woman's drudgery.*

The beliefs of all primitive peoples, men and women, concerning their spirit world are based upon their knowledge of this present world, of a very small portion of it—in truth, namely, the region where they have lived. Heaven has, therefore, its locality, natural history, and living beings or inhabitants. Of the last-named there are usually minute biographies, family trees, descriptions of households, equipages, servants, social life, and dealings with men. Human beings have also certain business with that world, which they may transact either with or without middlemen. Last of all, human destiny involves that world as well as this, because all mankind are going there some day. In all myths and all revelations there are most detailed and specific descriptions of this region. The fortunes and misfortunes of life follow the believer, and of the latter, women have had to take more than their share. A multitude of sects and creeds have been founded on the classification of spirits beyond the grave. The cults or worships of primitive peoples include a variety of activities, such as the dividing of society, the setting apart and furnishing of sacred places, the conduct of the clergy in these and elsewhere, the public and private acts of all, so far as they are impelled by this cult, such as penance, fasting, sacrifice, prayer, confession. This imitation of practical life in religious life, and attributing to all celestial things certain human characteristics is called anthropomorphism. And this long word covers a genealogy of ideas as extended as human history.

---

* "The women are then busy preparing the deerskins, for, on account of the requirements of their religion, the walrus hunt can not be begun until the deerskins which were taken in summer have been worked up for use."—Boas, Fifth An. Rep. Bur. Ethnol., p. 409. Consult also J. Anthrop. Inst., London, vol. xliii, p. 21.

The goddesses that thronged the elysiums of polytheistic nations in early historic times were the legitimate offspring of women in savagery and barbarism, through the operations of that primitive animism which endued all things here below with sentient life, and all beings in the spirit world with human characteristics. To these earliest worshippers all natural objects and all phenomena and all heavenly bodies were men and women, as was previously declared. They were men and women—nothing more. Which of them were men and which of them were women it will be interesting to inquire. It will be an important discovery if it turns out that the two fundamental ideas of militancy and industrialism, dwelt upon in the Introduction of this work, prevailed also in the skies, and set up the sexual distinctions which were plainly distinguishable on earth in primitive society.

All religions being more or less humaniform and anthropomorphic, there is nothing illogical in the opinion that the social structure of the spirit world ought to conform closely to the form and conduct of human society. So that there is little danger in asserting that the heavens militant were male, the heavens industrial were female.

The life of each people should be reflected in its mythology. The mythology of a people finds its explanation in their early history. The life also of a race or epoch should be similarly mirrored in its creeds and cults, and the creeds and cults of a race or people best understood by studying the daily life of that people.

With regard to women we are now ready to make the general statement that the daily life of a sex on earth will be the daily life of that sex in the spirit world. Moreover, if we know the goddesses of a mythology we may almost describe the women of a people among whom it arose.

Let it not be understood that the lines of sexual office are strictly drawn in heaven; they are not on earth. Therefore a goddess will now and then appear incased in armour, and gods will be busy about industrial pursuits. The assertion is a general one that the goddesses are the patrons of peaceful industries in heaven and on earth.

Mr. Lang says: "Everything in the civilized mythologies which we regard as irrational seems only part of the accepted and rational order of things to contemporary savages, and in the past seemed equally rational and natural to savages, concerning whom we have historical information. Our theory is, therefore, that the savage and senseless element in mythology is, for the most part, a legacy from ancestors of the civilized races who were in the intellectual state not higher than that of Australians, Bushmen, Red Indians, the lower races of South America, and other worse than barbaric peoples."*

In order, therefore, to understand fully the characteristics and conduct of the feminine half of the world of spirits, it was necessary in preceding chapters to acquaint ourselves with the lives of that half of savage humanity. Now it begins to dawn on our minds how most of the goddesses came to their heavenly home and duties, and why men as well as women have been only too glad to accord certain honours to them. It is seen how men deified women and their work, and thus unwittingly were creators of goddesses.†

---

* Encyc. Brit., 9th ed., New York, Scribner, 1884, vol. xvii, p. 142.

† In addition to the great classics on anthropology hitherto mentioned, the reader will consult with profit on this point the Hibbert Lectures of 1878, 1879, 1881, 1882, 1884, 1887, and especially of 1891, by D'Alviella, on the origin and growth of the conception of God as illustrated by anthropology and history. All of these vol-

A subtler question is, What are the views concerning the spirit world held in any tribe by the women as apart from the men? And we are bound to admit that the goddesses in the upper world are not only modelled after earthly women by men, but were modelled by women after their own image—that is, the beautiful conceptions of the ancient mythologies were as much the creation of women as of men. There is no time to work out this conception here, but on any theory of mythology and its origins there are points of view which women alone could assume and elements in the grouping which they alone would have contributed.

The psychological states of women, induced by many generations of inherited proclivities strengthened by use and seclusion, have also conspired to people their side of the heavenly world with some of its most distinguished and delightful inhabitants; have had a large share in the creation of primitive myths and cults; have left lurking around homes and wells and fields myriads of clever fairies, have sent to bloom in the gardens of the gods some of their loveliest flowers.

Women, far more than men, have enriched national and tribal mythologies with elements from other sources. Captured and carried from place to place all over the world, they have taken with them their stories, which, by removal from their indigenous soil, have assumed the form of myth.

Myths already made were carried in the same way, lent and borrowed, from tribe to tribe. This would give colour to the theory that there had been a common ground for all mythology.

On the contrary, there are certain occupations of women

---

mines abound in references to original authorities, which need not, therefore, be repeated.

common to the whole mass, so that if one could look with a little care he would find patterns and motives, hearth tenders and mother goddesses in every land and every age,

FIG. 37. MODERN WOMAN OF THE CROSS OF THE SAXONS.

are exceedingly similar tales about them. The sun god is everywhere — only sometimes it is a woman. We should be astonished to find a people who could not invent stories about the sun god. In the selfsame fashion, the universal tendency to attribute to the gods and goddesses our finest thoughts and feelings will give us pictures of the spirit world scarcely distinguishable from tribe to tribe. The doctrine of the latest school of mythology finds its verification in the apotheosis of women. But it must not be carried so far as to exclude the everlasting transfer and borrowing that went on wherever tribes were hostile and men were knocked on the head, while women were saved to be adopted into the households of the conquerors and win their favor by their tales of a Thousand Nights.

"Gypsies," says Leland, "have done more than any other race or class on the face of the earth to disseminate among the multitude a belief in fortune telling, magical or sympathetic cures, amulets, and such small sorceries as now find place in folklore. Their women have all pretended to possess occult powers since prehistoric times. By the exercise of their wits they have actually acquired a certain art of reading character or even thought, which, however it be allied to deceit, is in a way true in itself and well worth careful examination."*

This fact should be carefully noted in the light of what Buckle says on the conservatism of women and our own remark as to its causes.

In the curious persistence of custom among the folk, after the progressive portion of a people have risen above it, the worship of the ancient deities is one of the last relics to endure. But it is entirely in accordance with the theory of this work that the village goddess should be among the latest survivors.

Whether it be in southern India or nearer home in parts of Europe, the ceremony of paying devotions to her goes on from year to year.† Is it not a strange survival of this ancient fancy that the American people insist on calling Crawford's statue of armed Liberty on the Capitol in Washington " the Goddess of Liberty " ?

If there is one season or event that draws aside the curtain and lets us look upon the religion of a sex or a people, it is their conduct in the presence of death. Who has not watched with peculiar interest the vastly different behaviour of men and of women on such occasion? The former shrink away and almost hide themselves; the latter by an inexplicable fascination are drawn around the corpse. First at birth, last at death, they hail the young spirit at

---

* C. G. Leland, Gypsy Sorcery, p. xi.
† Compare Fawcett, J. Anthrop. Soc. Bombay, 1801, vol. ii, p. 261.

the opening of life and wave the last farewell to the departing ghost.

Could the reader walk along the trail of history back almost to the beginning, he would see at intervals a group of women sitting round a lifeless human body, on the boundary line of two existences, each one of which was to them as real as the other.

From daily experience it is known what the great body of women think and feel at such moments. The art and the literature of modern cultured and ancient classic nations abound with descriptions and illustrations of women in the presence of death, and it is the favourite theme of artists.

To complete the series so as to find the springs from which this marvellous conduct flowed in historic times it is necessary to observe carefully the behaviour of the savage and the partly civilized so far as their acquaintance can be made. The kingdom of spirits is indeed close about the imaginations of such people always, but there is, after all, a special sense in which each one becomes a citizen of that kingdom in crossing the boundary lines set by death.

Remembering that the citizens of that unseen country are men and women of some sort and guise, if our good offices are to attend our friends who emigrate thereto they must partake of the nature of our good offices at home. The less they change their form the more familiar do they seem. Men do not know how to perform such duties with skill. Indeed, some of the last rites would have to be omitted altogether on their account, since the performance of the duties which they mimic are tabooed to men in daily life.

Now, to a large extent, women in all lowly tribes set up the place of habitation and furnish it, clothe the family, and feed them. Nothing is more appropriate, therefore, than for them to perform the same functions for the dead.

The disposal of the dead, after all, is a weird sort of housekeeping, broken up only by those chemical changes that convert, sooner or later, each one to dust. When one died in a hut or wigwam all accustomed duties of life were laid aside that the savage woman might address herself to the necrotaxis.*

It is she that sits by the grave to keep burning the ghost fire, brings food and water for the hungering and thirsting manes and cuts off her hair, and mutilates her body if perchance she may persuade the homesick shade to depart in peace.

All her strange and seemingly foolish actions should be studied with greatest care in the light of her home life by those who would form true conceptions of beliefs and customs which thrust themselves upon our own firesides.

In one of the photographs taken by Powell during his geological survey of Utah a woman is shown sitting on a ledge of rock with an empty cradle at her feet.

Problem of problems! What has become of the living thing to which she gave birth and nourishment, and for which she would at any moment have laid down her life? The anxious face, so woeful and interrogative, links this poor savage with all women the world over who have seen her day. The weeping Magdalen, seeking the living among the dead, is the earliest and the latest picture of belief in immortals and immortality.

Among the Brulé Sioux all the work of winding up the dead in his best garments, building the scaffold, and placing the dead upon it is done by women only.†

---

* Yarrow, Mortuary Customs, etc., First An. Rep. Bur. Ethnol., Washington, 1881, pp. 89-203, 47 illustrations. Consult also Tegg, The Last Act.

† McKenney, Tour to the Lakes, 1827, p. 298. See also quota-

When an Indian dies, friends assemble in the lodge and indulge in heartrending lamentations. This crying is done almost wholly by women, and among them a few professional mourners. Those who wish to show their grief most strongly cut themselves with knives or pieces of flint.

The received custom requires of the women, near relatives of the dead, the following observances for ten days: They are to rise at a very early hour and work hard all day, joining in no feast, dance, game, or other diversion, eat but little, and retire late, that they may be deprived of the usual amount of food and sleep. During this time they do not paint themselves, but go to the top of some hill and bewail the dead. After the ten days they paint themselves and engage in the usual amusements of the people as before.*

The lighting of fires upon the graves of the dead had a widespread usage. And the lonely creature seated upon the mound happens always to be a woman. Yarrow has gathered references to Algonquins, Mexicans, and Californians.† There is something extremely pathetic in this watch fire. From time immemorial woman was the fire tender. It was her servant in cooking food for the dead ones while they were yet living, but it is known that the most ferocious beasts and therefore the most powerful spirits are afraid of it. No harm can come to the dwelling where this priestess maintains the ghost fire.

---

tion from J. L. Mahan to the same effect, in Yarrow, op. cit., p. 184, Fig. 53 and p. 185.

* Yarrow, First An. Rep. Bur. Ethnol., Washington, 1881, pp. 159-166, quoting Cleveland and others. Several excellent plates illustrate feeding the dead, self-lacerations by the living, etc. Catlin, Hist. N. A. Indians, 1844, vol. 1, p. 90. Ross Cox, Adventures on the Columbia River, 1831, vol. ii, p. 297. See also Brinton, Myths of the New World, 1868, p. 255.

† Yarrow, First An. Rep. Bur. Ethnol., 1881, p. 198 and Fig. 17.

FIG. 50.—SIOUX WOMEN CUTTING THEMSELVES FOR THE DEAD.

Among the California tribes the Yokaia mother who has lost her babe goes every day for a year to some place where her little one has played when alive or to the spot where the body was burned and milks her breast into the air. This is accompanied by plaintive moaning and weeping and piteously calling upon her little one to return, and sometimes she sings a hoarse and melancholy chant and dances with a wild, ecstatic swaying of the body.* The offering of milk to the dead babe would seem to be the very beginning of the entire class of food and meat offerings.

The author has received from Mr. Frank Cushing a most interesting account of the Zuñi woman and her dead. According to this observer, whose opportunities were of the rarest kind, the whole conduct of the woman is symbolical of her lifework. If she washed the head of the dead, it was because she performed always the same service at the opening of the gates of life. If her office was to break the water jar around the dead and pour out the water, it meant that she also first gave nourishment to the living from her milk, and now closed the scene by the destruction of the vase.

The Polynesian women on the death of a member of the family wailed in the loudest fashion, tore their hair, rent their garments, and cut themselves with sharks' teeth or knives in a shocking manner. The instrument usually employed was a small cane, about four inches long, with five or six shark's teeth fixed on opposite sides. With one of these every female provided herself after marriage. Some used a short instrument like a plumber's mallet, armed with two or three rows of sharks' teeth fixed in the

---

* Powers, Cont. to N. A. Ethnol., Washington, 1878, vol. iii, p. 104. Also Yarrow, First An. Rep. Bur. Ethnol., Washington, 1881, p. 195.

wood at one end. With this they cut themselves unmercifully, striking the head, temples, cheeks, and breast, till the blood flowed profusely from the wounds.*

The Andamanese mother, between the death and burial of her child, paints its head, neck, wrists, and knees, shaves off the hair, and folds the little limbs so as to occupy the least possible space, the knees being brought up to the chin and the fists close to the shoulders. The body is then enveloped in large leaves, which are secured with cords or strips of cane. The father digs the grave in the place where the hut fire usually burns. When all is prepared, the parents gently blow upon the face and bury their dead child. After a proper season the body is exhumed and the bones carefully washed. The mother, after painting the skull and decorating it with small shells attached to strings, hangs it round her neck. The next few days are spent by the mother in converting the bones into necklaces. When several are made, she and her husband pay visits to their friends, among whom they distribute these mementoes, together with any pieces that may remain over. In the dances of condolence which follow the women act the principal parts, continuing for many hours.†

When an adult person dies the women are alike undertakers and mourners, though the men perform the office of grave diggers and pall bearers. The last ones to leave the place of mourning always are the women.‡

The custom of slaying, or sacrificing, or burying alive women to accompany their deceased husbands has been found in many lands. In this matter their share in primitive cult was usually an involuntary one. The

---

* Ellis, Polynes. Researches, vol. i, p. 408; vol. iv. pp. 175, 183.
† Man, Andaman Islanders, London, 1883, Trübner, p. 75.
‡ J. Anthrop. Inst., London, 1881, vol. xi, p. 285.

Natchez Indians, the Oregon Indians, Aztecs, Tarascos, African tribes, and Hindu widows are examples.*

None of the great book religions of the world admit women to the priesthood, neither did the classic religions of the Egyptians, Mesopotamians, Semites, Greeks or Romans allow them to exercise the higher functions thereof. In savagery the case is somewhat improved, but even there the chiefs of religious organizations and directors of ceremonial are men. In the cult societies women occupy humble places. There is no difference between their organization and that of civil societies.†

But there are prophetesses. If there were sorcerers there were sorceresses, with wizards there corresponded witches, and for doctors there were doctresses. The function of these, one and all, is to look through windows or behind the scenes, and to report what is going on among the gods and what they have decided to do. Furthermore, these knowing and skilful ones undertake to influence, persuade, and compel gods and spirits to do their behests. For this kind of lobbying work between worlds women are thought to be more persuasive and acute and dangerous than men. They hear better, and sit, therefore, on the tripods of the oracles. They see better, and thereby become the knowing ones. They are better talkers, and for that they become the most successful conjurers. They cook better, so the witch is stronger than the wizard, and they are just as successful in denouncing and scolding, which qualifies them for doctors of a very old school.

---

* Cf. Bossu, Travels (Forster's Trans.), London, 1771, p. 38; Allen, Ten Years in Oregon, p. 891; Bancroft, Nat. Races, New York, 1875, vol. iii, p. 518.

† The reader should not fail to study the accounts of two ceremonial dances by Hopi women, by J. Walter Fewkes, Am. Anthrop., Washington, 1892, vol. v, pp. 105-130 and 217-246.

Why there should be anything uncanny about a very old woman no one knows, but so it is, and ever has been, whether she appears now in the form of an eagle, and then as an aged dame who lures away girls to a great cliff on the Gila River, or as the echo in the cañons of the Colorado. But this dread of the uncanny has acted as a powerful guard to women in troublous times and in the uncertainty of primitive society. Somehow or other it has crept into the belief of the race that there is a power which protects the weak, and in the long run they shall prevail.

"The women who follow the Cymbri to war are accompanied by grey-haired prophetesses in white vestments, with canvas mantles fastened by clasps, a brazen girdle, and naked feet. These go with drawn swords through the camp, and, striking down those of the prisoners which they meet, drag them to a brazen kettle holding about twenty amphoræ. This has a kind of stage above it, ascending on which the priestess cuts the throat of the victim, and from the manner in which the blood flows into the vessel judges of the future event. Others tear open the bodies of captives thus butchered, and from the inspection of the entrails presage victory to their own party."[*]

When Cæsar inquired of his captives "the reason why Ariovistus did not engage, he learned that it was because the matrons who, among the Germans, are accustomed to pronounce from their divinations whether or not a battle will be favourable had declared that they would not prove victorious if they should fight before the new moon."[†]

Among the Shastas of Northern California women doctors seem to be more numerous than men, acquiring their art in the *temescal* or sweat house, where improfes-

---

[*] Strabo, lib. vii. [†] Cæsar, Bell. Gall., Bk. 1, Harper's transl.

sional men are not admitted. Their favourite method of
cure seems to consist in sucking the affected part of the
patient until the blood flows. Sometimes the doctress
vomits some object to reassure the patient. She is frequently assisted by a second physician, whose duty it is
to discover the exact spot where the malady lies, and
this she effects by barking like a dog at the patient
until the spirit discovers to her the place. Gibbs mentions a case where the patient was first attended by four
young women, and afterward by the same number of
old ones. Standing around the unfortunate, they went
through a series of violent gesticulations, sitting down
when they could stand no longer, sucking with the most
laudable perseverance and moaning dismally. Finally,
when with their lips and tongue they had raised blisters
all over the patient, and had pounded his miserable body
with hands and knees until they were literally exhausted,
the performers executed a swooning scene, in which they
sank down apparently insensible.*

We come now to the second part of this study—the
description of the female inhabitants of the spirit world.
Our first steps must be through deep tangled wild woods,
in the midst of pure naturalism. The progress of belief
must be like the progress of arts—from the simple to the
complex, from nature to culture, through integrations of
structures and differentiation of functions. The one
law holds in all departments of human activity.

It will be a genuine surprise, and we shall fail after
a long inquiry, if the fundamental ideas of the female
pantheon in primitive life be not the four duties or functions that have been and must long remain the peculiar
province of woman's activity, to wit:

---

* Powers and Gibbs, quoted in Bancroft, Native Races, New
York, 1874-'75, vol. I, p. 355.

1. The bearing and nurture of children, the maiden, the wife, the mother.
2. The nourisher of the human family, the one who gives food.
3. The maker of the fireside, the house, the home.
4. The clothier of men, spinner, weaver, and, indeed, general guardian of peaceful industry and practical wisdom.

The existence of romantic love among the lowest of peoples and the amount of art and poetry dedicated thereto from purely æsthetic motives show how deep seated this feeling has always been. The deification of this sentiment is universal. The prominence given to the Roman Venus, the Greek Aphrodite, the Phœnician Astarte, the Assyrian Istar, the Egyptian Hathor in higher polytheism, and the excesses indulged in at their worship, might easily be matched by the annual customs of the Yuma and other Indian tribes, by the Polynesian *Areoi*, and by the African fetich societies. No other sentiment of earth in its good and bad embodiments has been so faithfully photographed on the skies.

Among the great gods of Greece and Rome having dominion over the elements of the universe—Demeter, the Latin Ceres; Poseidon, the Latin Neptune; Apollo, in both nations; and Athena, the Latin Minerva—two are women, the queen of the earth and the queen of the air. The poetic side of their several offices is worked out with much grace by Ruskin.*

But here there is space only to dwell briefly upon the primitive conceptions out of which their later honours arose, to treat of the womanly side of their natures. As to Demeter, was there ever a people so devoid of poetry as to miss the figure of calling the earth Mother, and

---

* Ruskin, The Queen of the Air.

the personification of the earth by some term akin to Demeter (γῆ-μήτηρ)? On the return of every spring, fructified by the sun and the warm rains, she gives birth to all life and all beauty. To the savage woman there is not a person called earth mother, who lives in the sky among the gods, born of Cronus and Rhea, and having a real daughter, Persephone. The earth itself is as much alive as we are, and has a mind and soul (*Erdgeist*), and is the real mother of all things. The earth mother's kind offices do not cease with giving us life. Every day she takes her burden basket upon her back and goes out, now to plant the good seed, or to weed and water and cultivate it, or to gather the harvest and grind it in the mill to make bread. Her functions are many, and to one who did not know the Greeks in their uncivilized state, when the maternal ancestors of Athenians were exactly like Zuñi Indians, these offices seemed strange and inexplicable. But Ceres in the sky is the reflection in the heavenly mirror of that good mother and sustainer whom no people has failed to honour.* And in the further myth of Persephone and the mother walking unconsoled until her return, there is a suggestion of the optimism which existed in early Greek mythology, when Mother Earth loved and grieved over her children when they were gone.† In this active imagination of the uncivilized they resemble children who are never unable to put themselves in possession of any kind of life they desire for the moment to lend.

The Zuñi say that the earth is the mother of all and the fire is the grandmother, for out of the earth comes

---

* In Egyptian mythology earth is the father of all things and heaven is the mother. Renouf, *Religion of Ancient Egypt*, New York, 1880, Scribner, p. 115.

† For connection of Demeter with the Greek mysteries, see Encyc. Brit., sub voce Mysteries.

the water we drink as the babe draws milk from the mother, and her flesh also furnishes food for man and beast. And our nourishment is no more cooked by the brand in the fire than it is by our mothers. Can any one hesitate to see the glorification of daily toil in this beautiful myth? The Indian woman's life is spent around springs of water and in the fields, and over the fire hearth among the brands. The seven varieties of corn are the flesh of seven maidens for whom prayer plumes were planted in the mythological age of the world.*

Previous to the birth of a child, if a daughter be desired, the Zuñi husband and wife proceed together to the mother rock, and at her feet make offerings and prayers, imploring her to intercede with the great father, the Sun, to give to them a daughter, and that this daughter may grow to be all that is good in woman; that she may be endowed with the power of weaving beautifully, and may be skilled in the potter's art.†

The following from Gatschet is interesting: "After Tecumseh had delivered a speech to General Harrison at Vincennes, in 1811, he was offered a chair by the interpreter, who said to him, 'Your father requests you to take a chair.' To this Tecumseh replied: 'The sun is my father, and the earth is my mother: on her bosom will I repose,' and immediately he seated himself in the Indian manner upon the ground." ‡ The Omahas worship corn as a "mother," according to Dorsey, and the descendants of the ancient Peruvians still pour libations of chicha to Puchamama or Mother Earth. The Klamaths say of the earth: "She deals out her bountiful gifts to

---

* F. H. Cushing, in The Millstone, Jan., 1884, p. 1.

† Mrs. Matilda R. Stevenson, Fifth An. Rep. Bur. Ethnol., Washington, 1887, p. 645.

‡ Gatschet, The Klamath Indians, Cont. to N. A. Ethnol., Wash., vol. ii, p. xcii.

her children, human beings, without envy or restraint, in the shape of corn, fruits, and esculent roots. Her eyes are the lakes and ponds disseminated over the green surface of the plains, her breasts are the hills and the hillocks; and the rivulets and brooks irrigating the valleys are the milk flowing from her breasts."[*] In the Egyptian religion the order was reversed, the earth (Seb) being the father, and Nut the heavens, the mother of all. From them sprung Osiris and Isis, wedded before they were born, and the fruit of their union was Horus, the sun, in his full strength.[†]

In each region of the world considered in its natural-history features there is some plant or means of subsistence that abounds. Perhaps it is maize, or manioc, or taro, or the palm tree. Now, in each case this plant is said to be the gift of some wonderful female who grows by and by to be goddess of all crops of food-producing plants. Frequently the earth mother is the same as the foster mother, and in the higher mythologies the two become blended. But the myths of the lower races are full of stories covering the whole art of food getting, assigning the rôle always to females. The Hindus celebrate Sita, spouse of Rama, rising brown and beauteous, crowned with corn ears from the ploughed field. She is the furrow (*sita*) personified.[‡]

The maize plant is associated in one tribe with the deification of woman, for the story is related among the Cañari Indians, who dwelt in the mountain of Huacapñan, south of Quito. At the time of a great deluge two brothers escaped to this mountain. On the subsiding of the waters they descended to lower ground, and, being

---

[*] Quoted in Gatschet, Cont. to N. A. Ethnol., vol. ii, p. xcii.
[†] Renouf, Religion of Ancient Egypt, New York, 1880, Scribner, p. 115.
[‡] Tylor, J. Anthrop. Inst., vol. x, pp. 74, 75.

pressed for food, two parrots in their absence entered their hut daily and prepared for them maize food and chicha. At length one of the birds, on being captured, changed to a beautiful woman, from whom the brothers obtained the maize seed, and learned the art of cultivating it. She subsequently became the ancestress of the Cañari tribe. Hence the reverence of this people for the mountain and the parrot, but it is to be feared they forgot to pay it to their women, who really gave the maize.*

The goddess Sekhet or Pasht, the daughter of Ra, equivalent to the goddess Diana, is represented with the head of a cat or of a lioness in Egyptian mythology. She was both a destroying deity charged with the torture of souls in hell and a protector of mankind. The cat tribe were specially sacred to her. There is little difficulty in watching the career of this divine woman, who was first in charge of granaries, preserver of life and destroyer of vermin, afterward the tamer of the cat for both purposes, and finally took up her abode in hell to torture souls, with time to spare for the help of mortals. And this brings us to the fire cult.

"The essential feature of the Greek prytaneum was its hearth (ἑστία), which differed from other hearths only in this, that it was pre-eminently the hearth of the city, the common hearth. On this there burned a perpetual fire. The prytaneum was sacred to Hestia, the personified goddess of the hearth. . . . Turning to Italy, we at once identify the Latin Vesta with the Greek Hestia. But, while in Greece the original identity of the goddess with the domestic hearth was still shown by the identity of their names, in Italy their relationship was so far obscured that the hearth had resigned its old name to the god-

---

* See Molina, ap. Markham, quoted in Payne, Hist. of Am., New York, 1892, p. 401.

does and was content to be known by the modest title of *focus*."*

Professor Frazer pursues the subject with great learning and shows clearly that the keeping up of perpetual fires and the ministrations of the vestals had their origin in those primitive times when this fire was in the chief's tent or hut with a hive-shaped dome and his wives and daughters were the priestesses of the precious element.

In her task of hearth builder the savage woman early encountered another problem—how to keep food over from one day to another. It is too late now to ask who discovered cooking; but, there never was known to history a people in which the presiding genius of the hearth was not a woman. It is well known that in great feasts and for special purposes men become cooks. But these are spasmodic efforts, not the steady pull. All travelers, historians, and opened sepulchers agree that Hestia, daughter of Cronus and sister of Zeus—

> Whose altar was the cheerful table spread,
> Whose sacrifice the pleasant daily bread,
> Offered with incense of sweet childhood's mirth
> And parents' priestly ministrations, worth
> More than all other rites that ever shed
> Light on the path that those young feet must tread †—

was also ancestress of that long line of busy women who tend the domestic fire.

It is said that Prometheus stole fire from the sky in a hollow fennel stick, which may mean that Prometheus or some one else of his sex really invented the fire sticks, the aboriginal device for recreating the element among most savage tribes. The reader will please remember that humanity had fire before that. A long time ago

---

* J. G. Frazer. J. of Philol., Lond., 1885, vol. xiv, pp. 145-172.
† Margaret O. Preston.

gods and men were disputing about the same questions that agitate men and women this very day—namely, what sacrifice to give to the gods and what to withhold. Prometheus, naturally enough, endeavored to keep the best for himself and cheat the divine beings. The result was disastrous—to wit, the withholding from mortals of that precious element whose uses had been discovered long before there were any fire sticks. Fortunately for us, we are not left in the dark regarding the last mentioned fact. A witness still exists to prove that a people may survive to our day with no knowledge of fire-creating or the trick of Prometheus.

Among the Damaras, in South Africa, a perpetual fire is kept burning about the chief's hut. Whenever the headman of a clan or kraal was about to move away to some distance, a portion of this holy fire was given to him with which to set up a vestal hearth upon the new village site. The same practice is to be seen among Russian peasants. When they move from one house to another they rake the fire out of the old stove into a jar and solemnly carry it to the new one, greeting it with the words "Welcome, grandfather, to the new home."*

The same thing was done by the ancient Greeks and Romans.

Women, the guardians of fire and water, mothers of all nymphs and vestals! Hovering about the clearest and coolest and shadiest springs of water in their savage home life and keeping alive the fire in the dreariest of all habitations! Whatever of their customs have passed away, these two have remained. Art and poetry have paid their homage to these essential elements in woman's industrial life. Is it any wonder, then, that the ministers of sacred fire on Roman altars and the happy spirits that

---

* Frazer, J. of Philol., vol. xiv, pp. 144-172.

frequent refreshing springs should all be women? So, the Zuñi Indian sings:

> The sun is the father of all,
> The earth is the mother of men,
> The water is their grandfather,
> The fire is their grandmother.*

Though it is a little difficult to make out how the water could be the grandfather of mankind, there is no doubt that it is the maternal grandfather. The family tree would be then complete as Zuñi genealogy goes. We should have Zuñi father and mother, and mother's father and mother. The sun-father, of course, belongs to another clan, the sky people, but the others are all associated with the earth mother.

A delightful allusion to the practical water goddess is found in Matthews. A Navajo family, consisting of father, mother, two sons, and two daughters, in their migrations came to a place where no water was, but one of the sons discovered a spring with his digging stick some distance from camp. The family had but one wicker bottle lined with pitch, so the woman, to lighten her labour, proposed to move to the vicinity of the spring, as it was her task to draw water. But the old man counselled to remain, since building material was so near by. They argued long, but the woman prevailed, and they carried their property near to the spring.†

Among the Australians of upper Finke River the sun is a woman with a great fire stick. When she puts on much wood the fire blazes up tremendously, and begets the excessive summer heat. In the evening the sun woman passes under the arm of an old woman and be-

---

* Cushing, The Millstone, Indianapolis, 1884, vol. ix. p. 1.
† Matthews, Fifth An. Rep. Bur. Ethnol., p. 368. Consult also Dorsey, Third An. Rep. Bur. Ethnol., p. 236.

comes invisible. Her nourishment consists of grubs feeding in timber.*

Really the sun is not the old woman, but her fire stick. The owner of the stick is invisible. Mythology, dealing with processes, makes visible only their phenomenal part. The passing of the light wood under the arm to keep it dry, as the old hunters did the locks of their guns, and the old woman's feeding in dead wood, out of which fire sticks are made, are charming bits of folklore.

The three Fates—Clotho, who spins the thread of life; Lachesis, who determines its prolongation; and Atropos, who severs this thread with remorseless shears—were necessarily women, and so represented in the mythology of Greece. In this same connection belongs Arachne, who challenged Athena to a contest in weaving and was turned by the latter into a spider.

> Her usual features vanished from their place;
> Her body lessened all, but most the face.
> Her slender fingers, hanging on each side
> With many joints, the use of legs supply'd:
> A spider's bag the rest, from which she gives
> A thread, and still by constant weaving lives.†

Sericulture has always been in China a national industry of paramount importance. Doubt seems to have been entertained by the people concerning the departed personage who in her lifetime had taken, more than any other, interest in the matter, and whose spirit was presiding over the silkworm rearing and silk industry. One thing is certain; as it was a feminine occupation, the tutelary deity could not be a man.‡

In the grounds of the imperial palace at Peking is an

---

* Schulze, Trans. Roy. Soc. S. Australia, 1891, xiv, p. 231.
† Croxall's Trans. of Ovid, Metamorph.
‡ Lacouperie, The Silk Goddess, London, 1891, Nutt, p. 10.

Fig. 15.—Seaside beacons set for thickly wet of ice.

altar forty feet in circuit and four feet in height, surrounded by a wall, and also a temple called the *ts'en-tsan-tso* (the early silkworm's altar), in the vicinity of which a plantation of mulberry trees and a cocoonery are maintained. It is dedicated to *Yuenfei*, otherwise First Wife, in her quality of discoverer of the silkworms, and annually, in April, the empress worships and sacrifices to her. The same goddess has several important temples in Tchehkiang, one of the provinces where the silkworm industry flourishes. Yuenfei is said to be the name of *Si-ling-she*, first wife of Huang-ti, civilizer of China.*

It must not be forgotten, as Brinton has well shown, that the use of figurative language enters very largely into savage mythology. This fact compels the ethnologist to move with caution in searching for a real and prosaic basis for every detail in a myth. The *temalucatl* or spindle stone, for example, in Mexican solar rites was doubtless so called from its resemblance in form to the whorl on the spindle used by women among all weaving tribes.

The primitive Minerva or Pallas Athena must be sought in the conceptions which uncivilized tribes have of the atmosphere. How did the air come to be a woman? There must have been some inseparable connection between what women had to do and what the air does. The air must be personified to be that woman, and then, with a capital letter at the beginning of her name, she must take wings and fly to high Olympus.

Stephen Powers says somewhere that he never saw an Indian woman that was not puddering at something, and it is this busy, bustling activity of the practical part of

---

* Lacouperie, Silk Goddess of China, London, 1891, Nuit, p. 3, and note 4 referring to Gray, Filkins, and Williamson. Cf. Gray, China, vol. ii, p. 220; Williamson, Journeys in North China, 1870, vol. ii, p. 283.

the universe that is Minerva's realm. She is represented with shield and spear in rest, and looks out over the earth as a superintendent of its industrialism. "The Greeks conceived that the light, the stars, the meteors drew nourishment from the waters and then returned it to the earth as moisture. The theory is favoured by such terms as 'bedewing stars,' 'heaven-producing dew,' etc. If this belief was at all general, it is not improbable that the goddess of light should be esteemed as the bestower of dew and fertilizing moisture." *

It might be rash to connect at once Minerva with a savage woman bearing a water jar on her head or, indeed, with a nomadic woman unsaddling her husband's horse on his arrival.† But there is no objection in this view to her being goddess of inventions, of practical wisdom and of art, of cheer to warriors, of protection to cities, of family and social order. If Athena first tamed horses, women tamed the first domestic animals. If Athena conquered Arachne and turned her into a spider, women have put to shame all spiders and worms and became princesses of spinners and weavers.‡

In her temple at Athens women worked. And at Athens women and girls wrought nine months to weave the peplos that was offered annually to Athena, and was carried in the Erechtheion. On the appointed day the peplos was unfurled like a sail over the sacred trireme, emblem of the maritime power which Athens owed to its tutelary goddess, and the ships moved by machinery ascended the Acropolis accompanied by the sacred cortège.

The gist of all this is that we have in the divine Minerva the human Minerva. Indeed, should one pro-

---

* R. O. Müller.

† One is here reminded of Juno, in the Iliad (v. 700), engaged in hitching horses.

‡ Consult Decharme, Myth. de la Grèce antique, p. 65.

nounce to-day the phrase "a sensible woman," "a practical woman," her qualifications would be found to be very similar to those of this ancient goddess. We are not at all surprised, therefore, to find in the Proverbs of Solomon this plain, every-day wisdom, commonly entitled "good sense," further personified.

Doth not wisdom cry? and understanding put forth her voice?
She standeth in the top of high places, by the way in the places of the paths.
She crieth at the gates, at the entry of the city, at the coming in at the doors:
Unto you, O men, I call; and my voice is to the sons of men.*

The great Egyptian goddess Neith, who at Saïs was worshipped as primordial deity, was, in addition to her higher attractions, the Weaver, and passed for having invented the art. Her most common hieroglyph—the one by which she was most generally designated—was the shuttle. In her temple at Saïs were large weaving establishments celebrated for their products, and one of the sanctuaries of Saïs is called in the texts "the house of textiles."†

In the temple of Neith were produced special textiles, used in sacred ceremonies,‡ and for priestly garments as well as for those of statues for mummies.

A papyrus" mentions that the hands and the feet of the mummy were wrapped "in a bandage of flax, of that kind which is manufactured at Saïs," etc.

These weaving establishments had evidently a sacred character, which was recognized throughout the land.|

---

* Proverbs, viii, 1–4.
† Denderah text of the mysteries of Osiris, Col. 28, cf. Mariette, Abydos, pl. lxlii.
‡ Mallet, Culte de Neït à Saïs, p. 242.
" Boulaq No. 3, iii, 15, Maspero, Mem. sur quelques pap. du Louvre.
| The author is indebted to Mrs. Sara Y. Stevenson, of the University of Pennsylvania, for this reference to Neith.

The connections of women with the myths of natural phenomena are innumerable.

The Ute women, according to Major Powell, say that the echo in their valleys is an old woman, who for some slight has taken refuge there out of the way of her persecutors, and mocks them day and night. This story tallies well with Ovid's account of the nymph Echo, who was deprived by Juno of the use of speech, except the power to pronounce the last word. Falling in love with Narcissus, she pursued him, but in vain.

> The nymph, when nothing could Narcissus move,
> Still dashed with blushes for her slighted love,
> Lived in the shady covert of the woods,
> In solitary caves and dark abodes,
> Where, pining, wandered the rejected fair,
> Till harassed out, and worn away with care,
> The sounding skeleton, of blood bereft,
> Besides her bones and voice had nothing left.*

Most of the inexplicable phenomena of Nature find their general raison d'être in the queer conduct of some ethereal old woman who for a long time seems to have kept the half-way house of science. The chirping of the cricket, the colour of birds, the spots on animals, the moisture on the stones—the list is endless and the venerable creature has been kept quite busy down to our time.

The primitive stone-cutting woman early found recognition in the heavenly company. The deity of stone workers and axe grinders is first known as a great priestess and magician. Once her brother Rata was not able to use the tree he had felled in making a canoe, because he had offended the wood fairies by omitting the proper invocation. So they set the tree up again every time he cut it down. His sister told him to sharpen his axe on her sacred body, and this had the desired effect. Hence

---
* Croxall's Trans. of Ovid, Metamorphoses.

the name of the priestess—The-Maiden-Whose-Back-Was-A-Whetstone. We next find this priestess installed in the Maori pantheon as the goddess or deified ancestress connected with stone axes.*

Whether the sirens were a three-headed rock, separating the Bay of Naples from the Gulf of Salerno, or not, the persons of whom they were the form, and whose bloody work they did, were women. The Lorelei in the rapids of the Rhine belongs to the same category—namely, of spirits who, by beauty of person and the gentle music of their voices, allure mariners, and other men as well, to forget their journey and to turn aside upon danger.† This set of characters, alas, link the heavens and the earth through that chapter in woman's history, hinted at in the introduction, too painful to write about—her rôle in the crimes of mankind.

Among the semicivilized races, especially those under Mohammedan influence, there seems to be small place for women in the ideal and artistic life on earth, and less in the life beyond. Among the more enlightened nations, however, the thoughts of primitive life survive in more rational form. It is true that the heavenly world of industrial goddesses has faded away; but from the crowning eminences of architecture, from pedestals along the greatest thoroughfares, from the costliest canvas in national galleries, from the richest pages of literature, from the highest prizes of industry, from thrones, from happy homes, from vigils by the dying—the forms of women, still called goddesses, shower their peaceful benedictions on our race and preserve the ideals most divine.

---

* Cf. J. Polynes. Soc., Wellington, 1892, vol. i, p. 82.
† See J. E. Harrison, Myth of Odysseus.

CHAPTER XII.

CONCLUSION.

CIVILIZATION is the composite result of progress from the purely natural life of the animal to the purely artificial life of the most enlightened individuals and peoples. This progress has always been made along the lines of satisfying human needs, of gratifying human desires. For bringing to pass this result Nature has contributed a great variety of materials from her three kingdoms, from time to time has furnished new forces to supplement human endeavour, and added the results of her experiences throughout all the history of the globe prior to man's arrival. She has occupied the position of almoner, prompter, teacher, and friend, saying at first what she says now: Occupy the earth, dress and keep it.

The human race faced this duty in the beginning with endowments that seemed to be entirely inadequate from a zoölogical point of view, but with more brain and mind than the mere bodily wants demanded. It is important to note this superabundance, since the highest development of the race has not been in those regions which naturally supply human cravings and offer the best security. With this extraordinary capital the man and the woman set forth hand in hand, the former to fight and outwit, the latter to conserve and elaborate the results of victory; the former to explore and wander, the latter to settle down and congregate; the former becoming dispersive or centrifugal, the latter unifying and centripetal; the former developing the militant spirit, the latter the industrial spirit. Many thousands of books have been written to set forth the gallant deeds of men, and these have stirred a noble emulation in youthful minds; but few books have been devoted to the patience and energy of the other actor in the drama.

To accomplish the object in view in this work there has been no necessity of eulogizing or depreciating the author's own sex. The past has been a mixture of good and evil, of light and darkness, of justice and injustice, of knowledge and ignorance. The former in each case, judging from the splendid results, has been growing more and more predominant—that is, the good has been slowly conquering the evil; light is coming over the minds of all, justice is the rule, and knowledge grows "from more to more." Life is now longer than it was and women live longer than men. Each moment brings a larger freight of joy, more to women than to men. There is at the present time a great awakening among women as to their own attributes and emotions and capabilities. They are seriously inquiring for the roads that will conduct them to their largest and noblest development. With eager eyes they look ahead to see whether they can discern the true outlines and character of that good life that is to be. With earnest sagacity they look around them as a merchant taking stock. But could any study lead them to truer success than the careful review of those activities and occupations through which they contributed so much to the general mass of happiness?

Long ago Buckle ventured the observation that women are more conservative than men.* It is one of the commonest of sayings that women arrive at conclu-

---

* Buckle, Fraser's Mag., April, 1858; Trans. Roy. Inst., 1858.

sions by a kind of instinct. But reflect a moment upon our savage woman. One has only to look around him in travelling through countries lately touched by civilization to notice that men have to drop their old occupations for new ones. In fact, not five men in a hundred in the most favoured lands are at this moment pursuing the calling for which they were educated. But in transitions from savagery to civilization, and in the vicissitudes of life, women go on housekeeping, spinning, demanding if no longer making pottery, using the same vocabulary, coining the same propositions, reproducing the same forms of ornaments, believing as of old, only making use of modified and bettered appliances. In this they are conservative, indeed, and the blood coursing through the brain tissue carries on the same commerce that has been familiar to women during many thousands of years.

Now the naturalists tell us that change in one bodily structure sets in motion a great number of co-ordinated changes throughout the entire system. The savage man in his normal life is ever changing. When a higher culture overtakes him it is worse. He must lay down a bow and arrow and take up the hoe, a woman's implement. In the struggles for a living in the best of surroundings the man is to-day a farm hand, to-morrow cutting wood, the next day in the crowded city. See how this racks his whole being, bodily, mentally, and spiritually. If he do not die under the treatment he must become adaptive, plastic, versatile. All the propositions and half-automatic activities that he acquires to-day are forgotten to-morrow, and instincts do not have time to mature. On the other hand, the women of a savage tribe, and the ordinary run of women in any civilized land, who change slightly the duties they have to perform, or their manner of doing them, need modify their conceptions and their opinions very little. The constant doing the same things and thinking the same thoughts from generation to generation pass the bodily activity and the mental processes on to a semiautomatic habit.

Very few men are doing what their fathers did, so their opinions have to be made up by study and precedents. Nearly all women, whether in savagery or in civilization, are doing what their mothers and grandmothers did, and their opinions are therefore born in them or into them. The same inheritances come to men also through their mothers, but they become like the muscles of the ear or of the nose, atrophied by almost entire disuse.

When a woman therefore expresses an opinion upon a subject whereupon she is entitled to speak at all—and this, as has been shown, covers a wide field—she utters the accumulated wisdom of the ages, and this is called her instinct. With reference to a gun or an object out of this long concatenation, she would be only bewildered, and say it is a horrid thing.

This progress of which we have been speaking may be said to have been the resultant of two forces. These forces are and have been animality and spirituality, and they are ever at war. The former is opposed to progress and favours dissolution. The latter is the genius of progress and set agoing those beneficent currents which have wafted and urged mankind to all the good they have attained.

When, therefore, one reads that a tribe or nation is immoral and brutalizes women, it is equivalent to saying that the guilty one has got out of the great stream of intellectual advancement and drifted into one of the eddies of animal existence.

If we should appeal again to the naturalists, they would tell us of a law of the survival of the fittest in the struggle for existence. In this, of course, they have reference to plants and animals. This law is one of severest retribution, and knows no exceptions. But there are social and moral retributions as well as physical, and there is a higher law as well as a lower law of the survival of the fittest. Even in the animal world, any species that would pollute the fountain and destroy the very foundation of life or in which the females committed suicide must speedily disappear. How much more fatal has been this defiance of law in the higher plane of existence! The intellectual races and nations when on the upward grade were never immoral or brutal. They were considerate toward their women in the daily walks of life. By a true poetic and æsthetic instinct they exalted every good and noble ideal by giving it the artistic form and grammatic garb of a female. They worshipped them in the skies.

It matters not whether we regard the history of the remotest past or the diverse civilizations of the present, the emancipation and exaltation of women are the synonym of progress. In the mind of the individual, in the family, and in the community alike the loss of veneration for women on the part of men and the loss of virtue and self-respect of women for themselves is the surest indication of destructive tendencies. We may look with pity for a moment upon such, but they have nothing to do with the subject under consideration here.

To sum up the results of our study, women in primitive life had their share in determining the relation of geography to history, in the conquest of the three kingdoms of Nature, in the substitution of other forces to do the work of human muscles, in the elaboration of industrial and æsthetic arts, in the creation of social order, in the production of language, in the development of religion. I mean that they had a peculiar part, aside from that they would have to play merely as human beings. To set forth this share the pages of this book are devoted.

The earth has long been divided by physiographers

into areas or regions going by different names, but each characterized by surroundings and resources of its own, capable of producing and sustaining a unique plant life, or animal life, or human culture. Climate is the chief factor in these areas, but elevation and slope, water courses and shore lines, have much to do with the flora, fauna, and culture. Now each of these regions has the power of deciding what a man shall eat and wherewithal he shall be clothed. It is true that weapons and tools for men must undergo some modifications from region to region, but the greatest changes are in the works of the tailor, the cook, the housebuilder, the maker of vessels.

Dealing with the mineral kingdom, it was woman's early function, using the same materials and means that men employed for their industries, to invent cutlery, hardware, mills, and the like. Of the four treatments of stone—chipping, battering, cutting, and grinding—they were familiar with the first for making knives and scrapers; with the second in the manufacture of mortars and other grinding stone; but the cutting and polishing of stone were the legitimate work of men. Women almost wholly were the patrons of water springs and wells. To this day on the old-fashioned farms the good wife dwells about the springhouse with her milk pans and washing apparatus. How common the picture of the African woman returning from the spring toting water in a jar on her head! The same is common in the arid region of the United States. Women were the first salt-makers and extracted nitre from the ashes of certain plants. They also understood thoroughly the quarrying and manipulation of potter's clay, mineral paint, and soapstone.

There is no end to woman's connection with the vegetal kingdom. It is peculiarly hers. Of the four main uses of plants as food, fibre, timber, and in landscape gardening, only a moment's thought is necessary to discern woman's varied relations. It was her duty to gather the roots, the fruits, and the seeds, to transport and store them, to cook and serve them. No one ever heard of savage men having aught to do with the food-plant industry. The same is true of plant medicines. The first empirical physicians were not the sorcerers, but the herb women. They gathered the first materia medica.

These good women made another journey. It was to collect flexible grasses and barks and roots and woods for basketry and cloth, to put this material through the tedious processes of dyeing, splitting, twisting, weaving, netting, embroidery. They laid the foundation of the great modern textile institutions. Rarely has one seen a man engaged upon such work in savagery, unless he be a squaw man, who has been adjudged unworthy of a place among the warriors and relegated to association with women. The tapa beaters in Polynesia, the mat weavers in Africa, the makers of basketry in America, are and have been women.

Women wrought in wood or timber sparingly. It is true that they gathered faggots, cut down tent poles, and made dishes of bark and logs by hollowing them, but the makers of dugout boats and the carvers of war clubs were more frequently men than women.

But it would be a reprehensible oversight to pass by the beginnings of agriculture and gardening. In point of fact, in the great savage arena at this very moment women are just beginning to discover that they can raise plants cheaper than they can gather the wild ones.

Of the animals woman was not generally the slayer, though she was expert in fishing and in the taking of land animals alive. But she was the butcher, the skin dresser, the curer and packer, the cook and the server, and all men and women now engaged in such work must look back to savage women as the founders of their craft. The whole clan of bonnet-makers, dressmakers, tailors, furriers, were originally of the gentler sex, and woman was the original St. Crispin. Domestic animals were first tamed not for men to ride, but for the service of women—for their fleece and milk and strong backs. The most eminent of these animals have a double and perhaps a triple function. The horse, camel, cow, ass, dog, llama, and reindeer are burden bearers, on to whose backs women shifted a portion of their wearisome loads. The first four also yielded milk, the dog assisted in hunting, and all of them had good skins, which the women at first converted into some form of leather. As for the sheep and the goat, they still live for spinners and dairy-women and cooks. The discovery that the horse, the camel, the cow, the ass, the goat, and the reindeer would yield milk was one of the most useful ever made. The race was multiplied more rapidly by the preservation of those that were born, by the increase of energy in men and women at smaller cost and risk, by the greater fecundity of women, and by the promotion of longevity. It can not be denied that the diversification of employment effected by domestication was a great stimulus to intellectual growth at the same time that it gave leisure for the perfection of women in the arts of refinement.

The physical forces and mechanical powers were at first unknown and entirely useless to both men and women. Only gradually were they brought within the area of intelligence and control. Savages know the inclined plane, the wedge, the lever, the lubricant, the roller, the pulley, in a crude form, but not the wheel in any of its combinations. For the most part men had to do with these. But we must not forget the landing of the Eskimo woman's boat on inflated seal skins, the hoisting of the skin tent by Sioux women, using a sort of pulley, the use of the wedge in setting up a loom, and, chief of all, should we keep in mind the fly wheel on the spindle, the first device ever made by human being for converting rectilinear into circular motion. This fly wheel is indispensable to the whole range of machinery in the world. The nearest approach to a compound pulley among savages is a sort of parbuckle arrangement by means of which the burden woman rolls her load up to her shoulders, doubling the time to decrease the effort. But I am inclined to think that woman's share in developing the mechanical powers was not great.

Of the utilization of Nature's forces to do work, much more may be said for the primitive woman. The fire industry, including its preservation, its use in heating, cooking, drying, smoking, was hers down to the age of metallurgy, and the Marquis of Worcester (1656) was the first to utilize steam in any other capacity than in getting a good dinner. Even in the spirit world woman does not relinquish her hold upon this element, where Hestia presides over the destinies of families and the exercise of hospitality, while Vulcan, as we have intimated, is only the celestial blacksmith or armourer.

Water power does not exist in savagery as a turner of wheels. The care of springs and the carrying of water is woman's constant employment. One of the earliest applications of water power is in this very occupation of transporting the element to irrigate the land. Agriculture, however, had begun to be an occupation for men as soon as they found tribute paying easier and cheaper than going to war. Here, again, is another example of the passing of an industry from one sex to the other in the course of history. The wind, however, appears first utilized in creating a draught to expel the smoke from a tent. This is effected by means of a movable fly. The freight boat in America also first appears driven by mat sails, made by the hands of women.

A careful study of the homely occupations of savage women is the best guide to their share in creating the æsthetic arts. Whether in the two Americas, or in the heart of Africa, or among the peoples of Oceanica, the perpetual astonishment is not the lack of art, but the superabundance of it. Call to mind the exquisite sewing of the Eskimo woman with sinew thread and needle of bone, or the wonderful basketry of all the American tribes, the bark work and feather work of Polynesia, the loom work of Africa, the pottery of the Pueblos, of Central America, and Peru. Compare these with the artistic productions of our present generation of girls and women at their homes. I assure you the comparison is not in favour of the labourers' daughters, or of the mechanics' daughters, or of the farmers' daughters, but of the daughters and wives of the degraded savage. In painting, dyeing, moulding, modelling, weaving, and embroidering, in the origination first of geometric patterns and then of freehand drawing, savage women, primitive women, have won their title to our highest admiration. The only regret is, that this deftness of hand, accuracy of eye, and communion with the beautiful no longer exist with the masses.

It is not necessary to repeat at length the many contributions which women have made to the creation, preservation, and spread of language. There is a language for every art of life, a vocabulary and a style of speech.* The blending of all these terms and phrases into a common fund of utterance constitutes the language as a whole. The arts practiced by women made their contribution to every tongue, the nurture of children almost wholly by women until their fifth year made the latter the transmitters of the common speech, and their forced wanderings from tribe to tribe constituted them the chief element in the commingling of languages.

All the social fabrics of the world are built around women. The first stable society was a mother and her

---

* Paul Ehrenreich, Ztschr. f. Etknol., 1894.

helpless infant, and this little group is the grandest phenomenon in society still. To attach the man permanently to this group for the good of the kind has been the struggle of the ages. No wonder that the mother goddess exists in all theologies, that savages worship the all producing earth as mother, that maternity has been ac-

FIG. 80.—KWAN-YIN, THE CHINESE FEMALE BUDDHA.

corded the highest place in prayer and adoration, that the Buddhists of China have changed one of the chief Bodhisattvas into the adorable goddess Kwan-yin, or Manifested Voice.*

---

* Samuel Johnson, Oriental Religions, China, p. 817.

John Fiske dwells upon the prolongation of helpless infancy as a chief factor in the elevation of humanity. Says he: "In order to bring about that wonderful event, natural selection had to call in the aid of other agencies, and the chief of these agencies was the gradual lengthening of babyhood."*

But the fact is that the progress of culture has shortened the period of babyhood. From primitive times to the taming of milk-yielding animals the baby had only the mother to depend on, and there are numerous testimonies to the suckling of children until they were five years old. The savage or the primitive mother had the brunt to bear. The use of milk from animals made an earlier transfer to the food of adults possible. The last steps in this proceeding are the substitution of a foster mother, and, last of all, an absolutely artificial supply from birth. At the same time intellectual and moral bonds have been strengthened, and the mother's control of the child increased.

In the monogamian family the attachment of the father to the initial group is most complete and the structure of the family is perfected. Under the patriarchal system, this stable element, the mother and child is one of several possible groups attached to the same father. It loses its dignity and identity.

Under the clan system paternity is of less consequence. The mother's name was the name of the *gens*, and the child took its title from her. The stable element was a group consisting of a supposed ancestress and her descendants along the female line. It will be seen, however, that though this is a comprehensive group, the bond is loosened. The mother and her sisters are all mothers

---

* Harvard Lectures, 1871; Cosmic Philosophy, pt. ii, chaps. xvi, xxi, xxii; Excursions of an Evolutionist, chap. xii.

of the child. The father is uncle of his sister's children, but has little control over his own. But in those early savage days, what a beneficent bond which held sisters together at least and mothers with their daughters! It furnished every child with a home and every individual with support. These young clan mothers, stimulated by maternal instinct, gentile pride, and devotion to the compact tribe, wrought day and night to bring to maturity the young lives they bore.

It is here and there affirmed that women are tiring of maternity, and that the progress of civilization and intellectuality are opposed to childbearing. When such a sentiment becomes prevalent in any tribe or region or state or nation, its doom is already in progress. In whatever actions the primitive women excelled—and the number is not small—they surely deserve the apotheosis they have received for their development of the maternal side of life. They prayed the gods for children, offered costly sacrifices for the honour of maternity, and even committed suicide when the blessing was withheld.

For the highest ideals in civilization, in humanitarianism, education, and government the way was prepared in savagery by mothers and by the female clan groups, and the most commanding positions are at this moment in their possession. Pedagogy and the body politic had their foundations laid there. Bebel says that "woman was the first human being that tasted bondage. Woman was a slave before the slave existed."* But this expression takes all the aroma from her fragrant life. She made a servant of herself, and willingly, before there was any slavery. The emancipation of woman is from a self-imposed bondage, as everybody knows.

---

* August Bebel, quoted by Helen Campbell, the Arena, Boston, 1893, vol. vii, p. 163.

In all religions the heavenly world is pictured as a reflection of our own. It may not be true that the goddesses were women in the sense that each one had been some noted person or holy saint on earth. Arachne was not a skillful young woman who was believed to have been turned into a spider. But the spider is a spinner, and Arachne is the composite deification of spinning women. She is the tribal or racial type of all women when they are engaged in that occupation. And so the sky people, by the tricks of human imagination, come to typify the terrestrial life. As in some placid mountain lake the woods and rocky cliffs and floating clouds are mirrored, so that one in gazing downward may behold the same pictures as though he were looking upward, so in all folklores and mythologies serenely lie the shadows of past civilizations and religions.

If women now sit on thrones, if the most beautiful painting in the world is of a mother and her child, if the image of a woman crowns the dome of the American Capitol, if in allegory and metaphor and painting and sculpture the highest ideals are women, it is because they have a right to be there. By all their drudgery and patience, by all their suffering and kindness, they have earned their right to be there.

In the World's Columbian Exposition the place of honour was occupied by the colossal statue of a young woman represented in burnished gold. In one hand she held the world, in the other the cap of emancipation or liberty. Upon her right hand stood the building devoted to manufactures and liberal arts, upon her left hand the temple of agriculture. In the distance the dairy, the leather, and the horticultural buildings. In the anthropological building, at the extreme south of the grounds, was an exhibit from the cemetery of Ancon, in Peru. One figure was of especial interest in this connection—the skeleton of an ancient Peruvian woman. It was in a crouching attitude, wrapped in the customary grave clothes, and about it were the spindles, cradle frame, pottery, and dishes of vegetables with which she was familiar in her life and from which her spirit was not to be separated in her death. Spontaneously the thoughtful mind connected this crouching figure with the statue in the place of honour, and with the noble buildings and scenes about her. How wonderful the transformation, wrought by no magic or legerdemain, but with woman's hands and heart and ingenuity!

It is not here avowed that women may not pursue any path in life they choose, that they have no right to turn aside from old highways to wander in unbeaten tracks. But before it is decided to do that there is no harm in looking backward over the honourable achievements of the sex. All this is stored capital, accumulated experience and energy. If all mankind to come should be better born and nurtured, better instructed in morals and conduct at the start, better clothed and fed and housed all their lives, better married and encompassed and refined, the old ratios of progress would be decupled. All this beneficent labour is the birthright of women, and much of it of women alone. Past glory therein is secure, and it only remains to be seen how far the future will add to its lustre in the preservation of holy ideals.

INDEX.

Acorn harvesting, 91.
Adair, James, 69.
Æsthetic elements in pottery, 171.
  evolution, 102.
Agriculture, primitive, 145.
Allison, Mrs. S. S., 90, 120.
Alviella, Goblet d', 246.
Animals furnishing hides for women's use, 71.
  woman's association with, 278.
Animism, 242.
Anthropoids carry their young on the hip, 119.
Apotheosis of women, 249.
Archæology, witness of, 11.
Arrowment still active, 2.
Art, analysis of its processes, 161.
  at first imitation, 163.
  its relation to geometry, 170.
Artists, women as, 164, 187, 291.
Athene, Pallas, 207.
Atkinson, J. J., 109.
Atolli, Mexican gruel, 27.
Australian relationship, 219.
Awl for basket-making, 42.

Back, carrying on the, 121.
Baker, Sir Samuel, 129.
Balfour, Henry, 109, 171, 177.

Bancroft, H. H., 8, 27, 55, 148, 150, 200, 214, 266.
Barbers, women, 183.
Bark-cloth making, 84.
Bartram, William, 10.
Basket work, 49.
Basketry, types of, 44.
  of Japan and Fuegia compared, 40.
  materials of, 50.
  uniformity of stitch, 59.
Baskets in shaping pottery, 90.
Baskets, water-tight, as cooking vessels, 32.
Beasts of burden, women the first, 114–128.
Beauty, personal, in art, 176.
Belief in relation to common life, 244.
Beliefs analyzed, 244.
Bigamy, 298.
Birds, only the male, sing, 174.
Boas, Franz, 10, 80, 244.
Bone-breaking tools, 29.
Bootmakers, 60.
Bossu, M., travels, 335.
Braiding, 56, 58, 163.
Brain of primitive woman, 4.
Brigham, William T., 63, 67, 190, 288.

(337)

236 WOMAN'S SHARE IN PRIMITIVE CULTURE.

Brinton, Daniel G., 180, 108, 197, 242.
Broom, early woman's implement, 88.
Buckle, Thomas, 201, 273.
Burden-bearing by modern woman, 130.
Burning pottery, 166.

Cacbes, woman's invention of, 18.
Campbell, O. W., 11.
Carr, Lucien, 148.
Carriage, erect, as a personal charm, 178.
Carrying devices, 115.
Casserrep in Guiana cooking, 28.
Cassava, preparation of, 89.
Cat, domesticated by woman, 18.
Cat goddess, 263.
Catlin, George, 123.
Cattle, hides of, replacing those of wild animals, 79.
Celibacy in savagery, 210.
Ceramic art and poetry compared, 172.
Ceres, type of herb women, 259.
Chewing skins to soften them, 73.
Childless mothers commit suicide, 207.
Chili, as food, 37.
Chimneys, woman's invention of, 235.
Civilization and artificialism, 279.
Clan and marriage, 218.
Clay, methods of treating, 96.
Cleaver, butcher's, origin of, 80.
Cliff dweller's textiles, 62.
Clothlets, 80.
Clothing, cutting and making, 66, more of, worn by women, 200.
Coiffures, 182.

Coiled basketry, 48.
pottery, 60.
Cullinson, T. B., 125.
Colour, how produced, 105.
in art, 152.
in pottery, 111.
in textiles, 85.
Communal marriage, 217.
Comparison of the sexes, 18.
Comprehensive work of women, 130.
Comprehensiveness in art, 162.
Conservation of language, 198.
Conservation of women, 278.
Conveyance of passengers, 115.
Cooking among the Mexicans, 37.
industries, 14.
modes of, and serving, 37.
vegetables, order in the inventions of, 20.
Co-operation of sexes, 10.
Cosmetics, 182.
Cotton in America, 64.
Courage among women, 265.
Couvade, 205.
Coville, F. V., 16, 20, 24, 50.
Cradle frames the first passenger cars, 116.
adapted to climate, 117.
Crantz, David, 73.
Crocheting, 67.
Cross, D. K., 287.
Cruelty to females not common among animals, 6, 275.
Cultivation of soil by gentes, 240.
Cushing, F. H., 100, 176, 200, 205.
Cutlers were women at first, 20.

Daily round of duties, 156.
Dall, William H., 150, 185, 207, 211.

Darwin, Charles, 223; 231.
Dead, disposal of the, 251.
Death, women in presence of, 249.
Deformations, 188.
Debarte drill among savages, 178.
Demeter typifies harvesting women, 239.
Design in art, 108.
 on pottery, free-hand, 112.
Disposal of the dead, 251.
Dissemination of language, 188.
Distaff, 58.
Ditmar, H., 6.
Diversity of occupation in cassava working, 39.
 of stonework by women, 141.
 of woman's work, 139.
Division of labour, 7, 231.
Divorce, 229.
Dodge, Colonel R. L., 27, 130, 154, 190, 285.
Domestication of animals, 149, 150.
Donlittle, J., 225.
Dorsey, J. Owen, 9, 27, 71, 85, 200, 215, 219, 265.
Drunkenness not known among savage women, 285.
Drying frames, 85.
Dumont, M., describes Choctaw method of making pottery, 105.
Duties of married women, 231.
Dyeing, 65, 105.

Earth mother, 259.
Echo, the goddess, 270.
Education of girls in savagery, 207.
Elevation of savages through women, 236.

Ellis, Havelock, 2.
Ellis, W., 53, 181, 212, 264.
Embroidery, 67.
Emmons, George T., 76.
Employments, circle of, in the butcher's art, 87.
Emulation of women at work, 88.
Endowments of primitive woman, 272.
Engineering, primitive, 128.
Ethnography, witness of, 12.
European women as burden bearers, 181.
Extent of the art of pottery, 91.

Family names in Australia, 220.
 woman the founder of, 219, 279.
Fat scrapers, 72, 75.
Fates, the three, 268.
Featherwork, 66.
Featherwork in art, 166.
Feeding the dead, 251.
Ferrywomen, 125.
Fewkes, J. Walter, 255.
Fibres, 55.
Figurative language, woman's, 191.
Fire kept burning at the grave, 251.
 peculiarly belonging to women, 82.
 woman's association with, 165, 264.
Fisherwomen, 132.
Fish ponds made by women, 152.
Fly wheel, invention of the, 67.
Folklore of women, 202.
 witness of, to woman's work, 12.
Food bringer, woman as, 14–49.
Form in art, 108.

Forms in pottery, 100, 108.
Fraser, J. G., 190, 242, 294.
Freighting on women's backs, 115.
French-Sheldon, Mrs., 165, 107.
Frijoles, Mexican food, 37.
Fringe of shredded bark, 65.
Fuel problem, 215.
Functions of pottery, 113.
Furs still gathered for women, 50.

Ganowanian marriage, 324.
Garrett, 153.
Garson, J. G., 19.
Gatschet, A. S., 198, 260.
Gentleness developed in women, 172.
Geometry originated by women, 58.
Gesture speech of women, 191.
Gibbs, George, 257.
Gloll, Prof., 132.
Girls in savagery, 302.
Glaze, substitutes for, 100.
Goddesses, types of woman's work, 245.
  with womanly traits and functions, 299.
Gomme, G. L., 199.
Goquet, M., 30.
Gourds, in shaping pottery, 96.
Grammatic gender, 192.
Granaries invented by women, 17.
Grandmother goddess, 259.
Grating cassava, 50.
Grinding seeds, woman's art, 12.
Gypsies, 246.

Habitations in relation to women, 132.

Hands, carrying in the, 19.
Hardisty, W. L., 155.
Hatters, primitive, 84.
Hearne, Samuel, 68, 108, 234.
Hearth goddess, 262.
Hides for canoes, 63.
Hindu women, a degraded type, 206.
History as a witness of woman's work, 17.
Holmes, W. H., 09, 116; 140–171 frequent references.
Holub, Emil, 17.
Honey industry, 24.
House building by women, 152.
  industrial part of, invented by women, 305.
Hunter, W. W., 286.
Husband, evolution of the, 213.
Husbands, number of, 215.

Im Thurn, E. F., 7, 38, 64, 158, 290.
Independence of females among animals, 281.
  of the savage woman, 282.
Industrialism, developed by women, 9.
  in religious belief, 245.
Infanticide in savagery, 208.
Infants, fate of, 206.
Inhabitants of the spirit world, their duties and functions, 257.
Initiation of young women, 210.
Intoxication, savage women free from, 315.
Intuition of women, 275.
Invention in the food arts, 14.
  of language, 188.

Jack-at-all-trades, woman a, 139–
  140.

Kapa-making, 54.
Kitchen, invented by women, 285.
Knapsacks for women, 124.
Knife, woman's invention, 26.
Knitting in art, 168.
Knottlon, Ludwig, 50.

Labrets worn by women, 134.
Lace-making, primitive, 168.
Lacework, 68.
Lacouperie, Terrien de, 267.
Lady, evolution of the fine, 177.
Lamp stoves, Eskimo, 93.
Landscape gardening, 160.
Lang, Andrew, 243, 246.
Language as a witness of woman's work, 11, 252.
  disseminated by women, 190.
  of women in harmony with their duties, 180.
  woman's share in, 188–204.
Lapidaries, women as, 180.
Leather industry, the, 70.
Leaven, origin of, 80.
Leland, Charles G., 249.
Lever used in pressing cassava, 90.
Ling Roth, H., 200.
Livingstone, David, ?, 26, 183, 207, 215.
Loads borne by women, 189.
Loan words in savage tongues, 198.
Looms and loom weaving, 59.
Looping, 58.
Love, language of, 196.
Lullaby, a Zuñi, 170.
Lummis, C. F., 210.

Machinery, women as inventors of, 156, 280.
Maguey fibre, 62.
Maize goddess, 261.
Mall, or common hammer, 20.
Mason, R. H., 7, 107, 156, 183, 210, 212, 217, 226, 234.
Markings of textiles on pottery, 57.
Marriage, kinds of, 216.
  relation to savagery, 212.
  relation to number of wives, 215.
Matrimony, its evolution in relation to woman, 213.
Mat robes in Polynesia, 53.
Matron, evolution of the, 159.
Matthews, Washington, 16, 37, 61, 156, 205.
McKenney, Thomas L., 251.
Medicine, practise of, by women, 149.
Medicine women, 256.
Melody older than harmony, 175.
Man in presence of death, 240.
Men's work regulated by women's, 9.
Metamorphosis of language, 188.
Metate and muller, 22.
Militancy developed by men, 3.
  in religious belief, 243.
  versus industrialism, 2.
Milk-yielding animals, 151.
Millers, women as, 112.
Mills, right and curved motion in, 22.
Mincing knife woman's universal knife in savagery, 27.
Minerals exploited by women, 25, 277.
Minerva, 267.

Mines, women in, 11f.
Mirrors, Nature's, 162.
Modelling in clay, 95.
Modern appreciation of savage woman's art, 172.
Moslem women's work, 133.
Modesty, development of, 237.
Monandry, 226.
Monotone the foundation of music, 174.
Monotony the beginning of art, 104.
Mooney, James, 104, 143, 174.
Moreist, Abbé, 189.
Morgan, Lewis H., 37, 231, 288.
Mortars and pestles, 10.
Mortuary customs, 251.
Mother goddess, 239.
Moulding in clay, 95.
Mourning for the dead, 252.
Murdoch, John, 5, 75, 80, 92, 126.
Music, theory of savage, 173.
  woman's sympathetic with her occupations, 173.
Musical composition not congenial to women, 174.
  Instruments not used by savage women, 174.
Musters, Lieutenant, 81, 182.
Mythical motive in pottery, 172.
Mythology enriched by women, 247.
Myths spread by women, 247.

Naming of girls, 250.
National life, women in, 240.
Natural objects, accessory to decoration, 109.
  suggest forms in pottery, 100.
Nature as food purveyor, 15.
Neith, patroness of weavers, 260.

Nets in shaping pottery, 96.
Netting, 50, 67.
  in art, 105.
Nursery tales, 202.
Nut, Egyptian mother goddess, 261.
Nuttall, Mrs. Zelia, 138.

Occupations in the preparation of food, 15.
Old women, numeracy, 256.
  in mythology, 271.
Onomatopœia, 101.
Ornamentation on pottery, 104.
Ovens, invented by women, 265.
  original, 32.

Pack women in Germany, 184.
Painting the dead, 254.
Papoose framer, 138.
Parkes, Bessie Rayner, 0.
Paste for pottery, 93.
Patterns of pottery in Nature, 109.
Payne, E. J., 8, 30, 189, 204.
Pemmican-making, 28.
Personification, 193.
Physiology of women, 1.
Pike, Warburton, 8.
Pits, cooking in, 85.
Plants, in relation to woman's work, 140, 207.
Ploss, Hermann, 1.
Plough, primitive, 25.
Plutarch, 12, 289.
Poison extracted from vegetables, 24.
Polyandry, 210, 221.
Polygamy, 210.
Polygyny, 222.
Pots for cooking, 84.

Potters, women the first, 91-113.
Potter's wheel wanting, 99.
 substitutes therefor, 100.
Pottery, occupations involved in, 102.
 savage uses for, 108.
 still made by savages, 92.
Powell, J. W., 250.
Powers, Stephen, 253, 257.
Presents to the bride, 214.
Price, F. G. H., 28, 129, 207, 209.
Primitive society illustrated in modern rural life, 242.
 woman poorly furnished, 3.
Privileges of married women, 230.
Promiscuity in marriage, 217.
Property of women, 240.
Prophetesses, 236.
Prytaneum, the, 208.
Psychology in relation to religion, 247.
Pulley, a rude form of, 154.
Pump, a very primitive, 87.
Punaluan family, 221.

Quarriers of soapstone, 30.

Rabbit-skin robes, 62.
Rawhide for lines, 75.
Refinement not born of cruelty, 7.
Relationship and marriage, 218.
Religion, defined, 241.
 in common life, 249.
 of women, 241-264.
Religious motive in pottery, 172.
Rights of married women, 232.
Rings, carrying, for the head, 123.
Roadwoman, the Dyak, 123.
Roasting seeds before grinding them, 30.

Rockhill, W. W., 181, 222.

Saddler's knife, woman's invention, 27.
Salt as food, 88.
Salt mining, 145.
Savage life a key to the religion of savages, 246.
Schweinfurth, Georg. 17, 20, 189.
Scissors, substitutes for, 85.
Scrapers for hides, 75, 77, 83.
Seed gatherers, 10.
Seething, primitive mode of cooking, 34.
Sokhet or Pasht, Egyptian goddess of the under-world, 262.
Selor, Cecilia, 2.
Sellers, George, 140.
Sewing, a skin-worker's art, 67, 85, 88.
Shamoying, 80.
Shells in pottery, 94.
Shoemakers, women as, 64.
Shoulders, carrying on the, 121.
Shredded bark for cinctures, 55.
Sifting, woman's art, 26.
Sign language of women, 195.
Silk as net material, 107.
 in mythology, 267.
Simon, Jules, 5.
Sinew, in textile work, 55.
Sirens, the, 270.
Sita, Hindu goddess of the furrow, 261.
Skin dressing, 70-90.
 among Eskimo, 73.
 among Sioux, 82.
 varieties of, 72.
Slavery, marriage relation in American, 219.
 of woman, 250.

Slip on pottery, 103.
Smoking food, 85.
Soapstone, cooking in, 145.
   woman's mineral, 56.
Social order founded on women, 205-240, 283.
Spindle, the, 58.
Spinning, 50.
Stevenson, James, 106.
Stevenson, Mrs. Matilda C., 260.
Stevenson, Mrs. Sarah Y., 269.
Stone workers, 73, 77, 270.
Storehouses invented by women, 18.
Sugar gathered from reeds, 24.
Sun worship, 205.
Survival of early arts, 4.
Syndyasmian family, 287.

Tacitus, 215, 230.
Tailors, women the first, 54, 55.
Tanners, women, 71.
Tapa cloth, how decorated, 107.
Tapa-making, 54.
Tattooing in relation to writing, 105.
Taylor, Isaac, 77.
Telegraphy, primitive, 106.
Tempering of clay, 94.
Tent-makers, women, 84, 153.
Textile art, 41-60.
   woman's invention, 171.
   woman's, up to the invention of machinery, 60.
Textile beauty, how secured, 105.
Textile material well known by savage women, 41.
Thomson, W. M., 28, 59, 95, 120, 168.
Time as an element in music, 175.
Torches, women makers of, 155.

Toting peculiar to women, 121.
Transportation, primitive, 114.
Tree-climbing for food, 23.
Trotter, Coutts, 7.
Turner, George, 33, 65, 235.
Twined basketry, 47.
Twining, a type of textiles, 50.
Twisting devices, 56.
Tylor, E. B., 190, 301.

Uniformity the foundation of art, 104.

Variety of corn preparations, 143.
Vegetable world explored by women, 16.
Venus, type of goddesses, 258.
Vermin as destroyers of granaries, 18.
Village goddess, the, 240.
Villages laid out by women, 84.
Vocal apparatus of women, 202.
Volubility of women, 201.

Wafer, Lionel, describes loom, 63.
Wailing for the dead, 268.
Wake, C. Stanilaud, frequently quoted, chap. x, 205-240.
Wallace, A. R., 120.
Wallace, Robert, 129.
War, women in, 288.
Ward, Lester F., 2, 281.
Wardrobe, Eskimo, 87.
Washerwomen, primitive, 155.
Washing the dead, 203.
Water goddess, 265.
Water vessels of bamboo, 85.
Weaving, woman's art, 41-60.
   in mythology, 263.
Weaving without loom, 58.
   with loom, 59.

Welding day, the, 212.
Whitney, William Dwight, 130.
Widows in savagery, 200.
Wife holding, methods of, 210.
Wife, value of a, 213.
Winnowing, woman's art, 21.
Wives, number of, 215.
Women, author of industrialism, 5.
   her feeble endowment, 3.
   in savagery not a brutalized slave, 6, 275.
   the best dictionary, 100.
Woman's boat, designed for freight and passengers, 130.
Women's work not always degrading to man, 10.
Women, as artists, 161-187.
   as beasts of burden, 114-138.
   as conservators of speech, 201.

Women as food bringers, 10-40.
   as jacks-at-all-trades, 180-160.
   as potters, 91-113.
   as skin dressers, 70-90.
   as weavers, 41-69.
   good on hunting parties, 8.
   in political life, 240.
   in religion, 241-285.
   made for work, 127.
   not musicians, 177.
   tenacious of language, 208.
Wood, J. G., 152.
Wood workers, women as, 150.
Working women, modern, 5.
Wright, Ashur, 10.
Writing, women as inventors of, 195.

Yarn-making, 50.
Yarrow, H. C., 251.
Yokes for women's shoulders, 121.

THE END.

www.ingramcontent.com/pod-product-compliance
Lightning Source LLC
Chambersburg PA
CBHW030744230426
43667CB00007B/830